THE HOLLAND HOUSE CIRCLE

HOLLAND HOUSE

THE
HOLLAND HOUSE
CIRCLE

BY

LLOYD SANDERS

BENJAMIN BLOM  New York/London

First Published 1908
Reissued 1969 by
Benjamin Blom, Inc. Bronx, New York 10452
and 56 Doughty Street, London, W.C. I

Library of Congress Catalog Card Number 70-82004

Printed in U.S.A. by
NOBLE OFFSET PRINTERS, INC.
NEW YORK 3, N. Y.

PREFACE

THIS book does not purport to be a connected account of Holland House, since that ground has already been covered by Princess Liechtenstein in her well-known work on the subject, by Faulkner, the historian of Kensington, in a chapter based on information supplied by the third Lord Holland, and by Leigh Hunt, who, in his pleasant, allusive style, recorded his personal impressions in "An Old Court Suburb." It is concerned rather with persons than the place. The earlier annals of Holland House have been rapidly summarised, and I have devoted my attention mainly to its most brilliant age; a period which may be defined, in general terms, as coinciding with the first forty years of last century. The materials for a survey of that famous society have been collected by a somewhat wide and minute study of contemporary memoirs and correspondence; but mere lists of those present at particular dinners have been omitted, as calculated to produce but little information and much tedium. Foreigners of distinction like Madame de Staël have not been excluded, though their association with Holland House may have been brief. Further, regarding the host and hostess as central and dominant figures, I have not thought it necessary to pursue to the end the careers of friends like Lord Palmerston and Lord John Russell, who long survived them. Instead of encumbering the page with references, I have compiled a bibliography arranged, so far as it was possible to do so without repetition, in sections embracing one or more chapters.

I must express my cordial thanks to the Committee of White's Club for enabling me to include in the illustrations a reproduction of Dighton's excellent caricature of Lord Alvanley, " Going to White's." Count d'Orsay's sketch of Henry Luttrell would also have been forthcoming for that purpose from their valuable collection, but it was not at the moment accessible. My gratitude is also due to Sir J. Tollemache Sinclair for permission to reproduce Upton's miniature of Princess Lieven, while the authorities of the British Museum, the National Portrait Gallery, and Sir John Soane's Museum have readily granted facilities for taking the various photographs enumerated in the list of illustrations.

L. S.

CONTENTS

PAGE

PREFACE . . . . **v**

SOME WORKS CONSULTED . . . . . . **xix**

CHAPTER I

INTRODUCTORY . . . . **I**

The founder of the Fox family—Sir Stephen's wealth—An elderly bridegroom—Henry Fox—A runaway match—Early history of the manor of Kensington—Cope Castle—The Earl of Holland—Under the Commonwealth—A house to let—Lady Warwick and Addison — The last of the Warwicks — A Royal suitor—Lord Holland's cupidity—A well-feathered nest—The beginnings of Charles Fox—His brother Stephen—Lord Holland's minority.

CHAPTER II

LORD HOLLAND'S YOUTH AND EARLY MANHOOD . . . **16**

Lord Holland's boyhood — Eton and the *Microcosm*—Lord Holland and Canning—Christ Church and Cyril Jackson—Travels in France and Switzerland—Germany and the French Revolution—Spain and Italy—Lord Holland's marriage—He takes his seat—The secession of 1797—A maiden speech—Fox's letters on literature—A visit to Paris—The First Consul—More visits to Spain—The "Lives" of Lope de Vega and Guillen de Castro — "A Dream" — Lord Holland as editor — Fox's history—Lord Holland as a memoir writer.

CHAPTER III

PAGE

LORD HOLLAND AS A STATESMAN 32

The Talents Administration—Lord Holland becomes Privy Seal
—Fall of the Government—The Whigs in opposition—Specula-
tions on office—Lord Holland's " protests "—Treason penalties
—Abolitionism — A visit to Naples — Napoleon's captivity—
Arguments *con* and *pro*—Lady Holland and Napoleon—An
historic snuff-box.

CHAPTER IV

UNDER GEORGE IV. AND WILLIAM IV.   44

Queen Caroline—An unflattering portrait—Creevey on the
situation—Holland House and the Queen—Collapse of the
Liverpool Ministry — Canning's Administration — A possible
Foreign Secretary—Navarino and its consequences—Chancellor
of the Duchy—Lord Holland and Reform—A Whig Nestor—
Peel's " Hundred Days " — The second Melbourne Ministry—
The Syrian crisis—Lord Holland's death—His political character
—Whiggism and Holland House.

CHAPTER V

HOST AND HOSTESS 58

Lord Holland at home—As a conversationalist—A man of many
friendships—Lady Holland's autocracy—Sir Henry Holland's
character of her—Historical retorts—Exercises of authority—
The dinner-hour—A crowded table—Good cheer—Lady Holland
in society—On her travels—Lady Granville's satire — Lady
Holland's correspondence—Byron's memoirs — " Glenarvon "
Calantha and Barbary House—Lady Holland's death—Guizot's
character—Servants and flowers.

CHAPTER VI

MISS FOX AND JOHN ALLEN   78

A cultivated maiden lady—Jeremy Bentham's only love—At
Paris and Combe Florey—Miss Fox's recollections—John Allen's
introduction to the Hollands—A philosopher on the trot—An
established institution—Passages of arms—Political and irreligious opinions—An armchair statesman — " The Rise and
Growth of the Royal Prerogative "—Fugitive writings—Allen
and Blanco White—The loss of a friend—Allen's death.

CHAPTER VII

PAGE

HOLLAND HOUSE AND FOX'S FRIENDS 90

The *salon* in England—The dining-room and library at Holland House—Wanted, a Boswell—Greville's record of conversation—Poets and women of genius—Lord Melbourne on theology—A tolerant atmosphere—General Fitzpatrick—Indolent but sagacious—Epigrams and the "Rolliad"—Hare's wit—An oracle of Brooks's—Lord John Townshend and Dudley North—Adair and the *Anti-Jacobin*—St. Petersburg and Constantinople—Adair and Stratford Canning—Lord Lauderdale—A violent Whig—Lauderdale's mission to France—A "cunning old renegade"—"Citizen" Stanhope—A Jacobin peer—Perverse inventions.

CHAPTER VIII

MORE FRIENDS OF FOX 108

The *Anti-Jacobin* on Erskine—A flippant conversationalist—"Trial by jury"—Impromptu verse—Erskine's eloquence—As Lord Chancellor—A graceless old age—Sheridan and the Whigs—His mystifications—Carlton House politics—An isolated politician—Drury Lane—Sheridan's last days—Sheridan in society—Sir Philip Francis and the Prince—A quarrel with Fox—"Junius Identified"—Lord Thurlow—An extinguished politician—Lord Macartney—"Solomon in all his glory"—Sir Gilbert Elliot—The Portland Whigs—The Grenvilles and the Whigs—Lord Minto in India—Georgiana, Duchess of Devonshire—The "Passage of the Mountain of St. Gothard."

CHAPTER IX

GRENVILLE, GREY, AND WINDHAM 129

"Our English Cato"—Grenville and Pitt—"Most affectionately yours"—The "Talents" Administration—The Regency Bill—Grenville's rupture with the Whigs—At Dropmore—Lord Grey's beginnings—His quarrel with the Regent—Grey and the Peninsular War—Madame de Lieven and Earl Grey—The Reform Cabinet—Life at Howick—Windham and his diary—His conversation and tastes—"Weathercock Windham"—As Secretary at War—"That excellent statesman"—Windham's death.

CHAPTER X

PAGE

WHIGS AND IRISHMEN   144

The third Marquis of Lansdowne—His junction with Canning
—A typical Whig—Bowood and Lansdowne House—Kindness
to Moore—Lord Moira—The negotiations of 1812—An unadroit
Mascarille—Thomas Grenville—Tierney—His duel with Pitt—
Leader of the House—Whitbread—" The Demosthenes of bad
taste "—An impossible Minister—Whitbread and the Princess of
Wales—The affairs of Drury Lane — Little Creevey—Lord
Sefton—An irresponsible politician—Grattan's maiden speech—
Catholic emancipation—Grattan in society—His attachment to
Rogers—" Longbow and Strongbow "—Curran's appearance—
Specimens of his wit.

CHAPTER XI

SOME MEN OF LETTERS   164

Dr. Parr—His correspondence with Lord Holland—The doctor's
retorts—His friends and his pets—" Monk " Lewis—A guest of
the great—His plays and ballads—Lewis and Scott—Hookham
Frere—His talk and his habits—Frere as a diplomatist—The
Anti-Jacobin and "The Monks and the Giants"—Frere as a
translator.

CHAPTER XII

ROGERS AND " CONVERSATION " SHARP   174

Samuel Rogers's good fortune—His house in St. James's Place—
—"A liberal host"—Rogers's intercourse with Fox—As brother
and friend—Rogers's jealousy—His caustic comments—His
cadaverous appearance—Built of a piece—" Columbus "—Lord
Dudley's review—"Human Life"—"Italy"—"Conversation"
Sharp—As host and politician—Sharp's " Letters and Essays."

CHAPTER XIII

HENRY LUTTRELL   185

The premiership of wit—Luttrell's social position—"A philosopher in all things "—London and Paris—Luttrell's epigrams
—" Letters to Julia"—Gifford's review—Almack's—The Park

PAGE

and Kensington Gardens—The Argyll Rooms and Brooks's—
An apostrophe to London—The dead season—Hunting and the
House—"Crockford House "—Luttrell's last years.

CHAPTER XIV

SYDNEY AND ROBERT SMITH   195

Sydney Smith on Luttrell—Foston—Combe Florey—As a social
reformer — The timidity of the Whigs — "Peter Plymley's
Letters "—"Persecuting Bishops " — "Letters to Archdeacon
Singleton "—A licensed jester—His letters to Lady Holland—A
parody of Mackintosh—A sermon on temperance—Sydney
Smith's wit—Bobus Smith—A suppressed individuality.

CHAPTER XV

MOORE, BYRON, AND SCOTT 206

Moore and Lady Holland—The "Twopenny Post Bag "—Moore
and Sheridan—Byron's "Memoirs "—"Tommy dearly loves a
lord "—Moore's independence of mind—"Lalla Rookh " and the
"Irish Melodies "—"English Bards and Scotch Reviewers "—
The Drury Lane Committee—Lady Caroline Lamb—"Glenarvon " — Byron at Holland House — His marriage — Lord
Holland's intervention — "Such a lovable person " — Scott's
quarrel with Lord Holland—His description of Holland House
—"Tales of my Landlord."

CHAPTER XVI

AUTHORS AND WITS 220

Campbell and the King of Clubs—A present from Lady Holland
—"A somewhat awful meeting "—An estrangement and reconciliation—Southey and Whig principles—From the *Edinburgh*
to the *Quarterly*—Hallam, the "bore contradictor "—His correspondence with Lord Webb Seymour—A domestic martinet—
Jekyll and his puns—A *protégé* of George IV.—Jekyll on Holland
House—Lord Alvanley and Talleyrand—Chief of the *ton*—
Alvanley's money affairs—His jokes and appearance—Alvanley
as a politician.

CHAPTER XVII

PAGE

AMATEURS, ARTISTS, AND ACTORS   233

Lord Egremont—Life at Petworth—Payne Knight—The Elgin
marbles—Lawrence and Lord Holland—Leslie and Holland
House—Hoppner—"Bilious from hard work"—Wilkie's preciseness—At Holland House—Wilkie's friends—Some sculptors
and   Canova — Kean — Jack   Bannister — John   Kemble — The
Kemble banquet.

CHAPTER XVIII

MEN OF SCIENCE   246

Count Rumford—"Useful" and "practical"—The arrival of
Davy — His   marriage   and   knighthood — Lady   Davy — Sir
Humphry's   carriage   and   four — Davy and Wollaston—"A
sporting Archbishop"—Faraday—William and Alexander von
Humboldt—Alexander in society—His reminiscences of England
—Charles Waterton—Sir Benjamin Brodie at Holland House—
Sir Henry Holland.

CHAPTER XIX

THE NEW SCHOOL OF WHIGS   255

Serious Whiggism—Dugald Stewart and Bentham—Jeffrey—
Mackintosh's beginnings—The King of Clubs—Mackintosh in
conversation—His residence in India—Mackintosh in the House
—In bondage to the Whigs—Ignored and slighted—A literary
lotus-eater—Francis Horner—His arrival in London—Horner in
society—As member for St. Ives—Nominee for St. Mawes—The
Bullion Committee—Horner's illness and death—Romilly and
Dumont—Romilly's parliamentary diary—The criminal law—
Romilly's   reforms — A   peace-at-any-price   man — Romilly's
character and death.

CHAPTER XX

LAWYERS AND RADICALS   272

Brougham's descent from the North—A breach and its cause—
Brougham in Parliament—His championship of the Princess—
A proposed settlement—Queen Caroline's trial—Brougham as a

PAGE

reformer — On the woolsack — Brougham's downfall — Lord
Melbourne's sentence—Brougham's eccentricities — His good
qualities—The rise of Denman—Solicitor-General to Queen
Caroline—His speech and its sequel—At Holland House—A
Whig dinner-party—Plunket and the Grenvilles—Irish Attorney-
General and Chancellor—Plunket's oratory and puns—John
Wishaw—"The Pope" and "the Mufti" — Hobhouse and
Byron—Hobhouse and Burdett—"Liberty candidates"—Ex-
hausted enthusiasms.

CHAPTER XXI

TORIES AT HOLLAND HOUSE 292

Wilberforce and Lord Eldon—Lord Stowell—A great character
—Stowell's penurious habits—As Judge of the Admiralty Court
—Lord Aberdeen — His relations with Pitt and Dundas —
"Athenian Aberdeen" — His varied attainments — As envoy
abroad—Aberdeen and Greece—His domestic afflictions.

CHAPTER XXII

THE CANNINGITES, PALMERSTON, AND MELBOURNE . 300

The friends of Canning—Palmerston—His slow advance—
Palmerston in society—As Foreign Secretary—His marriage—
The Syrian crisis—Palmerston's triumph—William Lamb, Lord
Melbourne—His marriage—Lamb as a student—A detached
politician—As a Canningite—Home Secretary—Lord Melbourne's
Premierships—His unconventionality—His character.

CHAPTER XXIII

OTHER COLLEAGUES OF CANNING 311

Melbourne's advice to Dudley—Dudley as Foreign Secretary—
"Ivy" and Bishop Copleston — Dudley's friendships — His
conversation—His relations with Holland House—George Ellis—
"The Rolliad" and the *Anti-Jacobin*—Ellis's friendships—The
sixth Earl of Carlisle—Lord Lyndhurst—A lawyer-politician—
"For 'views' read 'prospects'"—Lyndhurst's hospitality—His
conversion to Toryism—Scarlett, Lord Abinger—Scarlett and
the Whigs—*Qui s'excuse*—"Not at Home."

CHAPTER XXIV

PAGE

FOREIGN REFUGEES AND VISITORS .　　.　　.　　.　　. 323

Ugo Foscolo—A "tremendous" companion—" From a lion to a
bore "—Blanco White—His reception at Holland House—A
melancholy tutor—With Archbishop Whately—White becomes
a Unitarian—Calonne — His exit speech — Louis Philippe—
Etienne Dumont and Mirabeau—Dumont's worship of Bentham
—Madame de Staël—"The perpetual motion"—A welcome
outstayed'— Washington Irving — George Ticknor — His impressions of Holland House.

CHAPTER XXV

CONTINENTAL DIPLOMATISTS 　.　　.　　.　　.　　. 335

Metternich—Pozzo di Borgo and others—Van der Weyer—
Princess Lieven—A " *très grande dame* "—Her intimacies—The
eyes and ears of an Embassy—The Lievens' recall—Madame de
Lieven's last years—Talleyrand at Holland House—His appear-
ance and conversation—His affection for England — Count
Montrond—A salaried clubman—His relations with Talleyrand
—Count Flahault—A Paris salon—A figure of the Second
Empire—Guizot's mission — His stories of Lady Holland—
Holland House and the Syrian crisis.

CHAPTER XXVI

THE GREY AND MELBOURNE MINISTRIES .　　.　　.　　. 348

Old and Young Whigs—Spring-Rice and Abercromby—Lord
Duncannon—A healer of differences—The Duke of Richmond—
Lord Althorp's early years—His rooms in the Albany—The
leadership of the House—An indispensable man—Neighbour
and country gentleman—Lord John Russell and Holland House
—His literary efforts—The coming man—The Reform Bills—
Lord John upsets the coach—As leader of the House—Whig
legislation—Lord John at home—The Fox Club—John George
Lambton—" Radical Jack "—" A victim of temper "—A mission
to St. Petersburg—The Edinburgh banquet—The mission to
Canada—Brougham's revenge—The spoilt child of society.

CHAPTER XXVII

PAGE

A MISCELLANEOUS COMPANY   365

Jock Campbell—Elected to Brooks's—Visits to Holland House—
Norton v. Melbourne—The Irish Chancellorship—Macaulay
enters Holland House—Tears and a scene—A Cabinet Minister
—Macaulay as a talker—Charles Greville—A political factotum
—The friend of many—Poodle Byng and Albany Fonblanque—
The Grotes at Holland House—Monckton Milnes—Charles
Dickens—The next generation—Conclusion.

INDEX   377

LIST OF ILLUSTRATIONS

SOUTH VIEW OF HOLLAND HOUSE .   .   .   *Frontispiece*
> From an Engraving in Lysons' "Environs of London," 1795.

                                          FACING PAGE

THORPE'S PLAN OF HOLLAND HOUSE   4
> From the Book of his Designs in Sir John Soane's Museum.

LORD HOLLAND   5
> From the Painting by John Simpson, after Charles Robert Leslie, R.A., in the National Portrait Gallery.

NAPOLEON'S SNUFF-BOX   42
> In the Gold Room, British Museum.

JOHN ALLEN, M.D.   43
> From the Painting by Sir Edwin Landseer, R.A., in the National Portrait Gallery.

THE LIBRARY AT HOLLAND HOUSE   .   .   .   90
> From an Engraving in the Print Room, British Museum, after the Painting by Charles Robert Leslie, R.A.

THE DUCHESS OF DEVONSHIRE   91
> From an Engraving by G. Keating, after the Painting by Sir Joshua Reynolds, P.R.A.

WILLIAM WINDHAM   138
> From the Painting by Sir Joshua Reynolds, P.R.A., in the National Portrait Gallery.

THE MARQUIS OF LANSDOWNE   139
> From the Painting by Henry Walton, in the National Portrait Gallery.

SAMUEL ROGERS   174
> From the Painting by Thomas Phillips, R.A., in the National Portrait Gallery.

GOING TO WHITE'S   175
> From the Caricature of William, second Lord Alvanley, by Dighton. In the possession of White's Club.

FACING PAGE

SYDNEY SMITH 196
From the Painting by Henry Perronet Briggs, R.A., in the National Portrait Gallery.

THOMAS MOORE 197
From the Painting by John Jackson, R.A., in the National Portrait Gallery.

JOSEPH JEKYLL 228
From the Drawing by George Dance, R.A., in the National Portrait Gallery.

SIR DAVID WILKIE, R.A. 229
From the Painting by Himself, in the National Portrait Gallery.

SIR JAMES MACKINTOSH 256
From the Painting by Sir Thomas Lawrence, P.R.A., in the National Portrait Gallery.

FRANCIS HORNER 257
From the Painting by Sir Henry Raeburn, R.A., in the National Portrait Gallery.

SIR SAMUEL ROMILLY 270
From the Painting by Sir Thomas Lawrence, P.R.A., in the National Portrait Gallery.

LORD DENMAN 271
From the Painting by John James Halls, in the National Portrait Gallery.

VISCOUNT MELBOURNE 304
From the Painting by John Partridge, in the National Portrait Gallery.

PRINCESS LIEVEN 342
From the Miniature by Upton. By kind permission of Sir J. G. Tollemache Sinclair.

COUNT MONTROND 343
From the Pen-and-Ink Sketch by Count d'Orsay, published in " The Journal of Thomas Raikes."

LORD JOHN RUSSELL 364
From the Painting by Sir Francis Grant, P.R.A., in the National Portrait Gallery.

LORD MACAULAY 365
From the Painting by Sir Francis Grant P.R.A., in the National Portrait Gallery.

SOME WORKS CONSULTED

CHAPTER I

"Holland House." By Princess Liechtenstein. 1874.
"History and Antiquities of Kensington." By Thomas Faulkner. 1820.
"The Old Court Suburb." By James Henry Leigh Hunt. 1855.
"Kensington, Picturesque and Historical." By W. J. Loftie. 1888.
"Memoirs of the Life of Sir Stephen Fox." 1717.
"Diary and Correspondence of John Evelyn." Edited by W. Bray. 1850–52.
"Diary of Samuel Pepys." Edited by H. B. Wheatley. 1904.
"Memoirs of the Reign of George II." By Horace Walpole. Edited by Lord Holland. 1847.
"Memoirs of the Reign of George III." By Horace Walpole. Edited by Sir D. Le Marchant. 1845.
"The Letters of Horace Walpole." Edited by Mrs. Paget Toynbee. 1903–5.
"Life of the Earl of Shelburne." By Lord Fitzmaurice. 1875.
"Memorials and Correspondence of Charles James Fox." By Earl Russell. 1853–7.
"Life and Times of Charles James Fox." By Earl Russell. 1859–66.
"Memoirs of the Later Years of Charles James Fox." By J. B. Trotter. 1811.
"The Early History of Charles James Fox." By Sir G. O. Trevelyan. 1880.
"Charles James Fox: A Commentary." By Walter Savage Landor. Edited by Stephen Wheeler. 1907.
"The Life and Letters of Lady Sarah Lennox." Edited by the Countess of Ilchester and Lord Stavordale. 1901.

CHAPTERS II—VI

"Foreign Reminiscences." By Lord Holland. Edited by his Son, Henry Edward, Lord Holland. 1850.

"Memoirs of the Whig Party during my Time." By Lord Holland. Edited by his Son, Henry Edward, Lord Holland. 1852–54.

"Further Memoirs of the Whig Party." Edited by Lord Stavordale. 1905.

"The Opinions of Lord Holland." Collected and edited by D. C. Moylan. 1841.

"A Dream." [By Lord Holland.] 1818.

"A History of the Early Part of the Reign of James II." By C. J. Fox. [Edited by Lord Holland.] 1808.

"Lives of Lope de Vega Carpio and Guillen de Castro." By Lord Holland. 1817.

"Statesmen of the Time of George III." By Lord Brougham. 1843.

"Eminent Statesmen and Writers." By Abraham Hayward. 1880.

"The Works of Lord Macaulay." Vol. VI. Edited by his Sister, Lady Trevelyan. 1866.

"Napoleon : the Last Phase." By the Earl of Rosebery. 1904.

"Letters of Harriet, Countess Granville." Edited by her Son, the Hon. F. Leveson-Gower. 1894.

"Bygone Years." By the Hon. F. Leveson-Gower. 1905.

"Records of Later Life." By Frances Anne Kemble. 1882.

"Glenarvon." [By Lady Caroline Lamb.] 1816.

"The Works of Jeremy Bentham." Vols. X. and XI. (Life.) By Sir John Bowring. 1843.

"Inquiry into the Rise and Growth of the Royal Prerogative." With Biographical Notices. By John Allen. 1849.

CHAPTERS VII—X

"The Greville Memoirs." Edited by Henry Reeve. 1888.

"The Rolliad." 1795.

"Selections from the *Anti-Jacobin*." Edited by Lloyd Sanders. 1904.

"The Life of Lord Stratford de Redcliffe." By S. Lane Poole. 1888.

"Lives of the Lord Chancellors." Vol. VI. (Life of Lord Erskine.) By John, Lord Campbell. 1847.

"Life of Sheridan." By Thomas Moore. 1825.

"Sheridan : a Biography." By Fraser Rae. 1896.

"Memoirs of Sir Philip Francis." By Joseph Parkes and Herman Merivale. 1867.

"The Francis Letters." Edited by Beata Francis and Eliza Keary. 1901.

"Our First Ambassador to China." [George, Earl Macartney.] By Helen H. Robbins. 1908.

"Life and Letters of Gilbert Elliot, first Earl of Minto." By the Countess of Minto. 1874.

"The Two Duchesses : Georgiana, Duchess of Devonshire ; Elizabeth, Duchess of Devonshire." Edited by Vere Foster. 1898.

"Memoirs of the Court and Cabinets of George III." 1853-6. "Memoirs of the Court of the Regency." 1856. "Memoirs of the Court of George IV." 1858. By the Duke of Buckingham.

"Life of Pitt." By Lord Stanhope. 1861-2.

"Nugæ Metricæ." By Lord Grenville. 1824.

"Life and Opinions of Earl Grey." By Sir Frederick Grey. 1861.

"Correspondence of Princess Lieven and Earl Grey." Edited and translated by Guy Le Strange. 1890.

"Correspondence of William IV. and Lord Grey." Edited by Henry, Earl Grey. 1867.

"Diary of William Windham." Edited by Mrs. Henry Baring. 1866.

"The Creevey Papers." Edited by Sir Herbert Maxwell. 1903.

"The Reminiscences and Recollections of Captain Gronow." With illustrations from contemporary sources by J. Grego. 1888.

"Memoirs of the Life and Times of Henry Grattan." By his Son, Henry Grattan. 1839-46.

"Life of John Philpot Curran." By W. H. Curran. 1819.

CHAPTERS XI—XVI

"The Collected Works of the Rev. Samuel Parr," including a biography by John Johnstone, M.D., and correspondence. 1828.

"Life and Correspondence of M. G. Lewis." 1839.

"The Works of John Hookham Frere, with Memoir by Sir Bartle Frere." 1874.

"John Hookham Frere and his Friends." By Gabrielle Festing. 1899.

"The Early Life of Samuel Rogers." By P. W. Clayden. 1887.

"Rogers and His Contemporaries." By P. W. Clayden. 1889.

"Rogers's Poems," with Memoir by Samuel Sharpe. 1860.

Notices of Rogers in the *Edinburgh Review*, July, 1856 (by Hayward), and the *Quarterly Review*, October, 1888 (by Lady Eastlake).

"Letters and Essays." By Richard Sharp. 1834.

"Letters to Julia." By Henry Luttrell. 1822.

"Crockford House." [By Henry Luttrell.] 1827.

"A Memoir of the Rev. Sydney Smith," by his Daughter, Lady Holland, with a Selection from his Letters, edited by Mrs. Austin. 1855.

"Works." By the Rev. Sydney Smith. 1850.

"Sydney Smith." By G. W. E. Russell. 1905.

Memoirs, Journals, and Correspondence of Thomas Moore. Edited by Lord John Russell. 1853–6.

"Thomas Moore." By Stephen Lucius Gwynn. 1905.

"The Poetical Works of Thomas Moore," with Memoir by Charles Kent. 1879.

"Life of Lord Byron." By Thomas Moore. 1830.

"Works of Lord Byron." Poetry edited by E. H. Coleridge. Letters and Journals edited by R. E. Prothero. 1898–1904.

"Memoirs of the Life of Sir Walter Scott." By J. G. Lockhart. 1837–38.

"A Publisher and his Friends." By Samuel Smiles. 1891.

"Life and Letters of Thomas Campbell." By William Beattie. 1849.

"Correspondence of Robert Southey." Edited by the Rev. C. C. Southey. 1849–50.

"Correspondence of Two Brothers: the eleventh Duke of Somerset and Lord Webb Seymour." By Lady Guendolen Ramsden. 1906.

"Mrs. Brookfield and her Circle." By C. H. E. and F. Brookfield. 1906.

"Correspondence of Mr. Joseph Jekyll with his Sister-in-law, Lady Gertrude Sloane Stanley." Edited by the Hon. A. Bourke. 1890.

"A Portion of the Journal kept by T. Raikes, Esq." 1856–57.

CHAPTERS XVII AND XVIII

"Autobiographical Recollections of C. R. Leslie." Edited by Tom Taylor. 1865.

"Life of B. R. Haydon." Edited by Tom Taylor. 1853.
"Life of Sir David Wilkie." By Allan Cunningham. 1843.
"Memoirs of the Life of J. P. Kemble." By James Boaden. 1825.
"Collective Works of Count Rumford." Vol. V. Life by George E. Ellis. 1875.
"The Life of Sir Humphry Davy." By John Ayrton Paris. 1831.
"Life and Letters of Faraday." By Dr. Bence Jones. 1870.
"Lives of the Brothers Humboldt." By P. F. D. Klencke. Translated by Juliette Vauer. 1852.
"Autobiography of the late Sir B. C. Brodie, Bart." 1865.
"Recollections of Past Life." By Sir Henry Holland. 1872.

CHAPTERS XIX AND XX

"Life of Lord Jeffrey." By Lord Cockburn. 1852.
"Life of Sir James Mackintosh." By his Son, R. J. Mackintosh. 1836.
Lord Macaulay's Essay on Mackintosh's "History of the Revolution in England in 1688."
"Memoirs and Correspondence of Francis Horner." Edited by Leonard Horner. 1843.
"Memoirs of the Life of Sir Samuel Romilly." Edited by his Sons. 1840.
"Life and Times of Henry, Lord Brougham." By Himself. 1871.
"Lives of the Victorian Chancellors." Vol. I. By J. B. Atlay. 1906.
"Memoir of Thomas, first Lord Denman." By Sir J. Arnould. 1873.
"The Life, Letters, and Speeches of Lord Plunket." By his Grandson, the Hon. David Plunket. 1867.
"The Pope of Holland House." By Lady Seymour. 1906.
The *Edinburgh Review*, January, 1871. Containing Extracts from Lord Broughton's (John Cam Hobhouse's) "Recollections of a Long Life."
"Life of Francis Place." By Graham Wallas. 1898.

CHAPTERS XXI—XXIII

"Life of William Wilberforce." By his Sons, Robert Isaac and Samuel Wilberforce. 1838.

" Life of Lord Chancellor Eldon." By Horace Twiss. 1844.
" Sketch of the Lives of Lords Stowell and Eldon." By W. E.
Surtees. 1846.
" Life of Lord Aberdeen." By Lord Stanmore. 1893.
" The Life of Lord Palmerston." By Lord Dalling and Evelyn
Ashley. 1870–76.
" Lord Melbourne's Papers." Edited by Lloyd C. Sanders. 1889.
" Letters of Queen Victoria." Edited by Lord Esher and A. C.
Benson. 1907.
" Letters from the Earl of Dudley to the Bishop of Llandaff." 1840.
" Letters to ' Ivy ' from the first Earl of Dudley." Edited by S. H.
Romilly. 1905.
The *Quarterly Review*, December, 1840.
" Life of Lord Lyndhurst." By Sir Theodore Martin.
" Memoir of Lord Abinger." By P. C. Scarlett. 1877.

CHAPTERS XXIV AND XXV

" The Life of the Rev. Joseph Blanco White." By J. H. Thom.
1845.
" The Great Frenchman and the Little Genevese." Translated from
Étienne Dumont's " Souvenirs sur Mirabeau " by Lady Seymour.
1904.
" Madame de Staël." By Lady Blennerhassett. 1889.
" Madame de Staël and her Lovers." By Francis Gribble. 1907.
" Life, Letters, and Journals of George Ticknor." 1876.
" Mémoires etc. laissés par le Prince de Metternich." 1880–84.
" Letters of Dorothea, Princess Lieven." Edited by L. G. Robinson.
1902.
" Talleyrand." By Lady Blennerhassett. 1894.
" Mémoires pour servir à l'histoire de mon Temps." Tome 5. Par
François Pierre Guillame Guizot. 1858–67.

CHAPTERS XXVI AND XXVII

' Memoir of the fifth Duke of Richmond." [By Lord William Pitt
Lennox.] 1862.
" Memoir of Lord Althorp." By Sir Denis Le Marchant. 1876.

"The Life of Lord John Russell." By Sir Spencer Walpole. 1891.

" Life and Letters of the first Earl of Durham." By Stuart Reid. 1906.

"Life of John, Baron Campbell." Edited by his Daughter, the Hon. Mrs. Hardcastle. 1881.

"The Life and Letters of Lord Macaulay." By Sir G. O. Trevelyan. 1876.

"The Life and Labours of Albany Fonblanque." Edited by E. B. De Fonblanque. 1874.

"The Personal Life of George Grote." By Mrs. Grote. 1873.

"The Life of Richard Monckton Milnes, first Lord Houghton." By Sir Thomas Wemyss Reid. 1890.

"The Letters of Charles Dickens." Edited by his Sister-in-law, Georgina Hogarth. 1880–82.

THE

HOLLAND HOUSE CIRCLE

CHAPTER I

INTRODUCTORY

The founder of the Fox family—Sir Stephen's wealth—An elderly bridegroom—Henry Fox—A runaway match—Early history of the manor of Kensington—Cope Castle—The Earl of Holland—Under the Commonwealth—A house to let—Lady Warwick and Addison —The last of the Warwicks—A Royal suitor—Lord Holland's cupidity—A well-feathered nest—The beginnings of Charles Fox— His brother Stephen—Lord Holland's minority.

THE Fox family rose with a rapidity characteristic of the seventeenth century, when everything was possible to the adroit courtier. Sir Stephen, the founder of its fortunes, who was born in 1627, came from what his anonymous biographer calls "honest and approved parents of a middle station" in Wiltshire. He entered the household of the Earl of Northumberland, High Admiral of England, as a valet, and then passed into the service of that nobleman's brother, Lord Percy. After helping his master in the management of the Ordnance Board during the campaign of 1651, which ended in the overthrow of the Royalists at Worcester, he took an active part in smuggling Prince Charles out of the country, and was steward and collector of intelligence to the vagabond Court. Through the excellence of his information he was able to announce the news of Cromwell's death to the Prince six hours before any express reached Brussels.

After the Restoration, Stephen Fox stood high in the Royal favour and held various lucrative appointments. In 1680 his friend and admirer, Evelyn, reckoned him to be worth £200,000 or more, " honestly got and unenvied, which is next to a miracle." Honesty is a relative virtue. Fox's confidences to the sympathetic Pepys show that he farmed the Paymastership-General to some purpose, extracting a comfortable twelve per cent. interest on his outlay without any of the trouble that attended the like procedure at the Admiralty. He was, in fact, a typical placeman of the Restoration age, "as humble in prosperity," writes Evelyn, "and as ready to do a courtesy as ever he was." By judiciously absenting himself from Court during the last months of the reign of James II., he contrived to retain his appointments under William III., and, as member for Salisbury, led the procession of the House of Commons at Queen Anne's coronation. Part of his wealth was devoted to numerous and judicious benefactions. His chief memorial is Chelsea Hospital. Whatever may be the value of the story attributing the original idea to Nell Gwynn, Sir Stephen Fox was the leading spirit in the building and endowment of the college. He frequently consulted Evelyn during the progress of the scheme, and the diarist noted that its whole management was in his hands.

In his seventy-seventh year the veteran official found

himself with no prospect of direct descent in the male line, seven sons having died before him. Thereupon, being, as his biographer puts it, of "a vegete and hale constitution," he married Miss Hope, the young daughter of a Lincolnshire clergyman. They had five children, of whom the eldest became Earl of Ilchester and the second was Henry Fox, first Lord Holland. Sir Stephen Fox died on October 28, 1716, at Chiswick, in a country house built on property he had purchased not long before the Revolution,[1] and his wife survived him less than two years. The Foxes are said to have inherited from her their heavy eyebrows and dark complexions.

Henry Fox, with the possible exceptions of Carteret and Lord Shelburne, is the most conspicuous example in English political history of a great man *manqué*. Macaulay dismisses him, in one place, as a needy political adventurer. But that strictest of Whigs never gave quarter to a jovial reprobate, whether he was a party man or a man of letters like Steele or Goldsmith. Elsewhere Macaulay does Henry Fox more substantial justice in the sentence : " He was the most unpopular of the statesmen of his time, not because he sinned more than any of them, but because he canted less." Trained in the cynical school of Walpole, to whom he was a steady adherent, he lived on into an age elevated to higher aims by the moral earnestness of the elder Pitt. Judged by that standard Fox was found hopelessly wanting ; he sank, as Wraxall puts it in his memoirs, under the superior ascendant. Throughout the chaos of administration which ensued on the death of Henry

---

[1] This house stood near Chiswick House, Lord Burlington's villa. It was demolished and the grounds added to those of its neighbour in 1812, the Duke of Devonshire having acquired the property.

Pelham in 1754, he made ease and the emoluments of office his aims, justifying thereby Lord Chesterfield's censure that "he had not the least notion of, or regard for, the public good or the Constitution, but despised those cares as the objects of narrow minds or the pretences of interested ones."

The intimate of Horace Walpole, Charles Hanbury Williams, George Selwyn and the genial but unscrupulous Rigby, Henry Fox easily made his way in society. But he set the fashionable world by the ears when, in July, 1744, he perpetrated a runaway match with Lady Caroline Lennox, the eldest daughter of the Duke of Richmond. The stir was prodigious, and Carteret made it an excuse for hurling a characteristic jest at the first Minister, the Duke of Newcastle. When that emotional statesman was lamenting "this most unfortunate affair," Carteret affected to think that our fleets or our armies were beaten, or Mons betrayed to the French. "At last it came out that Harry Fox was married, which I knew before. . . And this man is Secretary of State!" The Duke and Duchess forgave the elopement after the birth of their first grandchild. Henry Fox and Lady Caroline occupied Holland House on a yearly tenancy in 1749. In 1767, after he had virtually retired from public life with the barony of Holland, which he attempted in vain to convert into an earldom, he purchased the property. Let us digress for a moment into its early history.

The manor of Kensington, on which Holland House was built, formed a portion of the estates belonging to one Edwin, described as a thegn, which were bestowed by the Conqueror on his follower Geoffrey de Montbrai or Mowbray, the redoubtable Bishop of Coutances.

THORPE'S PLAN OF HOLLAND HOUSE

LORD HOLLAND

FROM THE PAINTING BY JOHN SIMPSON AFTER CHARLES ROBERT LESLIE, R.A.,
IN THE NATIONAL PORTRAIT GALLERY

Under that bellicose prelate, " abler at war than at clerical business, and fitter to lead armed men in battle than to teach surpliced clerks to sing psalms," it was held by Aubrey de Vere, the founder of the line who were Earls of Oxford until well into the sixteenth century. Aubrey de Vere became tenant-in-chief, and in spite of alienations and forfeitures his descendants clung to a portion of their Kensington property. In 1626, how- ever, the poor remnant, reduced to the nominal rent of West Town, passed on the death of the fourteenth Earl, " little John of Camps," to his married sister. Thus it was owned by Sir William and Lady Cornwallis and their son-in-law, Archibald, seventh Earl of Argyll, before it became by purchase the property of Sir Walter Cope, Chamberlain of the Exchequer in the reign of James I. He had previously bought the manor of Notting Barns, but only to sell it again. However, he added to West Town the Earl's manor (Earl's Court) and the Abbot's manor (the land round St. Mary Abbot's church) and thus owned the greater part of Kensington.

The grandson of an Oxfordshire landowner, who employed his leisure in composing a work of religious meditation, and in compiling the " Historie of the two moste noble Captaines in the Worlde, Anniball and Scipio," Sir Walter Cope made his way through his friendship with the younger Cecil. In 1604 he com- missioned John Thorpe, the first architect of the day, to build a house which he called Cope Castle. The book of that assiduous worker's designs, which has found its way to Sir John Soane's Museum in Lincoln's Inn Fields, contains a ground-plan of the mansion with the identification—" Sir Walter Coapes at Kensington, perfected per me I. T." Building and lavish entertainment—for his Sovereign honoured him with a visit in 1612, and a somewhat doubtful tradition includes the Duke of Sully, the profoundly sagacious Minister of Henri IV. of France, among his guests [1]—exercised a baneful influence upon the finances of the owner of Cope Castle, and he died £27,000 in debt. But he had at least the consolation of having married his only child Isabel to Henry Rich, Earl of Holland, who, next to the Duke of Buckingham, was the most magnificent courtier of the time.

Thus Cope Castle became Holland House, and a scene of splendid hospitality. Rich added its wings and arcades, not altogether to the improvement of the original design, and erected a pleasing Inigo Jones gateway in the courtyard, which was subsequently removed to the entrance of the pleasure grounds. He also commissioned Francis Cleyn, a German artist of Italian training, to decorate the interior, and Van Dyck to paint his portrait. Dependent for his rapid rise on his handsome person and winning manners, Rich resembled Buckingham, the splendid being on whom he founded himself, in his inability to penetrate beneath the surface of events. As the representative of Charles, Prince of Wales, at the French Court he made love to Henrietta Maria with spirited ease ; but the negotiations for the marriage treaty were beyond him, and they passed into the hands of a safer diplomatist in Lord Carlisle. Buckingham contrived, nevertheless, to get

[1] Sully's mission to the Court of James I. was in 1603, a year or so before Cope began building, if the accepted date is correct. He was possibly entertained by the Chamberlain of the Exchequer at "the Moats" in West Town, where Cope lived while superintending the erection of Holland House, but his memoirs are silent on the point.

him raised to the rank of Earl, a little more than a year after he had been created Baron Kensington—a title derived from his wife's property. Holland intrigued against Strafford, and refused to join Charles I. at York, when affairs were hastening to a crisis, thus alienating the Court, without gaining the confidence of Parliament. " He was a very well-bred man," writes Clarendon, "and a fine gentleman in good times ; but too much desired to have ease and plenty when the King could have neither, and did think poverty the most unsupportable thing that could befall any man in his condition." This character explains the unhappy indecision which finally brought him to the scaffold in 1649, after he had appeared in arms for the King at Kingston-on-Thames and had been taken prisoner at St. Neots. He died gallantly, attired, an exquisite to the last, in a white satin waistcoat and white satin cap with silver lace.

Lord Fairfax occupied Holland House after the execution of the Earl, but his residence must have been brief, since he had his hands full with his campaign in the West. We may also believe, or disbelieve, the story that Cromwell held his conferences with Ireton on the lawn, the deafness of his subordinate rendering it expedient that they should be out of earshot. Sober history relates, however, that as it lay outside the entrenchments of Hyde Park, it was the spot where the baffled Corporation and Presbyterian remnant of the Commons met the all-powerful Army in August, 1647, after which the soldiers marched into the heart of the City " with boughs of laurel in their hats." The rulers of the Commonwealth had every reason for refraining from extreme measures against the family, since Holland's elder brother, the Earl of Warwick, was a staunch supporter of the Presbyterian party. The widowed Countess was permitted to return to her home, and even gave stage-plays, acted under the nose of an austere Government.

The Restoration failed to re-establish the fortunes of the family, though the second Lord Holland succeeded to the title and estates of the Earls of Warwick. The house, down to the middle of the eighteenth century, was not unfrequently let. Among its occupants was William Penn, when he was holding long audiences with James II. in order, as he hoped, to secure toleration for the Quakers, and at the hour when he rose it would be crowded by as many as two hundred suitors. Just after the Revolution Holland House narrowly escaped becoming a Court residence. It was renovated for the King and Queen in 1689, at the cost of some £1,500. But in the end William III. fixed his choice on Nottingham House, the suburban residence of the Earl of Nottingham, though the Court stayed at Holland House from October 14th to December 24th while Kensington Palace, as it became, was being prepared for its reception. In 1734 the *London Daily Mercury* of May 6th contained the following announcement: " Holland House and Gardens are put in order for the reception of lodgers there against the Court removes to Kensington Palace."

The Rich family, then, must have occupied Holland House but intermittently during this period of its vicissitudes. It was in the reign of William III. that John Aubrey, the antiquary, chronicles the death of the beautiful Lady Diana of small-pox, after her apparition had appeared to her as she was walking in the garden at eleven o'clock to take the fresh air before dinner. The

Earl of Warwick and Holland figures in " Esmond " as
Lord Mohun's supporter in the duel with Lord Castle-
wood, and history records that the pair were concerned
in a curious attempt to override the Bishop of London's
right of presentation and to impose a vicar of their own
on Kensington parish.   But the episode that stands out
from the annals of the house is the marriage of Addison
to the widowed Countess of Warwick on August 3, 1716,
and his subsequent residence and death at Holland
House.   According to a well-worn passage in Johnson's
" Lives of the Poets," the union resembled that in which
a Sultan gives his daughter a man as her slave, and it is
supposed to have resulted in unhappiness.   Macaulay
supports the story to the extent of saying that the tradition began early, and that we have nothing to oppose to it.
Yet Addison left his fortune at Lady Warwick's disposal,
and she, for her part, bequeathed one annuity of fifty
pounds to Mrs. Coombes, " the sister of my late dear
husband, Mr. Addison," and another of ten to the poor
of Bilton, where his only daughter lived.   In giving him
her hand she committed no pronounced act of condescension, since shortly after the marriage Sunderland
made him a Secretary of State, chiefly on account of his
personal charm and literary fame.   The rapid decline of
his health is the true explanation of any moroseness that
Addison may have imported into his relations with his
wife.   In 1719 came the " awful scene," as Johnson calls
it, immortalised by Tickell in a fine couplet, when he
summoned the young Earl to his bedside and said, " See
in what peace a Christian can die."

To what extent Lord Warwick stood in need of his
stepfather's lesson we cannot really tell.   Tradition makes
a rake of him, and he acted as talebearer to Pope during

the quarrel between Addison and that splenetic individual. But he died too soon to have done much harm, since he was called upon to carry the admonition into practice within three years of its delivery. The title and estates passed to a cousin, Edward Rich, who was last of his line. The property then went to his cousin, William Edwardes, who, in 1776, was raised to the Irish peerage as Lord Kensington, nine years after the sale of his estates to Henry Fox.

Under the ownership of Henry Fox, Holland House was enriched by numerous specimens of Reynolds's art, including the well-known painting of Lady Sarah Lennox his sister-in-law, Lady Susan Strangways his niece, and Charles James Fox his son.[1] Theatrical performances were also given there, which Horace Walpole greatly admired. "The two girls [Lady Sarah and Lady Susan] were delightful," he records, "and acted with so much nature and simplicity that they seemed the very things they represented." Lady Sarah, who lived under the guardianship of her eldest sister, Lady Holland, might have left Holland House to be married to George III. in Westminster Abbey, if she had not turned a deaf ear to the circumspect advances of her Royal suitor, always supposing, however, that she could have overcome the objections of the Princess-mother and Lord Bute. Henry Fox's attitude towards the affair amounted to no more than very benevolent neutrality, though Horace Walpole accused him of going off to his country house at Kingsgate, near the North Foreland, to hide his

---

[1] Princess Liechtenstein gives an animated description of the Reynolds pictures at Holland House. The famous portrait of Baretti, Dr. Johnson's friend, was acquired by the third Lord Holland in exchange from Lord Hertford.

intrigues, leaving Lady Sarah at Holland House, " where she appeared every morning in a field close to the great road (where the King passed on horseback) in a fancied habit, making hay."

Henry Fox's disinterestedness on this occasion comes as a rare relief to a career of persistent self-seeking. At the beginning of the reign of George III., his junction with Lord Bute, the best hated man south of the Tweed, brought upon him an odium which pursued him into retirement and embittered his last years. He heaped appointment on appointment ; forced the reluctant King to grant a peerage to his wife ; manœuvred Pitt and the Duke of Newcastle into resigning, and coerced Parliament and the Whig aristocracy by a judicious system of rewards and punishments. He was fully conscious of his unpopularity, though in a sanguine moment he wrote : " Instead of what I expected, I believe that in no fortnight since the year 1756 have I ever been less abused than in this last." Lord Shelburne, one of his confederates, declared that, having filled up the appointments from which the Duke of Newcastle's friends had been ejected, he no longer took any trouble with the business or the individuals of the House of Commons. His main object was to secure a safe retreat with his spoils. To that end he took a peerage, clinging the while to the lucrative post of Paymaster-General, though Shelburne, Rigby, and his faithful cousin Calcraft warned him that by so doing he would expose himself to the worst imputations. In 1765, however, the pertinacity of George Grenville, the First Lord of the Treasury, forced him to resign the appointment.

" Old and abandoned by each venal friend," according to Gray's biting lampoon, Lord Holland lived for nine

years longer, in constant apprehension of having to dis-
gorge his dubiously acquired gains. Proceedings were
actually begun against him in the Court of the Exchequer
and stayed only by a writ of the Crown, and in a petition
from the Livery of the City presented to the King he
was unceremoniously styled " the public defaulter of
unaccounted millions." His actual offence consisted in
holding the Pay Office during a prolonged period when
the existence of war rendered it unusually lucrative. In
making private profit by investing Exchequer balances
on his own account, and, as his detailed statement shows,
by selling out at judicious moments, he was only acting
as all his predecessors, except Pitt, had acted before him,
and Pitt's conduct was regarded as a miracle of disinterestedness. Still the public were justified in thinking
that he grew rich much too quickly. At his death, in
1774, he left his widow £2,000 a year, Holland House,
and Government securities amounting to some £120,000.
To his three sons he left £50,000 in money, and a sinecure worth £23,000 a year, and he had already paid at
least £200,000 of debts for Stephen, the eldest, and
Charles, the second. To Stephen, besides, he gave
between £4,000 and £5,000 a year in land ; Charles
received the Kent property and £900 a year ; Henry, an
estate in the North, and £500 a year. Lord Holland had
certainly feathered his nest to some purpose.

Gray exaggerated the reclusiveness of Lord Holland's
life after his retirement from politics. He had quarrelled
with Shelburne and Rigby, but he retained the friendship
of George Selwyn and Horace Walpole, and it was
transmitted to the second and third generations of his
family. Gardening and building in various eccentric
styles at Kingsgate seem to have been his favourite

occupations, and Charles Fox inherited the first of them.
Lord Holland's friend Charles Hamilton, of Pain's Hill,
laid out the grounds to the west of the house, turfed the
walks, and planted the cedars. His chief concern was
the forming of his sons, a duty he cannot be said to have
discharged to edification. He had provided Stephen and
Charles with tutors and sent them to Eton, where
Shelburne, no friendly witness, it is true, declared that the
" extravagant vulgar indulgence " of their father produced
a change for the worse in the morals of the school. They
were allowed to gratify every whim, and Lord Holland
even interrupted Charles's education at Eton and Hertford College, Oxford, to initiate him in the fashionable
dissipations of the Continent. His conception of parental
responsibilities began and ended with liberal supplies of
pocket-money and the discharge of liabilities whenever
they became pressing. As a matter of course, he bought
them seats in Parliament, and thus Charles became
member for Midhurst in March, 1768, though he had
barely turned nineteen and was wandering about Italy.
He lived partly at Holland House and partly in lodgings
with Stephen, and, after the latter had married, with his
cousin, Richard Fitzpatrick, for company. It was during
the first partnership that George Selwyn congratulated
the landlord, an Italian warehouseman by trade, on keeping two of the finest pickles in London. The easy-going
father of Charles Fox made no attempt to control either
his political escapades, which culminated in his dismissal
from the Treasury Board, "for great flippancies in the
House towards Lord North," as Horace Walpole put it,
or his gambling at Newmarket and his cards at Almack's
and Brooks's. But in the year of his death Lord Holland
saved his favourite son from ruin. The crash was

hastened by the birth of a son to Stephen, whereby
another life was interposed between Charles Fox and the
parental wealth. His jest that the boy was born, like a
second Messiah, for the destruction of the Jews, fell wide
of the mark. They came within a little of destroying
him, and Lord Holland had to provide no less than
£140,000 to save him from bankruptcy.

Stephen, the second Lord Holland, died within six
months of his father, leaving a widow and two young
children behind him. During his short life he pervaded
politics as an engaging and not too serious figure. In
the House he vied with his brother in audacity ; at
Brooks's he played as desperately. He was stouter
than Charles, but bore the infliction with indifference,
even though at a fancy ball, held in the Pantheon, a
Smithfield butcher took to following him about, feeling
him in the ribs and calculating his weight in stones.
Sometimes he despaired of the Republic, and Lord
Carlisle, a bosom friend of the two brothers, described
him as writing to the papers, and signing himself "A
Stander-by who has his doubts." His marriage with
Lady Mary Fitzpatrick, daughter of the first Earl of
Upper Ossory and sister of Richard Fitzpatrick, does
not seem to have overwhelmed him with a sense of
responsibility. They lived during the Parliamentary
recesses at Winterslow House, near Salisbury, and when
it was destroyed by fire, Lord Carlisle's unfeeling comment was, " If Lady Mary was much alarmed, or if
the birds were really burnt to death, I should be very
sorry. As this is the first misfortune to Stephen that
he did not bring upon himself, all compassionate
thoughts and intentions may be turned from Charles
to him." The catalogue of his library, which was sold

at his death, proves him to have been a discriminating collector of books.

During the minority of the third Lord Holland, Holland House was let, at one time to Lord Rosebery, at another to Mr. Bearcroft. Under such shifting conditions it fell out of repair, and much of Cleyn's decoration was irretrievably ruined. So late as 1804 Fox wrote to his nephew, "Poor Holland House is said to be in a bad way; I have not seen it; but I find there is a terrible outcry against its weakness, so that I fear it cannot stand." The observations of Sir Gilbert Elliot, afterwards Lord Minto, were to the same effect. But the presumption must be that rumour had exaggerated the state of affairs, since Lord Holland appears to have entrusted the restoration of the house several years before that date to George Saunders, a well-known architect of the day. Faulkner, the historian of Kensington, writing in 1820, alludes to a number of alterations which had greatly transformed the interior.

CHAPTER II

LORD HOLLAND'S YOUTH AND EARLY MANHOOD

Lord Holland's boyhood—Eton and the *Microcosm*—Lord Holland and Canning—Christ Church and Cyril Jackson—Travels in France and Switzerland—Germany and the French Revolution—Spain and Italy—Lord Holland's marriage—He takes his seat—The secession of 1797—A maiden speech—Fox's letters on literature—A visit to Paris—The First Consul—More visits to Spain—The "Lives" of Lope de Vega and Guillen de Castro—"A Dream"—Lord Holland as editor—Fox's history—Lord Holland as a memoir writer.

AFTER his brother Stephen's death Fox was an influence, rather than a presence, at Holland House. He acted as one of the guardians of his nephew, Henry Richard, who, born in November, 1773, was brought up chiefly by his maternal uncle, Lord Ossory, a friend of David Hume and a lover of letters and seclusion. From the fire to which Lord Carlisle lightly alluded the child was saved by his mother at the risk of her own life, but four years later she died. Lord Holland inevitably followed in his uncle's footsteps to Eton, and in due course became head of the school. He resided for nearly ten years, a period by no means uncommon before preparatory schools had assumed their present importance in the educational system. It was a period of brilliant boys, rendered remarkable by the literary beginnings of Canning and Hookham Frere in the *Microcosm*, but of undistinguished Masters and Fellows. Lord Holland's early days, like those of Sydney Smith at Winchester, were embittered by the most ruthless fagging. Samuel Rogers relates that he was forced to toast bread with his fingers for another boy's breakfast. A fork was sent him from home, but his fag-master broke it over his head and still compelled him to prepare the toast in the more primitive way. In consequence of this process, continues Rogers, his fingers suffered so much that they always retained a withered appearance.

Fox's correspondence with his " dear young one " is a model for elderly relatives. He discusses scholarship on equal terms, and politics without the smallest assumption of superiority. The letters begin in 1791, by which date Lord Holland had reached Christ Church, Oxford, where Cyril Jackson was Dean, and had become a hard-reading undergraduate with Canning, " Bobus " Smith, and Lord Morpeth, Lord Carlisle's son, as his intimate friends. An Eton "Montem" elicited one of the earliest of Fox's letters to his nephew. Mrs. Armitstead was his mistress, whom he married four years later :

" Mrs. Armitstead and I, and perhaps one or two more, mean to dine at Maidenhead Bridge on Saturday, and to go after dinner on the water to see the boys row up to Surly Hall, and I wish very much you would come and meet us. I know you would like to see whether things go on as well as in your time. Pray, come, and bring Canning with you, if he likes it."

From a subsequent letter it may be gathered that

Canning duly came, and won the hearts of Fox and
Mrs. Armitstead by praising Lord Holland's *jucunditas*.
The Oxford friendship, however, did not continue
beyond undergraduate days ; accident, not inclination,
caused the pair to drift apart. Meeting by chance
years afterwards, they dined together at Holland House,
in 1822, at an important crisis of Canning's life, when,
despairing of making his way in English politics, he
had accepted the Governor-Generalship of India. The
trick of mystification, for which his enemies reproached
him, disappeared before Lord Holland's geniality, and
he confided to his host that Catholic Emancipation
and other great Whig measures, including Parliamentary
Reform, must, in his opinion, be carried before his
return, though only after a struggle, which might
break up both the Whig and Tory Parties ; and
thus the field would be left open to him under advantages such as he had never enjoyed. Should, however,
the settlement of Parliamentary Reform fall upon him,
he would give the Radicals a dose too strong for their
stomachs. These calculations were thrown out by the
death of Lord Castlereagh, which placed the Foreign
Office in Canning's hands, and before even Catholic
Emancipation could be carried he had gone down into
the grave. But the confession, which is recorded in Sir
Denis le Marchant's " Life of Lord Althorp " and in
the " Greville Memoirs," throws an interesting light upon
the designs of a singularly detached politician, who was
more suited, perhaps, to the French system of government by group than to ours of government by party.

After taking his degree in June, 1792, Lord Holland
spent several years abroad, since his guardians wished
to avert his premature entrance into politics. He had

already paid a visit to Paris during the Long Vacation of
the previous year, where he heard the luckless Louis XVI.
profess attachment to the Constitution "in a clear but
tremulous voice and with great appearance of earnestness," and dined frequently with Lafayette, who appeared
to him full of private affection and public virtue, but
" apt to mistake the pedantry of liberty for its substance."
The most important of his boyish recollections, as published after his death by the fourth Lord Holland in the
entertaining volume entitled " Foreign Reminiscences,"
concerned, however, "Égalité" Orleans, whom he described as driven with extreme reluctance into democratic courses by the animosity of the Court, and
"indifferent alike to the pursuits of pleasure or vanity,
ambition or revenge, and solely intent on enjoying ease
and preserving existence." This was the opinion of
Talleyrand, with whom Lord Holland now formed a
life-long friendship, and who introduced him to Fouché,
a man "whose countenance, manner, and conversation
exhibited profligacy and ferocity, energy and restless-
ness." The tour was extended to Switzerland, and at
Lausanne Lord Holland met Lavater, the physiognomist,
whom he charitably and, probably with justice, set down
as the sincere dupe of his own pretended science. He
spent two days with Gibbon, and came away impressed
by the vanity and affectations of the historian, who, devoid
of human feelings, was "more like what he admired
and produced, a large book, than a living member of
society."

The late summer and autumn of the following year
were spent by Lord Holland in Denmark and Prussia,
whence he returned with an abundant crop of Court
anecdotage. But his impressions as to the state of

public opinion with regard to the possibility and propriety of suppressing the French Revolution by foreign
arms were of more permanent value. The military men
regarded the triumph of the Allies as inevitable. But the
people throughout the Protestant countries of the North
clearly wished, though they dared not hope, for success
to Revolutionary France. Before he left Germany he
received a letter from his uncle exultingly comparing the
Duke of Brunswick's retreat from the Ardennes to
Saratoga or Yorktown—parallels for which it is difficult
to forgive Fox. Reading between the lines, indeed, we
cannot fail to perceive that of the two the nephew took
the saner view of the progress of the Revolution ; he
was apprehensive of Jacobin excesses and of the war
being converted into one of aggression on the part of
the French, whereas even the September massacres
barely shook his uncle's optimism.

Court scandal, and very diverting it is, comes upper-
most in the " Foreign Reminiscences " when the traveller
reaches Spain and makes the acquaintance of that astonishing Court, which had as its leading personages the
simple Charles III., his immoral Queen, and her lover,
Manuel Godoy, the Prince of the Peace. The sympathies of the writer are naturally with politicians of the
type of the upright and austere Jovellanos, but they did
not blind him to the considerable abilities of Godoy,
who bore with philosophy the privations of his last
years, when he lived on a small pension from the French
Government. After settling for some time in Florence,
where he formed a poor opinion of our diplomatic
representatives in Italy, Lord Holland returned through
Vienna to England in the spring of 1796. We catch
a glimpse of him in a letter from Sir Morton Eden in

the "Auckland Correspondence" which is reminiscent of his uncle's days as a macaroni. He was dressed in the height of the prevalent fashion, "frocks and round hats, with his hair cropped as if round a bowl dish." He had, meantime, fulfilled his destiny as a Fox by eloping with Lady Webster, born Vassall, a great Jamaica heiress, and in July, 1797, her husband having obtained a decree for a separation, the pair were married at Isleworth. Their eldest son, Charles, afterwards well-known in society as General Fox, and to archæology as a collector of coins, was born out of wedlock.

The fortunes of the Whigs wore a dismal aspect when Lord Holland took his seat in the House of Lords. In the Commons, Fox, with some fifty followers, was still forcing division after division on the conduct of the war and the subsidising of the German Powers against Revolutionary France. But the secession of the Duke of Portland, Lord Fitzwilliam, and the other Whig magnates, had exercised a disastrous effect on the party in the Upper House. It was reduced to a mere handful of five or six. Lord Holland brought to the discomfited band the enthusiasm of youth, a strong belief in Whig principles, and considerable debating powers. As might be expected, he never overcame the disadvantage of entering upon public life in an assembly which had reduced discussion to a formality and which was decorously oppressive in its atmosphere. Brougham and Macaulay agree that in statement he suffered from hesitations due to a rush of ideas and, as Fox warned him, to an over-fastidiousness in the formation of his sentences. His voice, too, like his uncle's, was devoid of charm. But he shone in reply, for then he could expose the unsound points in an opponent's argument, and

illustrate their weakness from the resources of a cultivated mind. His contemporaries were of opinion that
none of his oratorical achievements gave a just measure
of his powers, and that, given the requisite stimulus, he
might at any moment have electrified the house by a
performance worthy of Charles Fox.

The first meeting of the party chiefs attended by Lord
Holland resolved upon the famous secession of 1797.
The plan was chiefly encouraged by Grey, always impulsive and querulous ; the Duke of Bedford and Erskine
regarded it as a feasible experiment. Fox, with his
thoughts centred in his home at St. Anne's Hill, longed
for it on personal grounds, but doubted its wisdom.
" He acquiesced in the idea," says Lord Holland in his
" Memoirs of the Whig Party," "more from indolence
than from judgment." The practical minds of Sheridan
and Tierney refused to be bound by an agreement which
Lord Lansdowne (formerly Lord Shelburne) censured
in a phrase of luminous felicity : " Is your uncle aware
of what he is doing ? Secession means rebellion, or it
is nonsense." The wisdom of the remark became manifest before many weeks had passed by. For the moment
Pitt was disconcerted by the absence of effective criticism, and by taunting the absent and extolling the
present, tried to win the wanderers back. But he soon
perceived the advantage of a free field for his measures,
which embraced an enormous increase of assessed taxation, and, by and by, the Act of Union with Ireland.
Fox warned his friends from the first that if he once
took leave of the House it would be no easy matter to
bring him back. He was as good as his word, since he
only spoke nineteen times between the secession of 1797
and his assumption of office in 1806. But the debates

on the Assessed Taxes Bill lured most of the other Whig malingerers back to the Commons, and drew from Lord Holland his maiden speech in Parliament. It was, he modestly wrote in his " Memoirs of the Whig Party "—

"hurried and confused ; my delivery at times rapid and unintelligible, at others hesitating and ungraceful. Yet I was told that parts of it, and yet more my reply, held out great promise of improvement ; and some of the older peers, though little disposed to encourage one of my principles and connections, flattered me by saying that my manner reminded them of my grandfather."

Posterity has little reason to quarrel with Fox for a retirement dictated, not by affectation, but by a sincere preference for lettered ease. Lord Holland has described how he came up to Holland House when the debate on the rejection of the peace overtures was imminent, how he stipulated for remaining only two nights, and how, when he heard that the debate was postponed in conse-sequence of Pitt's illness, he sat " silent and overcome, as if the intelligence of some great calamity had befallen him. I saw tears steal down his cheeks, so vexed was he at being detained from his garden, his books, and his cheerful life in the country." Yet his speech, when it came, was, in his own words, " his best." From St. Anne's Hill Fox poured out his thoughts on literature in unstudied letters to his nephew. He preferred the classics to the moderns, and our early writers to their successors, though he implicitly yielded incontestable superiority to Shakespeare. Philosophy did not attract him, and he valued history solely as a record of the actions of great men ; but all poetry, except that of

Germany, appealed to him. Thus, after extolling the
" Iliad," he writes :

" There are parts of Virgil (and among those, too, imitated
from Homer) which I think fully equal to Homer, but then
he has not in any degree approaching to his master that
freedom of manner which I prize so much ; and Milton, who
has some passages as sublime as possible, is in this respect
most deficient—or, rather, he has no degree of it whatever.
Ariosto has more of it than any other poet, even so as to vie
in this particular merit with Homer himself, and possibly
it may be that my excessive delight in him is owing to my
holding in higher estimation than others do the merit of
freedom and rapidity."

We find, rather to our surprise, that Fox was unac-
quainted with Boccaccio's " Griselda," but he was fully
aware of Chaucer's indebtedness to the "Decameron,"
though holding that he had improved on the original.
" What a genius Chaucer was ! " he adds in a postscript.
The following is a suggestive passage, dealing with some
of Chaucer's successors :

" I cannot help thinking that Dryden has not the exact
sort of playfulness, or levity, or familiarity of manner, or
easy grace which I mean, and which it is very difficult
rightly to define. Prior has more of it than Dryden, La
Fontaine more than Prior, and Ariosto and Ovid as much as
possible, which in them is the more remarkable, as I do not
think it often belongs to any great genius."

Fox's criticisms, it must be confessed, are generally
ab extrâ, and he but rarely attempts to put his authors
in relation to their time. Still, he was an inspiring pre-
ceptor, and to his influence was principally due the zeal
of Holland House for letters and erudition.

The resignation of Pitt, in 1801, failed at first to drag
Fox from his seclusion; he was much more interested in
Dryden than in Mr. Addington, whom he accepted on
the principle *quia impossibile.* But he spoke on the
preliminaries of peace, and after the Treaty of Amiens
had been signed, paid a short visit to Paris with Lord St.
John, Mrs. Fox, and his secretary, Mr. Trotter. Of his
conversation with the First Consul we have the record
preserved by the last enthusiastic gentleman. Napoleon
paid a florid compliment to the great statesman who
recommended peace because there was no just object
of war, who saw Europe desolated to no purpose, and
who struggled for its relief. Fox, who hated laudatory
addresses, said little or nothing by way of reply. The
party were joined by Lord and Lady Holland, Adair and
General Fitzpatrick, and the uncle and nephew dined
and spent the evening at the First Consul's Court.
From his conversation, Fox, always according to the
faithful Trotter, derived the impression that he was a
young man who was a good deal intoxicated by his
success and surprising elevation, and that he was sincere
as to the maintenance of peace. Lord Holland's recollections reproduce rather his appearance, voice, and
manner, and, appreciative though they are, virtually
confirm Talleyrand's opinion that Napoleon was *très
mal élevé.*

"The former [his countenance], though composed of
regular features, and both penetrating and good-humoured,
was neither so dignified nor so animated as I had expected ;
but the latter [his voice] was sweet, spirited, and persuasive
in the highest degree, and gave a favourable impression of his
disposition as well as his understanding. His manner was
neither affected nor assuming, but certainly wanted that ease

and attraction which the earliest habits of good company are supposed exclusively to confer."

Lady Holland appears to have previously conceived an admiration for Napoleon's genius, but it was thenceforth that Holland House developed the full measure of its sentimental devotion to the Emperor.

The Hollands remained abroad until the spring of 1805, spending much of their time in Spain and Portugal. She much preferred continental modes of living, while the Whig peer may have felt that attendance in the House of Lords was a profitless occupation. Lord Holland missed, therefore, the retirement of Addington, when the renewal of the war had thoroughly advertised his incapacity; the fruitless, though by no means the first, efforts to effect a junction between his uncle and Pitt, and the formation by the latter of a narrow Administration when the circumstances of the time clamoured for a strong Government. To this second visit, which was supplemented by a third in 1808, with the youthful Lord John Russell as one of the party—a tour much interrupted by the progress of the French arms—we owe more vivacious sketches of prominent Spaniards, the best remembered of whom, General Alava, became the intimate friend and guest of the Duke of Wellington. After he had escaped to England from the resentment of Ferdinand VII., the accomplished soldier was a great favourite with London society, though not with the Court. Lord Holland severely but justly remarks that "George IV., who wore his crown in virtue of the exclusion of the Stuarts, affected not to forgive a Spaniard for concurring, in a moment of national danger, in the temporary dethronement of a king more unwarlike than James I., more perfidious than either Charles, and more arbitrary and cruel than James II."

Besides making the acquaintance of individuals, Lord Holland collected many valuable manuscripts and printed works, some of which formed materials for his Lives of Lope de Vega and Guillen de Castro. The first was published anonymously in 1806, and reappeared with its companion, under its author's name, eleven years later. Taken in conjunction with his " Foreign Reminiscences," " Memoirs of the Whig Party," and " Further Memoirs," they fairly justify the praise lavished by Brougham on his prose. He certainly wielded an easy pen, whereas Charles Fox, oppressed by his models, composed his frigid " History of James II." " drop by drop," as Sydney Smith put it. The erudition is hardly equal to modern requirements, since Lord Holland candidly confesses that of Lope de Vega's five hundred extant comedies he had read but fifty. He places the famous dramatist, however, in instructive relation with his predecessors and contemporaries, notably with Cervantes, and shows how his strength lay not in the epics and novels by which he set store, but in the plays he affected to despise. Lope, he holds, resembled Shakespeare in his plots, but was inferior in all other respects : "a rapid succession of events and sudden changes in the situation of the personages are the charms by which he interests us so forcibly." The account of the writings of Guillen de Castro, and of the indebtedness of Corneille to him for " The Cid," is an even more satisfactory piece of criticism. It amounts to this, that the Frenchman greatly improved upon his original in point of literary judgment, but that in a passage or two the Spaniard must be accounted superior.

Lord Holland's other contributions to literature are not of much moment, with the exception of his "Memoirs." They include some graceful translations of Calderon and Ariosto, and various pamphlets bearing on politics, of which his "Letter to the Rev. Dr. Shuttleworth," on the Roman Catholic question, appearing in the critical year 1827, promptly ran into three editions. As an exercise of fancy, he addressed "A Dream"—an imaginary conversation between George III., Sir Thomas More, Bacon, Sir William Temple, and other illustrious dead, on education—to Rogers in the form of a letter. It cannot be said that much pains is taken in the trifle to preserve character; Addison talks much as Cowley, and Cowley as Berkeley. But the "Dream" contains several curious anticipations of modern educational developments, the Rhodes scholarships among them, thus:

" He (Sir William Temple) talked of three great universities, with respective dependencies of schools, military and naval academies, museums, libraries, galleries, gardens, laboratories, and observatories, to be established in three distinct quarters of the globe within the jurisdiction of the Crown of Great Britain. One was to be in Canada or the West Indies, another at Fort William in the East, and the third at Malta, Gibraltar, or some possession in the Mediterranean. They were to be connected with one another, as well as with the establishments of Marlow and Hertford; the colleges of Eton, Westminster, Winchester, and Maynooth; and the Universities of Dublin, Edinburgh, Oxford, and Cambridge."

The "establishment at Marlow" was the Royal Military College, subsequently removed to Sandhurst; that at Hertford evidently stands for the East India College, really situated at Haileybury, several miles away. The disputationists in the "Dream" finally decide on a

university at Malta, where modern Greeks could produce
new Aristotles and Platos, and Moors perfect themselves
in Arabic. Beneath this play of fancy we seem to
perceive those cosmopolitan sentiments which were
popularised by the French Revolution.

As an editor, Lord Holland gave to the world Lord
Waldegrave's " Memoirs," dealing chiefly with the confused period when Henry Fox, the Duke of Newcastle,
and the elder Pitt were struggling for the mastery, and
Horace Walpole's "Reign of George II.," which he
equipped with a workmanlike preface, setting forth its
authenticity and the obvious intention of its writer that it
should be published, and pointing out the unwarranted
bitterness of Walpole's strictures on individuals. Dr.
Smiles, in the entertaining volume " A Publisher and
his Friends," implies that Lord Holland drove rather a
hard bargain with Murray, the publisher. Byron was
of much the same opinion :

> " For Orford and for Waldegrave
>   You gave much more than me you gave,
>   Which is not fairly to behave,
>   My Murray ! "

But, even if the books did not prove profitable as speculations, they made valuable additions to the materials
for eighteenth-century history. The most interesting,
because the most personal, of Lord Holland's prefaces,
however, is that to Charles James Fox's " History of the
Early Part of the Reign of James II." In it he explains
how his uncle wavered between various projects, a
treatise on poetry, history, and oratory among them,
before he concentrated himself on the period before

the Revolution; how he spent much of his Paris
holiday in the Foreign Office with Lord St. John,
Adair and Mr. Trotter, examining and transcribing
Barillon's despatches, and how he wrote with painful
slowness, excluding every word for which he could not
find authority in Dryden, and studiously avoiding all
rhetorical effects. Lord Holland may be forgiven for
failing to point out that so laboured a performance
must necessarily be unsatisfactory. Few literary con-
trasts are more complete, indeed, than that between
the bald account of the execution of the Duke of
Monmouth, with which Fox's fragment closes, and the
treatment of that poignantly tragic episode by Macaulay.

Lord Holland's literary reputation ultimately depends
on his " Foreign Reminiscences," " Memoirs of the
Whig Party during my Time," and " Further Memoirs."
The first and second of these works appeared under
the editorship of his son, the fourth and last Lord
Holland; the third has recently been given to
the world by the present Earl of Ilchester. Written
with easy correctness, and with a constant sense of
humour, they supply a fund of information, political
and literary, from the beginning of the French Revolution down to the death of Queen Caroline. Lord
Holland can tell a story with point, nor does he mind
if its point is a trifle broad. The " Foreign Reminiscences " deal mainly, indeed, with the follies of Courts,
varied by admirable portraits of Talleyrand, Calonne,
and some of their contemporaries, and concluding
with facts about Napoleon assiduously collected and
stored in a retentive memory. The " Memoirs " and
" Further Memoirs " are open to the criticism that they
are concerned almost entirely with political intrigue,

and pay but little attention to popular movements. Lord Holland appears to have taken Horace Walpole for his model, and for him, of course, the people did not exist. Besides, in the days before the Act of Reform, the fate of parties hung to a considerable extent upon misunderstandings between the King and his ministers, or the undermining of responsible advisers by henchmen from Carlton House. Lord Holland cannot be blamed, therefore, for concerning himself with the accidents of politics, and it is a charm rather than a defect in his manner that a discursive, story-telling style develops those accidents at times beyond their proper proportions. Given an impressive incident, such as the death of Fox, he rises to genuine eloquence. The " Memoirs " are valuable, besides, as reflecting, though with a mitigating toleration, the passions and prejudices of the aristocratic Whigs. In them appears a curious leaning towards Republican principles, which, we may be sure, would never have been translated into practice, and a tendency to depreciate the actions of politicians like the Duke of Wellington who had the bad taste to be Tories. It must be added that Lord Holland's amiability sometimes appears to lack depth, and that an unexpected coldness pervades his characters of close political associates like Windham or intimate friends like Hookham Frere.

CHAPTER III

LORD HOLLAND AS A STATESMAN

The Talents Administration—Lord Holland becomes Privy Seal
—Fall of the Government—The Whigs in opposition—Speculations
on office—Lord Holland's " protests"—Treason penalties—Abolitionism—A visit to Naples—Napoleon's captivity—Arguments *con*
and *pro*—Lady Holland and Napoleon—An historic snuff-box.

LORD HOLLAND returned from Spain in time to
witness the junction of the Old Opposition, led by
Fox, and the New, under the conduct of Lord
Grenville, against Pitt's Government. The presentation
of petitions from the Roman Catholics, which they
selected as the point of their attack, resulted in animated
debates but disappointing divisions. He took part in
the discussion in the Lords, and discovered that want of
practice had not impaired his speaking as much as he
had apprehended. But the " Memoirs" naturally dwell
rather upon the two disasters—the exposure of Dundas's
irregularities as Treasurer of the Navy, and the defeat
of the Allies at Austerlitz—which dragged Pitt down to
the grave. A lively account is given of the formation of
the Ministry of All the Talents under Lord Grenville and
Fox ; the unfortunate admission of Lord Sidmouth and
his friends, with the additional anomaly of the Chief
Justice, Lord Ellenborough, as a member of the Cabinet,

because Fox thought that "it would stop all the earths,"
and the attempt to conciliate Carlton House by the
bestowal of the management of Scotland on Lord Moira.
Lord Holland's own preference was for diplomatic employment, but none happened to be vacant. He was
thus destined to witness Fox's gradual disillusionment as
to the sincerity of the French offers of peace, and the
rapid approach of his last illness. The uncle hoped that
the nephew would succeed him at the Foreign Office.
"But don't think me selfish, young one. The Slave
Trade and Peace are two such glorious things, I can't
give them up, even for you." That remark was made in
a sanguine mood; with clearer insight Fox confessed
that "it is not so much the value of the point in dispute"
—the future of Sicily—"as the manner in which the
French fly from their word that disheartens me." The
negotiations were virtually at an end as relations and
friends gathered round the bedside of the expiring
statesman, and Miss Fox, Lord Holland, and General
Fitzpatrick solaced his last hours by reading aloud to
him Virgil, Dryden, and Crabbe.

The death of Fox led to a Ministerial reconstruction,
in the course of which Lord Holland entered the
Cabinet as Privy Seal. But the Government only survived the removal of its most powerful member some
eight months. The King hated an Administration in
which the Whigs formed the predominant element; the
Prince, fancying himself neglected, developed Carlton
House politics upon tortuous lines of his own devising.
The people were alienated by the manifest incapacity of
the Government to carry on war, as displayed in the
frivolous expeditions to Buenos Ayres, Alexandria and
the Dardanelles. Even the Abolition of the Slave Trade,

highly though it must have gratified the Saints, failed to touch the imagination of the masses, who preferred the Radicalism of Sir Francis Burdett. It only needed the revival of the Catholic claims in a limited form to give the King the opening for which he was watching with narrow intentness, and he forced Ministers to resign by the unconstitutional demand that they should never press on him in future any measure connected with the question.

The Whigs, with the exception of those few who took office under Canning, were doomed to remain in opposition until 1830. Their greatest disaster was undoubtedly Grey's elevation to the House of Lords on the death of his father in the autumn of 1807. Thomas Creevey's opinions of "Snoutch" (Mr. Ponsonby) and " Old Cole" (Mr. Tierney), who successively undertook the thankless office of leading the Opposition in the Commons, were those of undisguised contempt ; give him, frank partisan as he was, the more robust faction of Whitbread. But a candid consideration of the efforts of the Whigs to return to power, from the proposal of an enlarged Administration in 1809 to the futile negotiations of Lord Moira in 1812, makes it clear that the tactlessness of their leaders in the Upper House, Grey and Grenville, protracted the misfortunes of the party rather than slackness in the Commons. They lectured the Prince Regent ; they ignored Sheridan, though his goodwill would have helped them much ; they raised needless difficulties ; they obtruded their principles.

Creevey furnished the low comedy of a succession of scenes in which the Regent was by far the most accomplished actor when he looked down the area of a Tory Prime Minister and watched the preparation of a dinner

by four men cooks and twice as many maids, at which
the perfidious "Prinny" was to be present. His *cri de
cœur*, "By God, this is too much!" was genuine, we
may be sure, since the Opposition, in the sanguine way
that Oppositions have, had already distributed office in
anticipation. Creevey was to have found a place at the
Admiralty Board with Lord Holland as First Lord.
Earlier in the Session, Speaker Abbot, afterwards Lord
Colchester, had predicted for Lord Holland an even more
important position; the premiership, he thought, lay
between him and Lord Fitzwilliam. This curious speculation implied, of course, the passing over of Earl Grey,
who was presumably expected to take the Foreign Office,
and the formation of a Government on a purely Whig
basis, to the exclusion of the Grenvilles.

The earlier part of the Regency must be pronounced
a singularly unattractive period of parliamentary history.
The Liverpool Administration, when deprived of the
services of Canning through his quarrel with Castlereagh,
possessed but little merit beyond a steadfast determination to continue the war in the Peninsula. Its finance
was inefficiently conducted by Vansittart, and it was
quite incapable of grappling with agricultural depression
or working-class discontent. The Opposition were in
no better plight; in a letter to Brougham written about
this time Lord Holland admitted that they were hopelessly divided. The Grey-Grenville *fiascos* had left
bitter memories behind them. Lady Holland requested
Creevey to spare the Government with his jokes, and to
begin on "those Grenvilles." Those were petticoat
politics. Her husband was much occupied during those
barren but momentous years in making his chiefs keep
step, and, out of doors, in inducing the Dissenters to

support the movement for Catholic Emancipation. The lot of political peacemakers is seldom blessed ; none the less, public life cannot afford to dispense with healers of differences like Lord Holland, Lord Duncannon, and the late Lord Granville.

Lord Holland's constancy to Liberal opinions was the more creditable, because that school of thought had fallen into general discredit. "It is certain," wrote Brougham in his "Statesmen of the Time of George III.," "that whensoever any occasion arose of peril to the great cause of toleration, the alarmed eye instinctively turned first of all to him as the refuge of the persecuted." The eulogy may appear at first sight overstrained, but a study of Holland's protests in the House of Lords, as collected and edited after his death by a barrister named Moylan, proves its substantial correctness. "The Opinions of Lord Holland," as the little volume is called, forms a text-book of Whig domestic policy. In drawing up his protests he took considerable pains, since Fox had taught him to regard them as excellent practice for seizing the point of an argument. They become genuinely eloquent when they touch upon the existence of oppression sanctioned by law. Thus the practice of imprisonment for debt was denounced by him on several grounds, notably because, the punishment being inflicted at the pleasure of the creditor, it sinned against the principle that "no man shall himself judge the extent of the injury he has received, or shall himself measure the degree of punishment to be inflicted on the offender." Romilly's Bill for removing the theft of goods from a shop, warehouse, coachhouse, or stable from the category of capital offences having been rejected in the Lords on the second reading, Lord Holland entered a pertinent protest : to assign the same punishment for heinous crimes and slight offences, he observed, "tends to confound the notions of right and wrong, to diminish the horrors atrocious guilt ought always to inspire, and to weaken the reverence in which it is desirable that the laws of the country should be held."

On his own account Lord Holland brought in several years afterwards, that is, in 1825, a Bill to take away corruption of blood from the penalties of treason. It was opposed by Lord Eldon, who had previously helped him to carry a Bill requiring the evidence of two witnesses to an overt act, and rejected by a majority of three. Yet a humaner age will cordially concur with Lord Holland's sententious observation that—

" The unjust and inhuman device of punishing the innocent heirs of a traitor for the treason of their relation or ancestor has, in all seasons of civil commotion, been found insufficient to deter men of strong passions, however elevated their fortune or their rank, from engaging in treasonable designs, and has an obvious tendency to shake the stability of property, to perpetuate the remembrance of political feuds, and to aggravate in individuals and families, in parties and sects, the turbulent vices of rapacity and revenge."

As Brougham appropriately noted, the West Indian interests of Holland House never prevented its master from being a strenuous advocate of the abolition both of the slave-trade and slavery. He earnestly supported Lord Grenville's motion for papers with the view of censuring Ministers for not having secured the cessation of the traffic by the Treaty of Peace with France of 1813. His zeal in the good cause delighted Wilberforce, to whom he wrote, while on a visit to Paris in 1814, that he was trying to make converts. Abolitionism was unpopular, however, with the French Royalists because it had been advocated by the Jacobins. "They make no difference," observed Lord Holland, " between you and me, or me and Tom Paine."

The Hollands extended this tour to Naples in company with Rogers, and they were joined by Dr. Holland, the physician and traveller. In a long letter to Francis Horner, the young hope of the Whig party, Lord Holland passed a penetrating judgment on the Court and people. He wrote on March 1, 1815, just four days before Murat, on hearing of Napoleon's escape from Elba, decided, to his own undoing, on throwing in his lot with his brother-in-law. Lord Holland perceived that King Joachim cherished ambitious designs ; he had too much of the spirit of a military chief *pour de pas dire un aventurier*. But he considered that England ought to support him rather than countenance a Bourbon restoration. Despite his good government, conscription and the heavy taxation rendered Murat's throne, in Lord Holland's opinion, none too stable. In person the King was " a fine, good-humoured soldier, too theatrical in his dress and mode of playing royalty, but even in his deficiencies calculated to put those with whom he converses completely at their ease." He was most friendly with the English, and lost, with great good humour, nine games of chess out of fourteen to Lord Granville Somerset, and two out of three to Lord Holland himself. The Queen is described as "pretty, though in bad health ; her manners are very agreeable and gentle, and she is said to possess her full share of the abilities and decision of character for which her family are remarkable." Rogers, in his " Table-Talk," furnishes a

characteristic incident. Lady Holland declined to go to
the Royal parties, until Murat gave a concert expressly in
her honour, when she had the gratification of sitting
between the King and Queen and putting to them what
questions she pleased. To the poet Murat used to be
most civil. "*Hé bien, monsieur*," he used to call out,
rising in his stirrups, "*êtes-vous inspiré aujourd'hui ?*"

Lord Holland's devotion to those humanitarian
principles which were the Whigs' chief virtue during
the long years of Opposition need not be laboured
further. He shared, however, that party's tendency to
Quixotic or obstructive views on the foreign relations
of the country. When Napoleon was finally consigned
to St. Helena, Lord Holland, with the solitary support
of the Duke of Sussex, recorded this protest against the
Bill introduced by the Colonial Secretary, Lord Bathurst,
"for the more effectual detaining of Buonaparte in
custody."

"To consign to distant exile and imprisonment a foreign
and captive Chief, who, after the abdication of his authority,
relying on British generosity, had surrendered himself to us,
in preference to his other enemies, is unworthy the magna-
nimity of a great country ; and the treaties by which, after his
captivity, we bound ourselves to detain him in custody at the
will of the Sovereigns to whom he had never surrendered
himself, appear to me repugnant to the principles of equity,
and utterly uncalled for by expediency or necessity."

To this pronouncement a later generation of Whigs
declined to subscribe. "We would not have signed it,"
wrote Macaulay in the *Edinburgh Review*, and Lord John
Russell took exception to it in his " Reminiscences."
The sentiment is honourable enough, but it inclines to

sentimentalism. Be it admitted that the consignment
of Napoleon to captivity might have been accomplished by any other Power with better grace than by
ourselves. But did any conceivable alternative exist ?
In reply to Lord Holland's private remonstrances,
Lord Liverpool defended himself by the extreme
difficulty of knowing how to deal with such a
prisoner.

The case was argued out at the time between Francis
Horner and Hallam, the former of them evidently
reflecting the sentiments of Holland House. "We
have been wanting in generosity," is the sum of his
argument. Hallam replied that in the unsettled state
of Europe Napoleon could not be left at liberty without a prodigious risk of exciting fresh disturbances.
He continued :

"I once wished that Buonaparte should have found a
tranquil asylum in this island ; but, when I see the foolish
admiration which many persons entertain for that man, and
the still more foolish association of his name with the love
of liberty, I cannot desire to see his Court, as it were,
frequented by all the discontented, as well as all the idle
and curious. Nor do I think it would be easy to obtain an
adequate security against his escape from the country,
except by measures almost as severe as those adopted at
St. Helena, of which I should be sorry to see a precedent
established in Britain. The condition of Ireland affords
another argument against allowing him to reside in this
country."

Hallam exhausts the common sense of the matter,
apart from the important question raised in another
of Lord Holland's protests, the restoration of the
Bourbons, "against the principles," as he put it in

the true Whig spirit, " on which the Revolution of
1688 and the succession of the House of Hanover
were founded." Here, again, the absence of an alternative stands out as an insuperable difficulty ; " everything else," said Talleyrand, " is an intrigue." To
permit Napoleon to return under restrictions, even
to place his son, the King of Rome, on the throne
with Marie Louise as Regent, would have been the
riskiest of expedients. Europe panted for peace, and
for peace a Bourbon restoration was the only
substantial guarantee, although in the event neither
Louis XVIII. nor Charles X. proved the most competent of sovereigns.

The admiration of Holland House for the fallen
Emperor came from a feminine rather than a masculine source. Lord Holland's analysis of Napoleon's
character in the " Foreign Reminiscences" does not
overstep the bounds of discrimination ; he extols the
vast administrative talents, but admits the lawlessness
of such crimes as the execution of the Duc d'Enghien.
Lady Holland set no limits to her hero-worship. In
July, 1815, just after Napoleon's fate had been decided,
Lady Granville found her at Holland House seated on
the grass with a plate of *baba*, " very cross and absurd
about Buonaparte, 'poor dear man,' as she calls him."
Still, her attentions assumed a harmless form, however
liable they may have been to misconstruction by contemporary gossip. During his captivity on Elba she
supplied him with newspapers under the sanction of
his gaolers ; after he had reached St. Helena she
forwarded books and delicacies to him at short intervals through the Colonial Office. The " pruneaux de
Madame Holland " were nearly the last article of food

he ever asked for. She is not to be blamed because Napoleon founded illusory hopes on her kindness, deluding himself with the idea that Lord Holland might become Prime Minister, and that then his own liberation would follow. Her correspondence with Sir Hudson Lowe shows that she took care to prevent anything of a dubious nature slipping into the packages addressed to the illustrious captive. The gifts must have gone some way towards mitigating the severity of an imprisonment which was the more deplorable because it was dictated, not by deliberate ill-will, but by conscientious pedantry. The presumption must be that Napoleon would have submitted with no good grace to restrictions, however lightly maintained. But the evidence collected by Lord Rosebery in " The Last Phase " proves conclusively that Sir Hudson Lowe behaved throughout as a suspicious martinet, and degraded his guardianship into an unworthy espionage. Lord Holland drew attention to his rigour in the House of Lords, and by private representations to the Colonial Secretary, Lord Bathurst, endeavoured to secure sufficient attendance for the captive, but in vain.

When Napoleon died the gratitude of those who still clung to his cause found expression in an anonymous note in pencil left on Lady Holland, who was in Paris, apprising her of the fact several hours before it was generally known. From St. Helena there arrived a snuff-box, in which was a piece of paper with the words, " L'Empereur Napoléon à Lady Holland, témoignage de satisfaction et d'estime." It had originally been presented to him by Pope Pius VI. at Tolentino in February, 1797, and she left it in turn

NAPOLEON'S SNUFF-BOX

JOHN ALLEN, M.D.

FROM THE PAINTING BY SIR EDWIN LANDSEER, R.A., IN THE NATIONAL PORTRAIT GALLERY

to the British Museum. The box was delivered in
great form at Holland House by Counts Bertrand
and Montholon, who had arrayed themselves in the
Imperial uniform. Lord Holland censured the display as an unworthy manner of honouring a great
man's memory, and the present they bore appears to
have created some dissension among his friends. Tom
Moore approved, and turned some easy verses in honour
of the occasion.   Upon Lord Carlisle it acted as a poetic
irritant.

"Lady, reject the gift, 'tis tinged with gore,"

he exclaimed, and much besides.   The effusion appeared
in the *Times,* and Byron in exile, mindful of old sores,
jotted down for the benefit of the receptive Medwin
the parody :

> " Lady, accept the box the hero wore
> In spite of all this elegiac stuff :
> Let not seven stanzas written by a bore
> Prevent your ladyship from taking snuff."

Lord Holland's comment was :

> " For this her snuff-box to resign,
> A pleasant thought enough ;
> Alas ! my lord, for verse like thine
> Who'd give a pinch of snuff ? "

CHAPTER IV

UNDER GEORGE IV. AND WILLIAM IV.

Queen Caroline—An unflattering portrait—Creevey on the situa-
tion—Holland House and the Queen—Collapse of the Liverpool
Ministry—Canning's Administration—A possible Foreign Secretary
—Navarino and its consequences—Chancellor of the Duchy—Lord
Holland and Reform—A Whig Nestor—Peel's "Hundred Days"—
The second Melbourne Ministry—The Syrian crisis—Lord Holland's
death—His political character—Whiggism and Holland House.

TO the captivity of Napoleon there succeeded, in
1820, as the popular topic of the day, the case of
Queen Caroline, and it placed the leaders of the
Whig party in a position of much difficulty. Though the
Regent, who had become George IV., had entirely transferred his confidence to the Tories, he still kept up social
relations with the Opposition, and frequently came to
dinners and receptions at Holland House and elsewhere.
Besides, they had been intimately concerned with the
" delicate investigation " held during the Talents Ministry,
which, while stopping short of finding the Princess of
Wales, as she then was, a guilty woman, recommended
that the Lord Chancellor should advise her to be more
circumspect in her behaviour. Lord Holland records, with
a shrug of amusement, in his " Memoirs of the Whig
Party," that in those days persons of rank plumed them-

selves on declining to meet the Prince at Holland House,
observing that he was no fit company for a gentleman.
His own sympathies, however, seem to have been rather
with the husband than the wife, of whom he set down a
character more faithful than flattering :

"She was, at best, a strange woman, and a very sorry and
uninteresting heroine. She had, they say, some talent, some
pleasantry, some good-humour, and great spirit and courage.
But she was utterly destitute of all female delicacy, and
exhibited in the whole course of the transactions relating to
herself very little feeling for anybody, and very little regard
for honour or truth, or even for the interests of those who
were devoted to her, whether the people in the aggregate or
the individuals who enthusiastically espoused her cause. She
avowed her dislike of many ; she scarcely concealed her
contempt for all. In short, to speak plainly, if not mad, she
was a very worthless woman."

Those who have studied the inner history of her case,
notably as it stands revealed in Sir J. Arnould's " Life of
Lord Denman," will be slow to quarrel with this estimate,
severe though it is.

Holland House had reasons for holding aloof from
the Queen's cause which were quite unintelligible to a
pronounced partisan like Creevey. They feared for the
State, whereas the "Mountain," or extreme Whigs,
cared little what became of the Crown, provided that
the Government were in the net result discredited.
Creevey looked on the trial exactly as if it had been a
rat-hunt with "Bruffam" as the most pertinacious
terrier. The Whig leaders tried to take away the vin-
dictive appearance of the proceedings by dividing against
Lord Liverpool's Bill for depriving the Queen of her

Royal titles and privileges and dissolving the marriage, while Lord Holland protested, on his own account, against the Ministerial plan of proceeding by way of committee and supported a regular legal procedure. Such moderation was far from suiting Creevey ; " as for the wretched dirt and meanness of Holland House," he wrote with his accustomed candour, " it makes me perfectly sick." He even carried his displeasure to the length of leaving Lady Holland's invitations unanswered, though he soon condescended to be flattered into a good temper. But then Creevey can pair off with Croker, on the Tory side, as political faction incarnate. When the interests at stake are considered, the responsible Whigs must be admitted to have extricated themselves with skill from the dilemma of abetting the King's vengeance, on the one hand, and lending fuel to popular passions on the other. If some of them made a mistake, it was in calling on Queen Caroline when the tide began to turn and the Government were evidently being driven to abandon their Bill.

Holland House took no part, however, in these eleventh-hour conversions. Lady Granville describes Lady Holland as " tapping her largest, most Italian fan with energy on the outside of the box " when the King at last ventured to appear at the play. Lord Holland illustrated the trial by various epigrams and puns which he tossed across the table to Lord Eldon, and these he seems to have repeated at home. One given by Lady Granville is of early eighteenth-century flavour. He also told an excellent story. The man employed in looking after the Italian witnesses, who was a bit of a dandy, happened to settle his cravat by running his fingers between it and his throat. The gesture, they thought, could have but one meaning.   Whereupon "they set up a horrid yell and plumped on their knees, crying "Misericordia."

Queen Caroline dead was speedily forgotten, as Lord Eldon predicted she would be, and thanks to the brilliant foreign policy of Canning and the wise administration of Robinson, afterwards Lord Goderich, at the Exchequer, and of Huskisson at the Board of Trade, the Government soon recovered strength.   In a familiar passage, Disraeli satirised the Liverpool Cabinet as one of mediocrities with an arch-mediocrity at its head, but the first part of the statement cannot be correctly applied to its later period.   On the contrary, by means of the convenient device of making Catholic Emancipation an "open question" Lord Liverpool enlisted the best talents of the Tory party in a Ministry of compromise.   The Prime Minister may not have been exactly a genius, but he was, as Twiss well calls him, the keystone of the arch, and kept the concern together.   When he was struck down by paralysis in February, 1827, no one was found capable of supplying his place.   Canning undertook the task, and all the Ministers who had resisted the Catholic claims promptly resigned.   He then attempted a coalition with the Whigs, but though Lord Lansdowne and Lord Carlisle entered the Cabinet, and Tierney became Judge-Advocate-General and William Lamb Irish Secretary, the magnates held icily aloof.   His Ministry, in fact, as the "Croker Papers" show, was formed rather on the principle of freeing the Crown from the rival aristocracies than on that of Catholic Emancipation. *Pourparlers* were apparently instituted with Holland House.   "What shall we do," was Canning's humorous comment, "with Lady Holland in the Cabinet?"   A corresponding distrust is to be discovered in the lady's shrewd summary of the situation in a letter to Lord John Russell.

"This confounded division of the country into Protestant and Catholic," she wrote, "makes the King as powerful as ever Henry VIII. was. He is at present as anti-Catholic as his father, and has assured the Archbishop that they may depend upon him as a Defender of the Church. The other sentiment that influences him is resentment against the seceders. . . Canning flatters this passion by obsequiousness to his will ; and, as I understand the matter, will dare to do nothing until time and his own dexterity overcome the scruples of H.M.'s conscience. This is a pretty state of things for Whigs to support, and nothing but fear of the seceders coming back to office and forming a thoroughly ultra-Tory and anti-Catholic Government could induce them to a coalition so utterly repugnant to all their principles and feelings."

Canning's ultimate policy must remain a matter of conjecture. Ill-health, the result of a cold caught at the Duke of York's funeral, and anxiety due to the instability of his position made an end of the Premier, after an acrimonious session, during which he was so irritated by the constant attacks of Lord Grey that he actually contemplated taking a peerage, so as to be able to meet them face to face.

Lord Goderich, the "transient and embarrassed phantom" of "Coningsby," succeeded Canning, and Lord Lansdowne tried to strengthen the Whig element by bringing Lord Holland into the Cabinet as Foreign Secretary. Lady Granville, an ardent Canningite, cordially hoped that the project would succeed. But the possible accession of so consistent a Whig alarmed the Tory wing of the coalition, most reactionary of whom was Herries, the new Chancellor of the Exchequer, and he was the King's nominee. The intrigue and counter-intrigue which raged round the unfortunate Prime Minister are developed at considerable length in the "Memoir" of Herries by his son. They virtually resolved themselves into a tussle whether Whig or Tory principles should prevail in a mixed Cabinet. "Lord Holland," Herries gloomily reminded Lord Bexley (formerly Mr. Vansittart), "took an opportunity, even so late as the month of May last, of solemnly declaring that on whatever side of the House he might sit, he would never fail to *vote for Parliamentary reform,* nor refuse to *move,* whenever called upon to do so, the *repeal of the Test and Corporation Acts."* Give him the peaceful spirit of compromise which prevailed under Lord Liverpool's late Administration. At last the King, become aware of the dissensions which were rending the Ministry, cut the knot by advising Lord Goderich to resign and charging the Duke of Wellington with the formation of a fresh Cabinet. "Lady Holland," wrote the wit, Joseph Jekyll, to his sister-in-law, Lady Gertrude Sloane-Stanley—

"is the only dissatisfied Minister out of office. She counted upon sailing down daily with her long-tailed blacks and ancient crane-necked chariot, to sit with Holland at the Secretary's office, to administer the affairs of Europe, and make Sydney Smith a bishop. As for him, he never cared twopence about the whole thing, and the delightful fellow was very wise in so treating it."

Jekyll read Lord Holland's mind correctly. In a letter to Plunket, the Irish orator, written so far back as the previous August, he had expressed his fears that the Ministry could not endure, if Herries was introduced into it as a disturbing element. If Herries was Chancellor of the Exchequer, not one-fifth or one-tenth of the Whigs would vote for the Government on questions of finance.

The Ultras, having discarded the Canningites, proceeded to surrender to O'Connell, and Catholic Emancipation was carried by the party which had uniformly resisted the principle. The Whigs, thus "dished"— not for the last time—directed their criticism chiefly to foreign affairs, now complicated by the battle of Navarino. "We have somehow or other," wrote Lord Holland to Lord John Russell, "exasperated the two greatest powers on the Continent, viz., the Cabinet of St. Petersburg and the public opinion of France ; and we have done so without serving ourselves or our pretended allies, and without ingratiating ourselves either with those we wished well to, or those who really benefited by the transactions. Neither the Greeks nor the Turks have to thank us." He made several incisive speeches against the Porte, advocating what was termed at a subsequent Eastern crisis a "bag and baggage" policy, and his friends expected that the rising tide of Liberalism would carry him into the Foreign Office.

But, when Lord Grey came to take his advice on the various claims for office, the ex-Canningite, Lord Palmerston, was given the appointment, and Lord Holland became instead Chancellor of the Duchy of Lancaster. Probably he did not regret the loss of the more important office, for he had long been a martyr to gout. With the Prime Minister in the Upper House, he played a secondary part in the debates on Parliamentary Reform.

But he kept on excellent terms with King William after the Royal anxieties as to possible Ministerial encroachments on the privileges of the Duchy had been overcome. In the Cabinet he counted for much, thanks to his rectitude of character and intimate knowledge of Whig traditions. His French predilections caused him to be sometimes at issue with Lord Palmerston, who came to cross purposes with that Power over the creation of Belgium, but, as he philosophically remarked, he would rather have twenty protocols than one bulletin. When the Reform crisis reached its height, gout kept him away from the Cabinet meetings at which the proposals of the "Waverers," Lord Harrowby and Lord Wharncliffe, were discussed. But he stood up stoutly for an immediate creation of peers, much to the disgust of Charles Greville, who set down in his journal several indignant entries against the stiffneckedness of Holland House. The diarist had appointed himself director-general to the Waverers, and failed to perceive that it was necessary to hold some kind of a rod *in terrorem* over the Upper House.

Lord Holland's position as a Whig Nestor became more assured as time went on. He kept the younger Ministers in order when they were disposed to raise difficulties, notably when in 1832 they wished the economies derived from the suppression of ten Irish bishoprics to be diverted to the general purposes of education. A letter, written at the instance of Earl Grey, in which he dissuaded Lord John Russell from resigning on the point is a model of commonsense applied to the quieting of an over-tender spirit. "The question you have to decide on conscience," he pointed out, "is not whether your plan or Stanley's is the right

one, but whether Stanley's plan, or your resignation, with
its consequences, is preferable." Unfortunately Lord
John could not keep his opinions to himself, and speedily
justified Lady Holland's shrewd prophecy, "Those young
men are breaking up the Government." Two years later
he repeated in the House his advocacy of the secularisa-
tion of the Irish ecclesiastical revenues, and Stanley
scribbled his historic note to Sir James Graham, "John
Russell has upset the coach."

Lord Holland continued to hold the Chancellorship of
the Duchy of Lancaster after Lord Melbourne had replaced Earl Grey as Prime Minister until William IV.
abruptly brought the Government to an end, in the
autumn of 1834, by dismissing it and sending for Sir
Robert Peel. Thus abruptly relegated to Opposition,
the Whigs had to think out a new line of policy. Lord
Melbourne, afraid of mob violence, was half inclined to
let matters be. Lord Holland's Liberalism, however,
was of stouter make, and he was more closely in touch
with the various sections of the party. They were all for
reprisals; thus, in the course of a long letter on the
situation, he quoted Alderman Combe, who said that the
Opposition wanted a focus, and "I in a saucy joke pretended he thought that word Latin for Fox, but what the
man meant to say was correct." He thought Lord John
Russell, much though he liked him, too cold for a leader,
and urged that the defect should be made good by meetings or consultations. An attempt should be made to
form a coalition with Stanley and his friends, who had
broken away from the Whigs, and that vast instrument
of mischief and annoyance, O'Connell, might be induced
to accept the Rolls or the Bench. As for general principles, he thought "necessity, honour, and even reason,

apart from passion, must make you try to do what you can to turn out a Tory Ministry, and to reinstate one in character, composition, and spirit like that over which Grey and you presided." Another letter in the same strain was addressed to Lord Melbourne early in February ; the Opposition were eager for battle, victory, and triumph, and the Fabian system would not serve. The acrimony of the debates during Peel's "Hundred Days" of office certainly proved him to have accurately gauged the feelings of the party.

The Whigs returned to power in April, 1834, and Lord Holland took up his old appointment again. He joined his colleagues in pressing Lord Grey to become Secretary for Foreign Affairs, but the ex-Premier declined, and Lord Palmerston secured the seals by declaring that if he were not continued he would sooner stand outside the Administration altogether. The Government was never strong, though the Lichfield House compact had disarmed the hostility of O'Connell. But Brougham's bitter resentment at being excluded from the Cabinet found vent in unscrupulous attacks on Lord Durham's mission to Canada, while the Lords freely mutilated such measures as were obnoxious to them. During the last years of his life, Lord Holland's chief efforts were directed towards keeping the party together ; more concert and consultation between the Government and its supporters, he wrote in 1839, must be without delay re-established, organised, and understood. He laboured hard to bring back Lord Althorp, who had become Lord Spencer, into politics, urging that his mere presence would keep Lord Brougham in order.

During the last months of his lifetime Lord Holland's feelings were deeply stirred, when Lord Palmerston developed the clever, but hazardous, policy of suppressing the ambitions of Mehemet Ali, the Viceroy of Egypt. Directly the subject of intervention was broached, the French Government hung back and made all sorts of difficulties. Palmerston then resolved on proceeding without it, and on July 15, 1840, concluded the Quadrilateral Treaty for the protection of the Porte between Austria, England, Prussia, and Russia, on the one side, and Turkey on the other. Lord Holland, true to the Whig traditions, clung to the French alliance, and it was not long before Lord John Russell and Lord Clarendon came over to his side. Resignations were imminent during the autumn, and it required all Lord Melbourne's tact to keep the Cabinet together. " Individual members of the Cabinet ought not," wrote Lord Palmerston to him, " as Lord Holland does every day of the week, to speak openly to all who come near them about the policy and measures which the Cabinet of which they are members is imbarked in, just as a member of Opposition would speak of the policy of an Administration which he was labouring to turn out." Lord Melbourne himself admitted that the talk at Holland House was irremediable ; " they cannot help it, and they are not themselves aware how much they talk."

But though the French leanings of Lord Holland may have been too strongly displayed, considering that Guizot, then French Ambassador, was his constant guest, and that Charles Greville was continually agog for news, his representations to Lord Melbourne were sound. If overtures were to be made to France, they should be conveyed to Paris speedily, and the Porte must be dissuaded from insisting on the deposition of the Pasha. But the prompt success of British naval measures against

Mehemet Ali soon solved the crisis, and with the resignation of M. Thiers, the bellicose French Premier, all
danger of a breach with France was at an end.   Before
that happy result was attained, however, Lord Holland
died after a few hours' illness, on October 22, 1840, and
it is conceivable that political anxieties cut short his days.
Just before he expired, he said to the page, " Edgar, these
Syrian affairs will be too much for me.   Mehemet Ali
will kill me."   The real charge against Palmerston's
policy was, of course, that he wished not so much to
ruin the Pasha of Egypt and to preserve the integrity of
Turkey as to humble France.   He undoubtedly isolated
and so helped to undermine the Orleanist monarchy, and
Lord Holland was right in contending that the disadvan-
tages of such a policy outweighed its benefits.

The attachment of the latter to the old school of
thought, both in domestic and foreign affairs, was
expressed in the lines found on his dressing-table after
his death :

> " Nephew of Fox, and friend of Grey—
>   Enough my meed of fame
>   If those who deign'd to observe me say
>   I injured neither name."

This self-appreciation defines Lord Holland's place in
the politics of his time at once modestly and correctly.
Circumstance and inclination made of him a follower
rather than a leader.   He entered public life as the pupil
of Fox : he continued in it as the second-in-command
to Lord Grey and Lord Melbourne.   Such ambition as
he possessed was mainly the creation of his wife ; for his
own part he was content to support Whig principles with

undeviating consistency in office and opposition. He
was the colleague to whom perplexed chiefs invariably
turned for advice, with the knowledge that it would
represent orthodox doctrine and that its motives would
be absolutely disinterested. With talents of a solid rather
than of a showy order, he counted for much more in
momentous decisions than the public of the day was
aware. What Dundas had been to Pitt, what Graham
was to be to Peel, such was Lord Holland to the statesmen under whom he loyally served. As an intelligence
officer he was without a rival, thanks to his wide social
relations. In the "tens" he could gauge the inclinations
of Carlton House; in the "thirties" he could forestall
the vagaries of Brougham. With much of his uncle's
inclination for political tutelage, it interested him to form
the minds of Horner and Lord John Russell.

Holland House was thus for years a political council-
chamber and meeting-place where the few matured plans
and the many made acquaintances. The value of such
a centre to a party under exclusively aristocratic leadership was almost incalculable; but for it, means of communication between the rank and file and the Whig
hierarchy would have been non-existent. Lord Grey
was a recluse by nature, and both he and Lord Melbourne
had to contend with the difficulty of directing a party
with a democratic element of rapidly increasing importance from the distant regions of the Upper House.
Their colleague, though essentially an aristocrat, had
acquired from travel and many friendships a larger
catholicity of taste, so that, though by no means devoid
of originality of intellect, he became a repertory, as it
were, of Liberal opinions. He shared the strength and
the weakness of the school which had grown up under

the shadow of the French Revolution. On questions of foreign policy he was prone to regard any movement as justifiable because it was insurrectionary, and to construe exercises of authority into acts of oppression. But his views on constitutional matters were such as have gained general acceptance to-day, though Tories of the Eldonian type regard them as identical with the worst excesses of Jacobinism. Religious disabilities, restrictions on free speech and a free press and taxes on articles of consumption found in him an unflinching opponent. He was, in Macaulay's suggestive phrase, a noble who in every crisis cast in his lot with the Commons, a planter who made manful war on the slave trade, a landowner whose whole heart was in the struggle against the Corn Laws.

CHAPTER V

HOST AND HOSTESS

Lord Holland at home—As a conversationalist—A man of many friendships — Lady Holland's autocracy — Sir Henry Holland's character of her—Historical retorts—Exercises of authority—The dinner-hour—A crowded table—Good cheer—Lady Holland in society—On her travels—Lady Granville's satire—Lady Holland's correspondence—Byron's memoirs—" Glenarvon "—Calantha and Barbary House — Lady Holland's death — Guizot's character — Servants and flowers.

LORD HOLLAND, though a more consistent politician than his uncle, regarded public life, it may be suspected, as a secondary pursuit. Affairs of State came to him as part of his birthright, and he carried out his duties conscientiously rather than with enthusiasm. Long years spent in Opposition blunted, in the end, an ambition which was less innate than inspired by those about him—by Fox and by his wife. His real interests lay elsewhere, in travel, reading, and above all in entertainment and the pleasures that entertainment supplies. He was not much of a club man, and went but rarely to Brooks's, though he was a fairly constant attendant both at the Literary Club, founded by Dr. Johnson, and the King of Clubs, of which Mackintosh, Bobus Smith and Romilly were the leading spirits. Lord Holland, who was totally devoid of affectation, fulfilled the ideal of a perfect host. It was among the least of his virtues that he kept an excellent table—"They live remarkably well" was the decision of Lord Minto—and of their intimates Luttrell, for one, was a confirmed epicure. Lord Holland possessed the far more essential qualities of a frank politeness and winning kindness which immediately set even the most timid of guests at their ease. Out of his own recollections Macaulay drew a lifelike picture of the venerable and benignant countenance and the cordial voice of him who bade them welcome. It at once relieved of all embarrassment the youngest and most timid writer or artist who found himself for the first time among Ambassadors and Earls.

Mere amiability can never win undisputed social leadership, even when, as in Lord Holland's case, there are added to it the claims of long suffering uncomplainingly endured. When in his best health he could only limp a hundred yards in a day ; he passed some weeks of every year in extreme pain. His most vigorous form of exercise consisted in sitting about the grounds on an old pony. In addition to a perfect temper, he possessed fine conversational qualities. Moore considered him equal to any talker of his time. He welcomed debate; he was, Macaulay tells us, most courteously and pleasantly disputatious, always beginning an argument by drawing down his shaggy eyebrows, making a face extremely like his uncle, and wagging his head. In other words, Lord Holland was well qualified to start a subject, and to keep it up, so long as it served its turn, with a constant supply of apt observation and anecdote. He was, in fact, better fitted for conducting the give and take of

conversation than any member of his circle, of whom
Mackintosh for one, and Macaulay for another, tended to
monologue, while Luttrell and Sydney Smith illustrated
by turns of fancy rather than originated. A well-stocked
political memory supplied him with endless stories, and
he told them with a mimicry as exquisite as the Regent's.
He could reproduce to the life the *staccato* accent of
George Selwyn and the broad Doric of Lauderdale.
His learning, though probably not very deep, was varied ;
he not only owned but studied the contents of a library
furnished with the most important historical works on
Italy, France and Portugal, with the classics, and political
tracts and pamphlets.

His intellect had its limitations, and they corresponded
to the gaps in the mental equipment of Fox. "Painting,"
said Rogers, "gives him no pleasure, and music absolute
pain." Pictures and busts he appears to have valued
chiefly as records of his friends, and to that end he
patronised the leading artists and sculptors of the day.
On the whole, however, he contended on equal terms
with those whose attainments in one direction or another
were much superior to his own, thanks to his *savoir faire*
and receptive curiosity. Though he chiefly cultivated
men's society, Lord Holland was most popular with the
ladies : "an angel," "a great grig and a great love," are
the endearments bestowed on him by Lady Granville in
her letters to her sister, Lady Carlisle. He delighted in
schoolboys, and Mr. George Russell has related how
pleased he was with the premature wisdom of a product
of Westminster. The youth, invited to spend a whole
holiday at Holland House, was told that he might have
what he liked for dinner. Wise beyond his years, he
chose duck and green peas, with an apricot tart to follow.

"My boy," said Lord Holland, "if in all the important questions of your life you decide as wisely as you have decided now, you will be a great and good man." Yet beneath the charming manners lay a philosophically detached temperament, compatible rather with many friendships than with a few deep affections. It was not without reason that Brougham wrote : "He surveyed mankind with the eye of a naturalist rather than a brother." His portraits confirm the statement that he came to look much older than his real age, thereby gaining himself the title of venerable by the time that he had reached fifty-five.

Lady Holland, though not without good qualities, inevitably provoked the critical faculties. Her imperiousness, not to say rudeness, gave birth to innumerable anecdotes, and even if many of them may have been improved in the telling, they convey the impression of a formidable character. She tyrannised over all who came in contact with her, including her husband, though it was all, no doubt, in the way of kindness. Lord Holland, on one occasion, was not permitted to dine in a white waistcoat, which loomed large upon his portly figure, suggesting, as Luttrell whispered in an aside, the image of a turbot standing on its tail. His wife declared that she would not sit down unless he changed it, and he was obliged to comply. Again, he was duly relieved of his crutches when they had ceased to be a necessity and had become a habit. "Put away your nasty crutches, Lord Holland; you look as if you were in prison." "Oh, dear woman, pray let me have them ; I like to have them near me." "Impossible. Mary, take away your papa's crutches." Lady Granville witnessed the scene, which was acted for the benefit of an audience of eight, including the Dutch Ambassador, M. Falck, and his attaché, the Prince de Chimay. As extreme measures Lady Holland would abruptly order the servants to take away her husband's plate, and even to wheel him off to bed when he was in the middle of a story; acts of autocracy which he bore with good-humoured philosophy.

Fearless and ready, Lady Holland brought what Hayward calls the police of the dinner-table to a condition of the utmost efficiency. "None but a masterhand," wrote a discriminating judge, "could have accomplished the result of so skilfully commingling English and Foreign Ministers and diplomatists, men of learning and of science, historians, poets, artists and wits." The author of this encomium was Sir Henry Holland, no relation, but the most sought-after physician of his time and the father of the present Lord Knutsford. He added very happily that she was—

" a remarkable woman in every way, well remembered by all who knew her—difficult to describe to those who did not. Supreme in her own mansion and family, she exercised a singular and seemingly capricious tyranny even over guests of the highest rank and position. Capricious it seemed, but there was in reality *intention* in all she did ; and this intention was the maintenance of power, which she gained and strenuously used, though not without discretion in fixing its limits. No one knew better when to change her mood and to soothe by kind and flattering words the provocation she had just given, and was very apt to give. In this latter case, indeed, she was aided by a native generosity of mind which never failed to show itself in kindness where kindness was wanted. In my long and intimate knowledge of Lady Holland, I never knew her desert an old friend, whatever his condition might be. . . . Her management of conversation at the dinner-table—sometimes arbitrary and in rude arrest of others, sometimes courteously inviting the subject— furnished a study in itself. Every guest felt her presence and generally more or less succumbed to it."

This corrective to the ordinary conception of Lady Holland as a person of merely purposeless rudeness is evidently truthful. She would never have exercised her social autocracy for forty years had it not been instinctively felt that there was method and reason in her castigations. They were undeniably administered without fear or favour, and neither the highest in the land nor the most confirmed *habitués* of Holland House escaped. Some of her retorts are historical. For instance, speaking of " Rejected Addresses," Monk Lewis remarked to her : " Many of them are very fair, but mine is not at all liked; they have made me write burlesque, which I never do." " You don't know your own talent," was the encouraging reply. Then there was the descent on Rogers : " Your poetry is bad enough, so pray be sparing of your prose." Even more characteristic was the comforting assurance to Moore, " This will be a dull book of yours, this ' Sheridan,' I fear," a prediction which, it must be confessed, carried with it the additional sting of exactitude. Much depends, of course, upon the time and place of the making of these amenities. They need not necessarily have been hurled across the dinner-table, or uttered in full conclave. Moore, most genial of beings, was far too much amused by her sallies at his expense to bear malice. Lord Holland's geniality could be trusted, too, to turn aside the biting edge of her comments. His warm praise of " Lalla Rookh " must have alleviated her equivocal compliment to the effect that, in spite of her objection to Eastern things, she must, some time or another, read it herself.

Lady Holland's autocracy becomes the more excusable when we remember that the foibles both of wit and authorship were represented at her table. The greater lights expected to rule not only the day but the night as well. A dominant individuality and an occasional display of the whip were needed to preserve the amenities. Lady Holland intervened with the calm assurance of an accepted dictator, and, if her manner was sometimes insolent, she always respected those who stood their ground. At the fitting moment there came the tap of the fan on the table, and, " Now, Macaulay, we have had enough of this; give us something else." Such exercises of authority could be overdone, and tiffs between Lady Holland and her intimates were not unfrequent. Visitors who entered Holland House for the first time surveyed the scene with open-eyed astonishment. Macaulay, when new to the surroundings, described in his letters how guests were ordered about as if they were servants, without any prefatory form of request. It was all rather absurd, but it was all good fun except for the victim of the moment. A tenable explanation of this brusqueness, partly natural and partly, no doubt, acquired, is that it served as an offensive-defensive cloak to a past which was never wholly forgotten either by great ladies like Lady Granville, or members of the strict professional classes like Denman, who, when they came to Holland House, left their wives behind them.[1]

[1] Sydney Smith wrote to Lord Denman in 1841 : " Lady Holland dines with us on the 17th. Does Lady Denman know Lady

The dinner-hour was the rallying-point of the Holland House circle. It was fixed in later years at five o'clock, *pour gêner tout le monde,* according to Talleyrand. This arrangement appears to have been made in the autumn of 1832, when Greville, too, strongly objected to it. "Lady Holland is unwell," he wrote in his journal on November 20th, "fancies she must dine at five o'clock, and exerts all her power over society by making everybody go there at that hour, though nothing can be more inconvenient than thus shortening the day, and nothing more tiresome than thus lengthening the evening." But the diarist was out of humour with his hostess, and on the eve of a quarrel with her which he kept up for two years. Deductions must in all fairness be made therefore from his sardonic account of "this strange house, which presents an odd mixture of luxury and constraint, of enjoyments, physical and intellectual, with an alloy of small *désagréments.*" He admitted, indeed, almost in the next sentence, that whenever, by the death of host or hostess, it came to an end, a vacuum would be made in society which nothing would supply. As for the constraints and *désagréments,* they seem to have consisted, for one thing, in the necessity of a formal invitation. Rogers used to tell how, as he was coming away one day from a call at Holland House, Lord Holland met him, and said, "Well, do you return to dinner?" The answer was, "No, I have not been invited," and the question was settled. Rogers handsomely added that he thought Lady Holland was right

Holland, and, if not, will that deprive us of the pleasure of Lady Denman's company? Lady Holland sinned early in life, with Methuselah and Enoch, but still she is out of the pale of the regular ladies, and the case ought to have been put."

in keeping the composition of her dinner-parties in her own hands, because Lord Holland was so good-natured hat he would ask any one whom he happened to meet in the course of the day.

Despite this regulation, her table was notoriously overcrowded. We find Lady Grey complaining to Creevey of having to dine sixteen at a table for nine, and Greville grumbling because, two more people arriving than there was room for, namely, Lord Melbourne and Tom Duncombe, Lady Holland had the pleasure " of a couple of general squeezes and of seeing our arms prettily pinioned." " Lord Holland sits at table," he continued, " but does not dine. He proposed to retire (not from the room) but was not allowed, for that would have given us all space and ease." Her proceedings at such crises were apt to be summary. " Luttrell," she cried one day, " make room." " It will have to be made," was the retort, " for it does not exist." Moore records how an unfortunate Mr. Gore was abruptly ordered to vacate his chair for some more favoured guest. Lord Melbourne once rose in his wrath, after she had fidgeted him by making him change when he was seated to his liking, and walked off to his house with, " I'll be damned if I dine with you at all." But here again Rogers is the apologist with the remark, made to Moore, that the close packing made her dinners agreeable, because, inconvenient though it was, a feeling of good-fellowship was the result. The same sort of enjoyment was supplied, in fact, as attends the skirmishing and scramble of a picnic.

Lady Holland brought to the furnishing of her table the talents of a commissariat officer. She levied contributions of fish and game from the owners of salmon rivers and well-stocked preserves. The present of a haunch of venison was a sure way to her good graces ; and Hayward tells how Sydney Smith made up one of their occasional squabbles by the offering of a sucking pig. Her foreign guests were expected to supply the delicacies of their respective countries. Some Dutch herrings were once recommended by her for the odd reason that they had arrived in an Ambassador's bag. M. Van der Weyer, the representative of the newly constituted Court of Brussels, imperilled his diplomatic reputation in the eyes of his serious fellow-countrymen by his zeal in procuring for her some *mouton des Ardennes*. Half a sheep was left at the Brussels Foreign Office, marked "très pressé" ; and the clerks, mistaking it for a bundle of despatches, forwarded it by special messenger. Gifted with a robust appetite, she was quite free from any squeamish affectation of disliking to discuss food and its preparation. On the contrary, she engaged Motteux, an epicure alleged to dispose of sixteen *entrées* at a meal, in a hot discussion on the ingredients of cock-a-leekie soup, the point in debate being whether prunes were an orthodox addition to it or not.

Supreme in her own home, Lady Holland expected, and generally contrived, to obtain unquestioned defer- ence when she went into society, which, previously to her husband's death, was but rarely. In her later years she usurped the privileges of Royalty, and required to be informed beforehand of the company she was to meet. On her arrival she altered the places so as to give herself the most entertaining neighbours available. She paraded her opinions without the smallest reserve ; and in Macaulay's Life is to be discovered a capital description of a dinner at Rogers's, where she became so "outrageous " that the party combined to suppress her. She received the correction in good part, no doubt. With her own sex, however, she was hardly a favourite, more especially when she took upon herself to keep its younger members in subjection. Mrs. Norton, being gifted with a sense of humour, merely laughed when Lady Holland abruptly removed some roses from her head, considerably disarranging her hair in the process, with the remark that they did not suit her style. Though the process was summary, the result, as its victim admitted, was an improvement. But Fanny Kemble, when a bouncing and high-spirited girl, bitterly resented her dictation, and in the "Records of a Later Life" reproduced her mannerisms in passages written with gall rather than ink.

They first met at Rogers's, when she drank out of Sydney Smith's glass, and otherwise behaved like a spoilt beauty of eighteen. Some years afterwards they dined together at the same table. Lady Holland dropped her handkerchief, and when Adelaide Kemble, who had joined the party, picked it up, the only thanks she received was : "Ah, I thought you would do it." After that we are not surprised to learn that, when Lady Holland had become a widow, Lady Morley and other social leaders only tolerated her for the sake of Lord Holland's memory. From Greville and Sir Henry Holland we gather, however, that, after Lord Holland's death, far from being, as Fanny Kemble asserted, "the most miserable woman in England" and "left utterly alone," she made her dinners at South Street as popular as those at Kensington had been, and that, down to her last illness, she gathered her old friends around her, and even extended her acquaintances. There remains the abundantly confirmed detail of behaviour that Lady Holland's *im-*

pedimenta served, much as his handkerchief did to Napoleon, as a test of authority. Count d'Orsay, so the story goes, emancipated himself from her by a joke. After he had picked up her fan several times, when sitting next her at dinner, he suggested that he should spend the rest of his time on the floor, so as to be thoroughly prepared for each crisis.

On her journeys to Ampthill, Brighton, and the houses of her friends, Lady Holland, before the invention of railways, affected the state of the eighteenth-century *grands seigneurs*. In December, 1815, she arrived at Woburn with a train of sixteen people, imposing thereby a severe strain even upon ducal hospitality. She also insisted that her nerves would not permit her to travel faster than a few miles an hour, a fancy which protracted her expeditions abroad into the most deliberate of pilgrimages. She made the coachman put on the drag while driving on the Paris boulevards. When Sir Henry Holland went with the Hollands, General Fox and Lord John Russell to Pæstum from Naples, the trip took from four to five days. After railways came in she exerted the powers of her will to discomfit the dangerous invention. On returning from Chippenham by the Great Western Railway after a visit to Bowood, she compelled Brunel to limit the speed of the train to less than twenty miles an hour, much to the indignation of the other passengers.

In foreign capitals Lady Holland exacted the same degree of homage as in London, and society submitted in sheer astonishment. Lady Granville's descriptions of her in Paris are so cleverly done, that they would be spoilt by any attempt at paraphrase. The first relates to the year 1825 :

"The Hollands have a good apartment and an excellent cook. She is very well, and to me all smiles, but to her *alentours* rather more in the termagant line than common. To the awestruck world who frequent her house (the most strict, undivorced and ultra-duchesses now go there) she appears encompassed by a solemnity and state of fan and elbow-chair and shaded light which makes them suppose themselves in the presence of Maria Theresa at least."

Thirteen years later occurred an even more characteristic scene :

"Madame de Lieven and she are great friends. 'Ma chère, j'étais chez elle. Il y avait Mme. Durazzo, Molé, Humboldt. On annonce Pasquier. Elle a l'air tout charmé, tout flatté. Elle me dit : " Restez, je vous supplie ; causez avec le Chancelier." Je résiste ; elle m'implore de ne pas l'abandonner. Je cède. Pas plutôt assise avec tout cet entourage qui nous regarde, qu'elle laisse tomber son sac. Elle me tape sur l'épaule : " Pick it up, my dear ; pick it up "—et moi, tout étonnée en bonne bête, me plongeant sur le tapis pour ramasser ses chiffons.' Is not this a true and incomparable Holly-ism, taking out of Lieven's mouth the taste of the little flutter at the visits and the *besoin* of her support, by treating her like Antonio, and showing off, what I believe never was seen before, Mme. de Lieven as a humble companion ? "

Traits more distinctly feminine were a fear of thunder and lightning, expressed by closing the shutters, drawing the blinds, and ordering candles in broad daylight ; and a terror of the cholera, a sentiment that stood, no doubt, in need of considerably less excuse.

A person of Lady Holland's unruly tongue inevitably appears in a juster light in correspondence than in conversation. The specimens of her letters which have

been published show her to have been gifted with a
happy faculty for hitting the taste of those she addressed.
Whatever her opinion of Sir Hudson Lowe, as Napoleon's
gaoler, may have been, she remembered that, dwelling on a
lonely island, he must be thirsting for news. Lady Holland
gave him, therefore, a racy account of the state of public
feeling created by the trial of Queen Caroline. She considered it by no means impossible that a junction of mob
and soldiery would be formed in her Majesty's favour,
adding that "it is a singular fact that these persons
cannot be made to understand the difference of Queen
and Queen Consort, and fancy it is no departure from
their allegiance to prefer Queen to King, pretending their
rights are the same." Just as characteristic are her letters
to Mrs. Creevey; they range over every conceivable topic,
including the disbanding of his followers by Canning in
1813, when Ward (Lord Dudley) remarked that it was
hard to serve a year without wages, but he hoped he
should get a good character from his last place; the
entrance of Mme. de Staël into London society; various
marriages, some respectable, others not; a visit to Lord
Grey at Howick, where his countenance "exhibited
gaiety and smiles which never were seen this side of
Highgate Hill"; and an illness of the Regent treated,
after the drastic methods then in vogue, first by drawing
60 ounces of blood, then by administering laudanum
and cordials. The tone is that of an accomplished
woman of the world, fond of gossip, but not to the extent
of straying beyond good nature and good breeding.

Lady Holland's warmheartedness comes out most
strongly, however, in her letters to Francis Horner,
whom she and her husband regarded almost as a son.
When, in 1816, the health of that Marcellus of the

Whig party broke down, she hastened to put three rooms in Holland House at his disposal for the winter, where he could have his time, company, and occupations all to himself. "Pray spare me," she wrote, "all the commonplace compliments of giving trouble and taking up too many rooms. What you know I feel towards you ought to exempt me from any such trash." The doctors, however, decided that Horner must winter in the South, and he went to Pisa to die. But she kept up a correspondence with him to the last, persuading him to reconsider his opinion of Sismondi, the historian, whom he had condemned as " a very poor writer, greatly below the name he had got," and forwarding to him the " Tales of My Landlord." " No one," the grateful patient declared, "knows half so well what to write, or how to write it."

When Moore was entrusted with Byron's " Memoirs," and contemplated their publication, he took the prudent course of disarming her possible resentment. Thus on July 6, 1821, he wrote in his journal :

" By the bye, I yesterday gave Lady Holland Lord Byron's ' Memoirs ' to read, and on my telling her that I rather fancied he had mentioned her name in an unfair manner somewhere, she said, ' Such things give me no uneasiness : I know perfectly well my station in the world, and I know all that can be said of me. As long as the few friends I am really sure of speak kindly (and I would not believe the contrary if I saw it in black and white), all that the rest of the world may say is a matter of complete indifference to me.' "

An excellent maxim, though one more easily laid down than carried out. She had greater cause for resentment when Lady Caroline Lamb, fresh from her rupture with Byron, proceeded, in the notorious *roman à clef*, "Glenarvon," to satirise Holland House as Barbary House, and its mistress, to the undying joy of Creevey, as the Princess of Madagascar. Lady Holland, however, took the spiteful attack with an unconcern which appears the more praiseworthy when we remember that after Byron's farewell letter the feature in the book which attracted most attention was the spiteful caricature of Holland House. The portraiture was unmistakable, and in addition Barbary House was identified as "an old-fashioned Gothic building three miles beyond the turnpike." The "pale poet" of the following extract is, of course, Rogers; Hoiaouskim, John Allen; Luttrell is supposed to have stood for Mr. Filmore, while Calantha, Lady Avondale, is Lady Caroline herself.

"Calantha now, for the first time, conversed with the learned in the land : she heard new opinions started and old ones refuted ; and she gazed unhurt but not unawed upon reviewers, poets, critics, and politicians. At the end of a long gallery, two thick wax tapers rendering 'darkness visible,' the Princess was seated. A poet of an emaciated and sallow complexion stood beside her ; of him it was averred that in the kindest and most engaging manner he, at all times, said precisely that which is most unpleasant to the person he appeared to praise. This yellow hyena had, however, a heart noble, magnanimous, and generous ; and even his friends, could they but escape from his smile and his tongue, had no reason to complain. Few events, if any, were ever known to move the Princess from her position. Her pages—her foreign attire, but genuine English manners, voice and complexion, attracted universal admiration. She was beautiful too, and had a smile it was difficult to learn to hate or mistrust. She spoke of her own country with contempt, and even in her dress, which was magnificent, attempted to prove the superiority of every other over it. Her morals were simple and incorrupt, and in matters of religious faith she entirely surrendered herself to the guidance of Hoiaouskim. She inclined her head a little upon seeing Lady Avondale ; the *dead*, I mean the sick poet, did the same ; and Hoiaouskim, her high priest, cast his eyes with unassuming civility upon Calantha, thus welcoming her to Barbary House.

" The Princess then spoke a little sentence—just enough to show how much she intended to protect Lady Avondale. She addressed herself, besides, in many dialects to an outlandish set of menials, appointing every one in the room some trifling task, which was performed in a moment by young and old, with surprising alacrity. Such is the force of fashion and power when skilfully applied. After this, she called Calantha : a slight exordium followed, then a wily pointed catechism, her Highness nodding at intervals, and dropping short epigrammatic sentences, when necessary, to such as were in attendance about her. ' Is she acting ? ' asked Calantha, at length, in a whisper, addressing the sallow-complexioned poet, who stood sneering and simpering behind her chair. ' Is she acting, or is this reality ? ' ' It is the only reality you will ever find in the Princess,' returned her friend. ' She acts the Princess of Madagascar from morning till night, and from night till morning. You may fall from favour, but you are now at the height : no one ever advanced further—none ever continued there long.'

" ' But why,' said Lady Avondale, " do the great Nabob, and all the other Lords-in-waiting, with that black horde of savages——' ' Reviewers, you mean, and men of talents.' ' Well, whatever they are, tell me quickly why they wear collars and chains round their necks at Barbary House ? ' ' It is the fashion,' replied the poet. ' This fashion is unbecoming your race,' said Lady Avondale ; ' I would die sooner than be thus enchained.' ' The great Nabob,' quoth Mr. Filmore, joining in the discourse, ' is the best, the kindest, the cleverest man I know, but, like some philosophers, he would sacrifice much for a peaceable life. The Princess is fond of inflicting these lesser tyrannies : she is so helplessly attached to trifles —so unweaningly fond of exercising her powers, it were a pity to thwart her. For my own part, I could willingly bend to the yoke, provided the duration were not eternal ; for observe that the chains arc well gilded ; that the tables are well stored ; and that those who bend the lowest are the best received.' 'And if I also bow my neck,' said Calantha, 'will she be grateful ? May I depend upon her seeming kindness ? ' The poet's naturally pale complexion turned to a bluish green at this inquiry."

By way of adding a genial touch or two, Lady Caroline, in the course of the novel, describes Lady Holland as travelling with "twenty-three attendants and fifty-four domestic friends," as deserting the fallen and silencing the most contemptible scribblers with the grossest flattery, as fearing death and yet dying with the word "cook" on her lips.

Lady Holland survived her assailant by a good many years, and when death drew near her in the autumn of 1845, she faced it with much courage. Greville asserts that she never gave the least sign of religious feeling or belief, yet "evinced during her last illness a very philosophical calmness and resolution and perfect good-humour." She consoled herself with the reflection that during her existence she had done as much good and as little harm as she could. Greville devotes to her one of his most elaborate characters, and does her substantial justice, though he seems at all times to have been rather afraid of her. She was "always intensely selfish," and "a woman for whom nobody felt any affection, but she entertained feelings of friendship as strongly as her nature permitted." Hers was, in fact, a hard masculine intellect, accustomed to domineer, and intent on getting her own way. General Fox, as a boy, complained that she showed less affection to her children than to their young friends who were invited to the house, and a condition of her will by which she left her property at Kennington to Lord John Russell for his life was generally blamed. Yet Lady Holland could be amiable when she chose, and her severest critics agreed that she was unremittingly kind to her intimate friends when they were ill and suffering. Lady Granville, who did not like her, gave as a final verdict : "That woman has suffered much, and I will never again say she has no heart." With all her absurdities she was an able woman, well read and receptive of information. She was proud of her position, the more so, no doubt, because it had taken much pains to gain, and she was far from being a mere promiscuous angler after social celebrities, except, perhaps, after her husband's death, when she seems to have developed a craving for fresh faces and new houses. In her best days she selected her court with care, and would have cashiered an unsuitable addition to it without much ceremony and, indeed. with no ceremony at all. The most pleasing portrait of her is Guizot's, drawn when he was in London as French Ambassador. Calling and finding her alone, he asked if she often was so. She answered :

"'No, very seldom ; but when it occurs I am not without resources,' and, pointing to the portraits, she observed : ' I ask the friends you see there to come down ; I know the place that each preferred, the armchair in which he was accustomed to sit : I find myself again with Fox, Romilly, Sheridan, and Horner ; they speak to me and I am no longer by myself.' "

Guizot, as became a Frenchman, was much *attendri* by these remarks, and took away a favourable impression of this "haughty, imperious and capricious woman, who, in the midst of the triumphs she had won by her beauty and talents, yet retained the reputation of coldness and egotism."

Among Lady Holland's amiable qualities were kindness to servants and fondness for flowers. Greville describes her as making a great fuss over the illness of her page, called Edgar, though his real name was Tom or Jack, and termed a "little creature," though he was a hulking fellow of twenty. Her guests were compelled to sit by his bedside and amuse him, not a little, one would imagine, to the mutual embarrassment of would-be entertainers and entertained. The fact remains that Lord Holland's death sixteen years afterwards found Edgar still in their service. As a horticulturist Lady Holland reintroduced the dahlia, in 1804, a plant which the Marchioness of Bute had failed to establish in 1789. Her attempt was only attended, however, by temporary success, and it was not until 1815 that a permanent stock was introduced from France. She planned the small formal gardens on the western side of the house, and of them the Dutch garden with its pattern of straight paths bordered by box is praised by Leigh Hunt in "The Old Court Suburb" as a fitting accompaniment to the old building.

CHAPTER VI

MISS FOX AND JOHN ALLEN

A cultivated maiden lady—Jeremy Bentham's only love—At Paris
and Combe Florey—Miss Fox's recollections—John Allen's introduction to the Hollands—A philosopher on the trot—An established
institution—Passages of arms—Political and irreligious opinions—
An armchair statesman—"The Rise and Growth of the Royal
Prerogative"—Fugitive writings—Allen and Blanco White—The
loss of a friend—Allen's death.

MISS FOX, Lord Holland's only sister, died in
March, 1845, eight months before Lady Holland,
and Greville regretted her as a most amiable
woman, with excellent abilities. She lived for many
years at Little Holland House with her cousin, Miss
Vernon, as her companion, until the death of the latter
in 1830. Her days seem to have flowed tranquilly and
happily away, among such interests as were accessible
in those days to a maiden lady of cultivated and active
mind. An early glimpse we catch of her is by the
bedside of Charles James Fox, when she soothed his
last hours by reading aloud, chiefly from novels. "I
like your reading, young one," said Fox to Lord Holland,
"but I liked it better before I heard your sister's. That
is better than yours, I can tell you." Various accidents,
it appears, had prevented his seeing much of her until

some three years before his death. "But," wrote Lord
Holland in his "Memoirs of the Whig Party," "all her
excellent qualities of mind and heart came upon him
at once, and endeared her, as well they might, most
sincerely to my uncle." Macaulay, too, praised her
reading ; it was more quiet and less theatrical than
the general run.

The romance of Miss Fox's life, if romance it can be
called, occurred, however, some twenty-five years earlier,
when she became the first and only love of the philosopher, Jeremy Bentham. They met at Bowood as
guests of Lord Shelburne, in 1781, and in a letter
to a friend the future reformer of our jurisprudence
described how they spent their evenings together over
the chess-board. "She seems a good-natured, pleasant
kind of girl ; but has not much to say for herself, as yet,
as you may imagine. Her face—I had like to have forgot
her face—is far from being an unpleasant one ; but the
form of it, which is rather too long ; a mouth, which is
the Fox mouth ; and a set of teeth, which, though white.
are rather too large, save her from being a beauty."
By and by Bentham began to survey her with a less
severely critical eye ; he was glad to possess a sketch of
her in *crayons* executed by a lady staying in the house,
and when he left he sent her ponderous compliments
through Lord Shelburne. "Missing the chess-board,"
he wrote, "it is possible that, for a week or so, she might
be led to bestow a straggling thought on the once happy
man who used to sit on the other side of it." But he
never told his love, and his biographer, Bowring, records
the half-pathetic, half-grotesque sequel. A short time
before his death in 1832 he sent a playful "love epistle"
to Miss Fox, speaking of the grey hairs of age and the

bliss of youth. " I was with Bentham," writes Bowring, " when the answer came to this letter—that answer was cold and distant—it contained no reference to the state of former affections ; and he was indescribably hurt and disappointed by it."

Miss Fox might well be excused from fully appreciating the importance of what had evidently been a suppressed adoration. In those precise days the son of a city attorney, however eminent, could never have aspired to the hand of a peer's daughter. She had, besides, set her affections on her brother, whom she nursed during his many illnesses, and her brother's family. " Aunt Ibby " or " Little Aunty " is to be discovered in Lady Granville's correspondence staying with the Hollands in Paris, where Lord Holland promised her a dinner at Robert's. She paid a visit to Sydney Smith at Combe Florey, and he sent her nephew, General Fox, an account of her being foiled by a gate with a double latch, made to stop donkeys, " till Bobus and I recalled her with loud laughter, showed her that she had two hands, and roused her to vindicate her superiority over the donkeys." When six months before her death she was attacked by a stroke of paralysis, the Canon of St. Paul's called her " a most beautiful specimen of human excellence." She abounded in reminiscences of Mackintosh and Dr. Parr ; she heard Coleridge descant on German literature during a whole dinner at Bowood, and afterwards recite " Christabel," then unpublished, without a pause. She described Bentham's manners, it is satisfactory to know, as quite unlike those of any one else, but there was a singular charm about them, they were so perfectly natural and simple. Unlike her brother and sister-in-law, she was a person of sincerely religious feeling.

John Allen completed the household, combining the positions of librarian, steward, and inseparable friend. The relationship was more common a century ago than it is to-day. Dumont, the Swiss publicist, occupied at one time a similar place at Bowood, and Crabbe was foi some years domesticated at Belvoir. Allen, together with Mackintosh and Horner, was, no doubt, in Lord Brougham's mind when he remarked that, whereas Fox had cultivated the society of Irishmen, Lord Holland preferred to associate with Scotsmen. Born in 1771, and the son of a writer to the Signet, he took a medical degree from Edinburgh University at the age of twenty. A professor of Whig opinions at a time when to hold those opinions was risky, he took part in a dinner held to celebrate the fall of the Bastille, and associated with the brilliant band which acknowledged the intellectual influence of Dugald Stewart, and which subsequently combined to found the *Edinburgh Review*. Sydney Smith, while staying in the Scots capital during the days of his early poverty with his pupil, Mr. Beach, also joined the set, and he it was, according to one account, who introduced Allen to Lord Holland. General Fox asserted, however, that the two were brought together by Lord Lauderdale. The explanation may be that Allen, hearing that Lord Holland was looking out for a medical man to accompany the family to Spain, armed himself with letters from both of them. Anyhow, he made his first appearance at Holland House in 1802, when General Fox remembered him as a "stout, strong man, with a very large head, a broad face, enormous round silver spectacles before a pair of peculiarly bright and intelligent eyes, and with the thickest legs I ever remember. His accent Scotch, his manner eager but extremely good-natured, all made a lasting impression on me, then a boy of six years old." Landseer's portrait attests the fidelity of this description as regarded the upper part of Allen's person. Sydney Smith poked fun at his legs when, some forty years later, he wrote to Lady Holland that " they are enormous—they are clerical ! He has the mind of a philosopher, with the legs of a clergyman ; I never saw such legs—at least belonging to a layman."

During the Spanish tour Allen could work his legs to some purpose. General Fox remembered that he used to start, book in hand, in front of the train, consisting of three large English carriages, and frequently arrived at the end of the next relay before it. If he was in danger of being overtaken he ran, swaying his body from side to side in the oddest manner. A philosopher on the trot must in truth have been a strange sight. Travel lasting nearly three years made Allen indispensable to Lord and Lady Holland, and when they returned home he joined their household, never to leave it. His medical qualifications passed out of sight, and, as Greville says, he became established permanently as a friend and looked upon as an immense literary acquisition. His duties embraced the preparation of the lists of those who were to be present at dinner, while during that meal he sat at the foot of the table and carved, often with a running commentary on his handiwork from Lady Holland, under which he was known to turn restive. He also arranged what rooms those staying in the house should occupy, though the more privileged, such as Rogers and Frere, had their own reserved for them. Out of doors he accompanied Lady Holland when she drove, and was usually invited with her and Lord Holland when they

dined with friends. He went abroad with them, and
Lady Granville describes how, in Paris, Lord Holland
roared with laughter when, at a sign from Lady Holland,
he meekly rose from the dinner-table to go with her to
the Théâtre Français.

Such an existence implies a complete surrender of
individuality rare among bachelors, since Allen was
never allowed to absent himself from Holland House
except for the few hours in each week when his
attendance at Dulwich College, where he was Master
for twenty-two years, was imperative. Yet, within the
prescribed boundaries, he managed to get pretty much
his own way. Completely in the confidence of Lord
and Lady Holland, he was treated by the master of the
house, says Greville, with uniform consideration, affection, and amenity, while its mistress worried, bullied,
flattered, and cajoled him by turns. To Macaulay, in
the early days of their acquaintance, he appeared to be
used by her " worse than a Nubian slave," but Sir Henry
Holland declares that she appeared to regard him with
"a certain dim fear." In their frequent sparrings he
seems to have got the better of it as often as not.
When, after the Restoration of the Bourbons, he commented on the age (forty) under which deputies were
not allowed to enter the Chamber, Lady Holland
descended on him with, " Come, come, Mr. Allen, for
the sake of a coarse epigram making a most brutal
remark ! " But he won a signal victory in an encounter
thus retailed by Lord Sefton to Creevey. She talked
about ages, and observed that Lord Sefton and Lord
Holland were of the same age—about fifty-six : " For
myself," she said, " I believe I am near the same." And
then the page, being called, was told to ask Allen how

old she was. The house, a "nutshell" she was occupy-
ing during a temporary absence from Holland House,[1]
being small and the rooms near, they heard Allen holloa
out in no very melodious voice, "She is fifty-seven."
But Lady Holland was not content with this, said it was
too old for her, and made the page go back again ; and
again they heard Allen roar, in a much louder voice, "I
tell you she's fifty-seven !" Altogether, there seems no
reason for finding fault with Greville's estimate that Allen
was "a mixture of pride, humility, and independence ;
he was disinterested, warm-hearted, and choleric."

Allen is chiefly remembered as the literary oracle of
Holland House. His learning and general knowledge
were extensive, and, living in a library, he was perpetually
adding to his stock. Byron, in his enthusiastic way,
described him as "the best informed and one of the
ablest men I know—a perfect Malliabrecchi ; a devourer,
a *heluo* of books, and an observer of men." He was
the universal referee, when discussions arose, on questions of fact, and he was never found at fault. Allen
was very Liberal, even Republican, in his political
opinions, and in religion a confirmed sceptic, whence
he was called in derision, "Lady Holland's atheist."
But theology was not touched upon at Holland House
except rarely and incidentally ; and besides, Allen did
not take much part in general conversation, though he
was naturally vivacious, and through long association
with wits became something of a wit himself. The
compactness of his knowledge was, however, his most
remarkable gift. Brougham, in a warmly eulogistic

[1] Evidently the house in South Street, where Guizot tells us that
Lord Holland had to dress in the dining-room and could find no
place in which to bestow his books.

notice of him to be found appended to the article on Lord Holland in the " Statesmen of the Time of George III.," declares that he had "the rare faculty of combining general views with details of fact, and thus at once availing himself of all that theory or speculation presents for our guide, with all that practical experience affords to correct those results of general reasoning." He was esteemed an authority on the politics of the day, though the instance of his wisdom given by Brougham will fail to impress most people by its profundity. It was to the effect that a negotiator ought not to display earnestness and anxiety, however necessary those qualities might be to one addressing a popular assembly. Allen's value as a political adviser consisted chiefly, it may be suspected, in the historical allusions he provided to Lord Holland's speeches and in the criticism he applied to his protests.

Brougham sneers at the "ruling caste" because Allen never filled any place in public life except for a few months in 1806, when he acted as Under Secretary to the Commissioners treating with America, of whom Lord Holland was one. But it is pretty certain that, if he had so desired and Lady Holland had so permitted, Allen would have experienced no more difficulty in finding a seat than Horner, Mackintosh, Romilly, Macaulay, or, for that matter, Brougham himself. He evidently loved his ease much more than he cherished his ambition, and found his time amply occupied with a multitude of small duties. Besides, his politics were always of an impracticable kind. A theoretical Republican, he ardently advocated that form of government until his eyes were opened by Napoleon's assumption of the purple. The limitation of liberty with which the Restoration of

the Bourbons was accompanied, and the reactionary
tendencies of Lord Liverpool's Ministry, so disgusted
him that he abandoned modern politics, for the time
being, for early constitutional history. But he emerged,
if Brougham is to be trusted, from the Heptarchy to
express his strong disapproval of the Reform Bill of
1831–32 ; he regarded it as all but revolutionary and as
having in the result worked great mischief in the composition of the House of Commons, whatever benefit it
might have secured to the Whigs as a party measure.

With his time much occupied in looking after the
concerns of others, he left nothing behind him worthy
of his reputation. His most important work, an " Inquiry
into the Rise and Growth of the Royal Prerogative in
England," published in 1830, stands at a disadvantage
nowadays because of the great advance in the study of
the origins of English history that has been accomplished
since it was written. The treatise, besides, hardly corre-
sponds with its title. It is not exactly an attempt to trace
the vicissitudes of the idea of kingship from the pure
despotism of the Conqueror or Henry II. and the
authority assumed by Henry VIII., when the *lex regia*
gave his proclamations the force of law, down to
its supersession by the " Venetian oligarchy " of the
eighteenth century. Allen sets himself to prove rather
that the actual power exercised by the monarch had
never squared with the legal fiction of an ideal king—as
stated by Blackstone—a statement too obvious to require
much demonstration. He puts, however, the Whig
theory which triumphed at the Revolution of 1688 with
clearness and sobriety :

" It is a rare fortune, and peculiar to England, that we have a family on the throne who have no legitimate pretensions to the Crown but what they derive from Parliament. The Act of Settlement, which is the sole foundation of their title, has cut off all obsolete claims, whether derived from Egbert or the Conqueror. . . . When we hear of a prerogative interest in the Crown, which the King has no legal means of exercising, we may be certain that it has no existence but in speculative notions of government. Emergencies may arise when it is necessary for the safety of the State to commit additional powers to the person intrusted with its defence. But when such cases occur, we are to be guided by considerations of reason and expediency in the power we confer and not by vain and empty theories of prerogative, which the very act we are called on to perform proves to be futile and unfounded."

All this is true enough, but Allen was too much disposed to quote Saxon precedents as if they had been the sole influence to colour the monarchical idea throughout English history.

The rest of Allen's writings are concerned mostly with controversial points whence the interest has evaporated. His patriotic pride having been touched by Sir Francis Palgrave's assertion that his country was subject to England from the seventh to the fourteenth centuries, he published in 1833 a "Vindication of the Ancient Independence of Scotland." He also carried on a pamphlet duel with Dr. Lingard, firing the first shot in the *Edinburgh Review* on the credibility of that Catholic historian's account of the massacre of St. Bartholomew. Of his other contributions to the *Edinburgh,* a review of Warden's letters from St. Helena astonished Napoleon when it reached that island by its intimate knowledge of his early life. The number which was forwarded to the Emperor, and which he marked approvingly in the margin, is now in the Holland House library ; the information was derived by Lord Holland from Cardinal Fesch. But a study on the interior economy and administration of Spain under the different periods of her history, the materials for which he collected during the tour of 1807 with the Hollands and Lord John Russell, was never finished, and some " Suggestions for the Cortes" were printed for private circulation only, though Dr. Parr decided he had never read anything " with such unhesitative approbation." His sympathy with Spanish Liberalism induced him, however, to give constant assistance and advice to Blanco White when that refugee was producing his propagandist paper, the *Español*, and he subsequently persuaded the unhappy being to stand, though without success, for the organist fellowship at Dulwich. " With your knowledge of music I have no doubt that you will learn to play the organ in a much shorter time than a few months" is an encouragement which reads rather oddly in these days of acute competition. Allen had evidently forgiven Blanco White his " Evidences Against Catholicism," which, on its appearance in 1825, made him explode with comical wrath :

" Since we last parted, I have read your book with very great pain, and no small degree of mortification. I was grieved you should have written a book, the tendency of which was to defeat an object to which so many of your friends have devoted their lives and sacrificed every worldly prospect, and I was surprised and mortified, after so many years' acquaintance, to discover, for the first time, that you were an enemy to Catholic Emancipation. Notwithstanding your hatred of the Church of Rome, I believed you a sincere friend of religious liberty ; but now I find that, after all your

efforts to divest yourself of the rags of Popery, the mantle of
Father Torquemada still cleaves to you like the shirt of
Nessus.   I have not the vanity to suppose that I can disrobe
you, and as our last conversation might lead you to imagine
that I would make the attempt, I write chiefly to assure you
that, after reading your book, I have no thoughts of review-
ing it, nor of recommending to any other person to review it,
hastily, or at all."

Very different in tone from this irate rebuke were
Allen's letters to Horner during the last week of the sick
man's life; they were cheery and considerate.   To that
estimable politician's father he wrote a model specimen
of that difficult form of composition, a letter of
condolence:

"I have lost a friend of twenty years' standing, whose
advice I have for many years been accustomed to use on
every event and project of my life, to whose appreciation I
looked forward as the reward and incentive of all my labours
and occupations, in whose judgment I had the most perfect
reliance, and whose integrity of character and benevolence
of heart I had every day more reason to admire.   The
prospect of life before me, though uncertain, is long enough
to make me feel severely the loss of such a friend and
counsellor, and too short to allow me to indulge a hope that
I can acquire another of the same value, if such another as
he was is to be found."

When Allen died, in April, 1843, he was buried at
Millbrook, close by Lord Holland and a daughter of the
house, who found an early grave and to whom he had
been much attached.

CHAPTER VII

HOLLAND HOUSE AND FOX'S FRIENDS

The *salon* in England—The dining-room and library at Holland House—Wanted, a Boswell—Greville's record of conversation—Poets and women of genius—Lord Melbourne on theology—A tolerant atmosphere—General Fitzpatrick—Indolent but sagacious—Epigrams and the "Rolliad"—Hare's wit—An oracle of Brooks's—Lord John Townshend and Dudley North—Adair and the *Anti-Jacobin*—St. Petersburg and Constantinople—Adair and Stratford Canning—Lord Lauderdale—A violent Whig—Lauderdale's mission to France—A "cunning old renegade"—"Citizen" Stanhope—A Jacobin peer—Perverse inventions.

THE *salon*, as Hayward has remarked, is a social institution which cannot be said to have prospered largely out of France. It is essentially feminine, and demands a *femme d'esprit* for its head. It also implies intimacy between a small set of persons, who are accustomed to meet without any formal invitation. The nearest approach to an English *salon*, if we except the gatherings organised by Mrs. Montague and Miss Chapone, was made by the Miss Berrys, who were not unfrequently content to light the lamp over the door of their house in Curzon Street, by way of notice to their friends that they were at home. The society at Holland House was not conducted on these simple principles, which had indeed become impracticable, even in the London of the Regency, a London bounded on the

PORTRAIT OF ADDISON   LORD HOLLAND   JOHN ALLEN   LADY HOLLAND   DOGGETT (LIBRARIAN)

THE LIBRARY AT HOLLAND HOUSE

FROM AN ENGRAVING AFTER THE PAINTING BY CHARLES ROBERT LESLIE, R.A.

THE DUCHESS OF DEVONSHIRE

FROM AN ENGRAVING BY G. KEATING AFTER THE PAINTING BY SIR JOSHUA REYNOLDS, P.R.A.

south by Pall Mall, on the north by Oxford Street, on the east by Regent Street, and on the west by Park Lane. It thus escaped the narrow preciosity of a *coterie*, while a permanent element, Allen, Rogers, Luttrell, and—though probably to a less extent—Lord Melbourne, prevented its dinners from assuming an appearance of undue promiscuousness.

The dining-room was the rallying-point, described by Princess Liechtenstein as cheerful and convivial in appearance. "Besides many likenesses speaking to us from its crimson damask walls, it has a sideboard rich and glittering with venerable family plate, a great looking-glass in which a merry party may have the satisfaction of finding itself repeated, and a gay china closet, filled mostly from the East." It was, by a curious contradiction, the room in which Addison breathed his last. The pictures included Kneller's portrait of Lady Fox, Sir Stephen's second wife, Reynolds's of the first Lady Holland, and Fagan's of Elizabeth Lady Holland, and the likenesses of friends such as the third Lord Lansdowne after Lawrence, Moore by Shee, Rogers by Hoppner, and Lord John Russell by Hayter—an interesting group. The library, "that venerable chamber," as Macaulay calls it, with "shelves loaded with the varied learning of many lands and many ages," and portraits "in which were preserved the features of the best and wisest Englishmen of two generations," was originally a portrait gallery. Lord Holland's accumulated books banished the pictures into other rooms, though he still put many portraits above them, of friends, kinsfolk, and men of letters with Addison at their head.[1] Leigh Hunt gives

[1] This portrait is of dubious authenticity, and is supposed to be that of Addison's friend, Sir A. Fountaine.

the dimensions of the library as upwards of 90 ft. long, by only 17 ft. 4 in. wide, and 14 ft. 7 in. in height. "The moment one enters it," he continues, "one looks at the two ends and thinks of the traditions about Addison's pacings to and fro," with a bottle of wine to fortify him at each end of the room. Leigh Hunt took exception to the vaulted compartments of the ceiling, with their groundwork of blue relieved by gold stars, as unsuitable to the winter's enjoyment of a book by the fireside. But the library looks cosy enough in Leslie's picture, which engravings have rendered familiar; and it is superfluous to dwell on its historical and literary associations.

Greville is the only diarist who chronicles with any minuteness the conversation at Holland House. The entries in Moore's journal are interesting enough so far as they go, but they are chiefly concerned with scraps of conversation which relate to himself and his projects, and Mackintosh is even less illustrative. Macaulay, amusingly though he writes about Holland House, is chiefly concerned with "her" oddities, her oppression of Allen, and her perturbation when the French cook was ill. But he makes no attempt to give the range of the conversation or the part taken in it by the various speakers. Holland House, in short, never had its Boswell. Yet Lord Holland himself kept a six days' record of the conversation in 1814, as an experiment of what could be done in that direction, which he showed, amongst others, to Jeffrey. " It is very entertaining," writes the latter, "and contained some capital specimens of Grattan, Parr, Frere, Windham, and Erskine, but I quite agree with him that it would not have been fair to continue it." A continuous chronicle, had its existence become generally known, would certainly have acted as a damper to the talk of all except the most hardened of drawing-room declaimers. But it would have been invaluable as illustrating just that period of the existence of Holland House which it is, most difficult to reproduce from the contemporary memoirs and diaries, the period when the Regency had attained the height of its prosperity, and when the contemporaries of Fox were rapidly being replaced by the contemporaries of Brougham and Melbourne.

Greville's record is chiefly concerned with conversations in which Macaulay and Lord Melbourne played the principal parts. Readers of the journal will remember how, meeting the historian for the first time, the diarist set him down as a dull fellow, how that opinion was modified by an allusion to the wounding of Loyola at Pampeluna, and how Lord Auckland's challenge, " Mr. Macaulay, will you drink a glass of wine ? " produced final enlightenment. The incident occurred in 1832. Two years later Greville made three elaborate attempts to chronicle the conversation. On the first evening there were present Lord Melbourne, Spring Rice, who was to succeed Lord Althorp as a Whig Chancellor of the Exchequer, and his son, and Lord Palmerston. They were subsequently reinforced by Allen and Bobus Smith. The talk turned on literature, Lord Melbourne expressing the unexceptionable opinion that Taylor's "Philip van Artevelde" was superior to anything in Milman. They held Wordsworth cheap, except Spring Rice, who was enthusiastic about him. Lord Holland thought Crabbe the greatest genius among modern poets. Lord Melbourne replied, with much pertinence, that he degraded every subject. After stories

had been told of Edward Irving and his followers, Lord
Holland took them back to the age of George III. and
Lord North. The Duke of Richmond told the King,
after an audience, that "he had said that to him which,
if he was a subject, he would not scruple to call an
untruth." A discussion on women's works elicited the
opinion that there were only three *chefs d'œuvre*, those
of Madame de Sévigné, Madame de Staël, and Sappho.
Mrs. Somerville was great in the exact sciences, and
Miss Austen's novels were excellent. Lady Holland
would not hear of Madame de Staël, and she certainly
seems outclassed in merit by her rivals. From women
writers the conversation passed to the early English kings
and Klopstock, the mystic.

Two nights later Lord Melbourne shone in a disputa-
tion with Allen :—

"After dinner there was much talk of the Church, and
Allen spoke of the early reformers, the Catharists, and how
the early Christians persecuted each other. Melbourne
quoted Vigilantius's letter to Jerome, and then asked Allen
about the 11th of Henry IV., an Act passed by the Commons
against the Church, and referred to the dialogue between the
Archbishop of Canterbury and the Bishop of Ely at the
beginning of Shakespeare's ' Henry V.,' which Lord Holland
sent for and read, Melbourne knowing it all by heart, and
prompting all the time. Lingard says of this statute that the
Commons proposed to the King to commit an act of spolia-
tion on the clergy, but that the King sharply rebuked them,
and desired to hear no more of the matter. About etymo-
logies Melbourne quoted Tooke's ' Diversions of Purley,'
which he seemed to have at his fingers' ends."

Less than a week later theology was again in the ascendant. Lord Melbourne, who, as Greville says, loved

dashing opinions, swore that Henry VIII. was the greatest man that ever lived, and Allen declared that if he had not married Anne Boleyn we should have continued Catholics to this day.

Lord Holland's contributions to these debates would have been interesting if they had been preserved. If we may judge from a letter of his to Blanco White, after that theological rake had completed his progress from Roman Catholicism, through Anglicanism, to the cold shades of Unitarianism, his opinions were practically those of an eighteenth-century Theist, unable to accept either the Athanasian interpretation of the New Testament or the Divinity of Christ. The atmosphere of Holland House was, however, essentially tolerant. Among its *habitués* were several clergymen besides Sydney Smith—for instance, Dr. Shuttleworth, Warden of New College and Bishop of Chichester, who as a young man had been tutor to General Fox.

The friends of Fox formed the nucleus of Holland House society. Rogers, it is true, was an early accession, and " Monk" Lewis was another man of letters who joined the circle before the close of the eighteenth century. But even John Allen, as we have seen, as well as Luttrell, Sydney Smith, Moore, and Mackintosh, were later additions. General Fitzpatrick, on the other hand, as Lord Holland's uncle by marriage and the most intimate friend of Fox, ranked as one of the family. Few men have ever enjoyed a higher social reputation, though it had reached its climax before the nineteenth century dawned. In his youth he was the inseparable companion of Fox, a partner in his ventures at Newmarket and at cards, his fellow-traveller on the Continent, and a sharer in his taste for the classics, private theatricals and polite conversation. He was much in the company of David Hume, of whom he used always to speak as "a delicious creature"; and he remembered the tears of gratitude shed by Rousseau in his Chiswick lodgings when Hume succeeded in recovering a favourite dog that had been lost. His dandyism was of a quieter kind than the florid style affected by his friend; indeed, so exquisite were his manners considered that the Duke of Queensberry—"Old Q," no mean judge on the point —left him a handsome legacy as the finest gentleman of the day. Fitzpatrick's progress in the army was chiefly due to his family connections. But though he strongly disapproved of the American War, he played a brave part when ordered to the front with a relief of his battalion.

It was to please Fox that Fitzpatrick entered the House in 1774, the Duke of Bedford having provided him with a seat at Tavistock; and as Irish Secretary under the Duke of Portland and Secretary of War in the Coalition with Lord North he displayed ability and even some aptitude for business. His constitutional indolence, however, got the upper hand; as the years went on he withdrew from debate, though his speech of 1796 in pro-test against the imprisonment of Lafayette by the Allies was a parliamentary event. If we may judge from his calling the altercation between Burke and Sheridan, which preceded the final breach between the first of the pair and Fox, "a fine race for the Curragh," he took politics jocularly even in serious times. None the less Fox poured out his most private thoughts to his "dear Dick," and depended much on his judgment as to matters and men. Upright and devoid of enthusiasms, he acted as a drag on his cousin's impetuosities; a profound judge of character, he diverted Fox from misplaced trust in various adventurers, of whom a journalist named O'Brien appears to have been the most dangerous.

"A man of pleasure, wit, eloquence, all things," wrote Byron, who only saw him in his decline, of Fitzpatrick. Pleasure visited on him a shattered constitution which rendered him a cipher when he became Secretary at War, for the second time, in the Administration of 1806, and his political interests expired with the death of his friend. Of the eloquence of his single great speech we have spoken already. As to his wit in society, there is Madame du Deffand's opinion that he was a cleverer talker than Fox, and Rogers's that he was nearly the equal of Hare. Adair's verdict was practically the same : Fitzpatrick the most agreeable of all the friends of Fox, Hare the most brilliant. But even in his lifetime his reputation depended chiefly on his ready pen. Horace Walpole circulated his riddles, though he neglected to supply the answers. No album, not even the immaculate Brummell's, was complete without a set of verses by Fitzpatrick. He scarified his political foes ; the youthful Canning for one, when he decided on throwing in his lot with the Tories :

> "The turning of coats so common is grown
>   That no one would think to attack it ;
> But no case until now was so flagrantly known
>   Of a schoolboy turning his jacket."

He extolled his friends, as in his well-known, though not very appropriate, lines on Nollekens's bust of Fox :

> "A Patriot's even course he steer'd
>   Midst Faction's wildest storms unmov'd,
> By all who mark'd his Mind, rever'd ;
>   By all who knew his Heart, belov'd."

Lord Holland's coming of age was celebrated, too, by some neat verses written for the temple built by Fox at St. Anne's Hill.   But the savour has inevitably departed from much that Fitzpatrick wrote.   "Dorinda, a Town Eclogue," is a facile, though fairly spirited, account of the boredom endured by fine ladies during their banishment to the country at the close of the season.   He put his talents to better purpose in the "Rolliad," the pungent satire composed by himself, George Ellis, Sheridan's friend Richardson, and others on the Tory majority of squires, nabobs, and City aldermen who supported Pitt, and more particularly on Mr. Rolle, the unsophisticated Devonshire member, whose most important contributions to debate took the form of trying to cough down Burke.   Ellis contributed the wittiest pieces, such as the burlesque of the Rolle pedigree at the commencement and the happy attack on the young Prime Minister, beginning—

"Pert without fire, without experience, sage."

But the twelfth number, which Lord John Russell identifies as Fitzpatrick's, fully sustains the level of the whole, as in its description of Mr. Rolle, who—

"Majestic sits, and hears, devoid of dread,
The dire Phillippicks whizzing round his head.
Your venom'd shafts, ye sons of Faction, spare :
However keen, ye cannot enter there."

Alderman Watson, whose leg had been bitten off by a shark, is thus commemorated :

" 'One moment's time might I presume to beg !'
Cries modest Watson, on his wooden leg ;
That leg, in which such wondrous art is shown,
It almost seems to serve him like his own.
Oh ! had the monster, who for breakfast eat
That luckless limb, his nobler noddle met,
The best of workmen, nor the best of wood,
Had scarce supply'd him with a head so good."

About the time that Lord Holland was gathering
his friends round him, Canning satirised the Bench of
Wit at Brooks's :

"Where Hare, Chief Justice, frames the stern decree,
While with their learned Brother sages three,
Fitzpatrick, Townshend, Sheridan, agree."

Of them, James Hare—" the Hare of many friends " as
the Duchess of Gordon called him—made his wit tell
by his manner of uttering it.   Fox, Rogers relates, was
once sitting at Brooks's in a very moody manner, having
lost a considerable sum at cards, and was indolently
moving a pen backwards and forwards over a sheet of
paper.   "What is he drawing ? " said some one to Hare.
" Anything but a draft," was the reply.   Again, when
Sheridan, in the course of his speech against the Union,
boasted that he was a descendant of the Irish kings and
" an old Milesian," Hare readily remarked that he
evidently alluded to his connection with Miles's
gambling-house.   " He was one of those men," wrote
Lord John Russell in a note to Moore's diary, " who
glittered with wit and humour in their day, but whose
fame *caret vate sacro.*"   He also characterised Hare's
wit as being, like Sydney Smith's, of the sparkling order

in contrast to Talleyrand's and Sheridan's, which was dry.

Hare was, in short, a striking instance of how far agreeable manners and a ready tongue could carry a person of obscure origin in the eighteenth century. The son of an apothecary, who sent him to Eton, he was a poor man throughout his life. Hare was often on the lookout for employment, but Fox was only able to help him during the brief period (October, 1779, to January, 1782) when he served as British Minister at Warsaw. The story of his failure in the House is familiar. "Wait till you hear Hare," said Fox when receiving congratulations on his maiden speech. The House did hear Hare, when he rose to defend his friend, but with such impetuosity that rage almost choked his utterance. Hare, therefore, was reduced to become the oracle of Brooks's, and to inspire the young Whigs with the parliamentary courage which Nature had denied him. Behind the scenes he counted for much. His association with Holland House in the days of the third Lord Holland cannot have been a very long one, for when Fox visited the French capital in 1802 he found Hare there a hopeless invalid, and two years later the end came at Bath.

Lord John Townshend survived Fox many years, and died in 1833. In the House he was a characteristic specimen of the aristocratic and silent Whig who could be trusted to stand by his party in troublous times. In private life Jack Townshend, as became a member of his family, was a merry man, who called a spade a spade and Sheridan a liar. As a repository of Whig tradition, it was to him that Lord Holland applied for information about Sir Robert Adair's visit to St. Petersburg on the outbreak of the French Revolution, which the Tories asserted to have been due to his chief's desire to thwart the foreign policy of Pitt. Eighteenth-century diaries frequently allude to Lord John Townshend in association with Dudley North, another social wit who failed to make a figure in the House, but who is dimly remembered as a mourner at the funerals of Sir Joshua Reynolds and Burke, and as one of the daring few who ventured to question Sir Philip Francis on the authorship of "Junius."

Adair, who lived on until 1855, was actually the last survivor of Fox's friends. Moore's diary records him as dining frequently at Holland House in the year 1825, and as telling on one occasion a capital story about a peer who kept on saying in one of his speeches, "I ask myself so and so." "Yes," said Lord Ellenborough, "and a damned silly answer you'll get." By that time he had come to be in great request as giving what Moore calls an agreeable whiff of the days of Fox, Tickell, and Sheridan. He might also consider himself as something of a martyr to the Whig cause. His intimacy with Fox had earned him in 1728 unmerciful roasting from the *Anti-Jacobin*. He was the Rogero of the "Rovers" who loved "sweet, sweet Matilda Pottingen"; he was the Bobba-dara-adul-phoola of the satire on Sir John Sinclair's Association for Promoting the Discovery of the Interior Parts of Africa, and his visit to the Court of the Empress Catherine was quizzed in "A Bit of an Ode to Mr. Fox" as well as in the lines :

> "Or is it He—the Youth whose daring Soul
> With *Half a Mission* sought the Frozen Pole ;
> And then, returning from th' unfinish'd work,
> Wrote *Half a Letter*—to demolish Burke ?[1]

[1] The real title was "Part of a Letter from Robert Adair to C. J. Fox, occasioned by Mr. Burke's mention of Lord Keppel in a recent Publication."

Adair's friendship for Fox, which began before he was twenty, constituted his chief, if not his only offence in the eyes of Canning and his associates.   His journey abroad, mysterious though it was, does not really seem to have been a mission of anti-patriotic intrigue.   In after years Adair asserted that he wished to qualify himself for diplomatic employment.   As young men will, he aired his Whiggism by rudeness to the British Minister at St. Petersburg, while his inexperience contended on unequal terms with the consummate cunning of the Empress Catherine.   When his knowledge had hardened, Fox employed him, in 1806, on a mission to warn the Austrian Government against the aggressive intentions of Napoleon.   The Court of Vienna objected to him as not being of a sufficiently good family until some one, remembering that he was the son of a famous surgeon, answered, " Mais c'est le fils du plus grand saigneur de l'Europe."   He was avenged of the *Anti-Jacobin* on his return, for Canning, recognising his ability, despatched him to Constantinople to renew relations with the Porte.   Diplomatically the mission was a success, socially it is remembered for the quiet firmness with which Adair suppressed Lord Byron's attempt to take precedence at some reception of various dignified Ambassadors, a lesson which the poet at first resented and afterwards acknowledged to be just.

Adair's greatest service to his country consisted in the training of young Stratford Canning, afterwards Lord Stratford de Redcliffe, who, as an undergraduate-diplomatist, accompanied him to Constantinople.   With Napoleon triumphant in Europe, he had a most difficult task, but, as his subordinate observed, he brought to it " a conscientious zeal and a liberal intelligence, accompanied by an amount of strenuous practical upright ability much above par." His mission came to an end in July, 1810 ; and he left Canning, aged twenty-four, behind him as Minister Plenipotentiary. Adair's last mission abroad was in 1831, when Lord Palmerston sent him to the Netherlands, where he prevented a general war between the Dutch and Belgian troops. When he died in October, 1855, at the age of ninety-two, his pupil, become Lord Stratford de Redcliffe, and within a year of seventy, mourned him with tears, as he used to mourn Fox. It was while walking through Chiswick House that Adair asked Rogers in which room it was that Fox had died. "In this very room," was the answer, and Adair burst into tears. That tribute of affection, notes Macaulay, was paid to Fox but not to Byron. Allowance should also be made, however, for the propensity to conceal the natural tearful man, which increased with the advance of the nineteenth century.

Adair was fond of telling how Sheridan once said, on entering a room, " By the silence that prevails, I conclude Lauderdale has been cutting a joke." On another occasion he is supposed to have answered the Earl's request for permission to repeat one of his stories with, " I must be careful what I say, for a joke in your mouth is no laughing matter." Lord Lauderdale was a typical Scot in his lack of humour, his broad accent, and his choleric temper. His violence of language twice led to challenges ; and he fought a bloodless duel, Fox acting as his second, with Benedict Arnold, the American renegade soldier. In his early days, as member for Newport, Cornwall, he was an extravagant opponent of the American War, and later an out-and-out supporter of the East India Bill and the impeachment of Warren

Hastings. Election as a Scottish representative peer, after the death of his father in 1789, was far from tranquilising that restless spirit. On the contrary, he scandalised the House of Lords by appearing in the "rough costume of Jacobinism," and, during a visit to Paris, held familiar intercourse with Brissot and other political leaders. He was one of the founders of the Society of the Friends of the People, and though Francis, Duke of Bedford, began by objecting to that imitation of the French clubs, Lauderdale was not content until he had dragged him into revolutionary politics. He was, in short, among the most indiscreet of Fox's supporters. In rasping and ungrammatical Scotch he denounced the hostilities with France, brought forward a motion in favour of peace which received only eight votes, and was clamorous against the Habeas Corpus Suspension and Treasonable Practices Bill. His fellow-peers avenged themselves by declining to re-elect him, whereupon Lord Lauderdale seems to have contemplated ridding himself of his nobility.

Violent Whig though Lord Lauderdale may have been, he was unselfish. No room could be found for him in the Grenville and Fox Administration. " It is a damned thing," said Fox, " but it could not be otherwise. I saw it would not do, and one must not be impatient." Lord Lauderdale took his exclusion in perfect temper, and accepted the office of Keeper of the Great Seal of Scotland, a mere sinecure, to show that he was not out of humour. Another disappointment awaited him when the Directors of the East India Company declined to accept him as Governor-General, but he cheerily relinquished the object on which he had set his heart. He accepted, instead, the position of joint-commissioner, to negotiate peace with France, with Lord Yarmouth as a singularly incompetent colleague. The mission was, of course, a failure; but Lord Lauderdale, though disputatious in form, was conciliatory in substance. His tenacity about the *uti possidetis*, and his frequent recurrence to that phrase, led Napoleon to reproach him with an adherence to "des formules Latines," which, commented Lord Holland, "to those well acquainted with the nature of Lauderdale's acquirements in classical phraseology, was diverting enough."

To all appearance Lauderdale's Whiggism suffered no abatement for several years after the death of Fox. The town rang with his speech in support of Queen Caroline; and Lady Granville, who met him at Holland House during the trial, relates how he and Brougham compared the abuse they received in the shape of anonymous correspondence. She wondered if it was the extreme of honesty, or its opposite, that made him always hold his ground on every occasion. The doubt was justified by events, for his interests as a landlord had already made him the open champion of the restrictive Corn Law passed by the Liverpool Government, and by 1825 he was regarded as the confidant and adviser of the Cabinet. About that time, when the King's reigning favourite went to hear Edward Irving, he declared, with pawky humour, that the preacher had talked not of the heavenly mansions, but of the heavenly Pavilion. Lord Lauderdale's last public appearance was as an opponent of the Reform Bill; and so skilful was the manœuvring of the "cunning old renegade"—the expression is Lord Cockburn's—that out of the sixteen Scottish representative peers, twelve voted with the Opposition. It was a strange political end for one of

whom Fox had said, " I wonder how the world went on
when there was no Lauderdale to help it, or what will
become of it when he leaves it."

Charles, third Earl Stanhope, was a more considerable man than this pragmatic Scot. As the brother-in-
law of Pitt, he gave that statesman vigorous support in
the days when he was a parliamentary reformer ; and,
while still Lord Mahon and a member of the House of
Commons, he vehemently attacked the Coalition and the
East India Bill. But the French Revolution completed
an estrangement that the institution of the sinking fund
had begun. " Citizen " Stanhope flung himself into
democratic extravagance ; he became chairman of the
Revolution Society, and fathered some of its most in-
expedient addresses of congratulation to the French
Assembly. From his father and mother he had inherited a love of Liberty with a large L, and education
at Geneva had perfected that disposition. His principles
deserted him, however, when his third daughter eloped
with the family apothecary, and Gillray saw his chance
and took it in the caricature "Democratic Levelling :
Alliance à la Française ; the Union of the Coronet and
Clyster-pipe."

Lord Stanhope's opposition to the war with France
left him, on a famous occasion, January 6, 1795, in a
minority of one. After a five years' secession from Parliament, he reappeared to propose peace with the enemy,
and secured a solitary supporter, as eccentric as himself,
in Lord Camelford. Impervious to criticism, given to
making mischief, coarse in his anecdotes and ungainly
in his gestures, he was more at home at the "Crown and
Anchor " than in the House of Lords. Yet the Peers
laughed with him, when they were not laughing at him,

and he was missed when he succumbed to dropsy in the winter of 1816. Lord Stanhope was, in short, an irresponsible genius, who handed on his contempt for conventionality, though in a nobler form, to his daughter, Lady Hester, the mystic of Mount Lebanon, whom Lamartine and Kinglake have immortalised.

Stanhope's devotion to science was marked by the same perverse ingenuity as his politics, though he generously placed his inventions at the public disposal, without a thought of private gain. He effected a substantial advance in stereotyping, and a microscopic lens still bears his name. But his attempts to apply steam to land and water carriage were failures, despite their cleverness. A vehicle tried on the road between Calais and Boulogne, some ten years before the beginning of the nineteenth century, ran up hill with extraordinary rapidity, went along with some difficulty on the level, and stopped at every incline. In 1792 he built a steam collier of 200 tons which, according to Lord Holland, would have consumed its cargo before it reached its destination; nor were his "ambi-navigator" and other experiments more successful. It is worth mention that the friendship of Holland House descended to Citizen Stanhope's grandson, the historian, who, as Lord Mahon, had already made a reputation by his careful and impartial handling of the events of the eighteenth century, when the period under my survey came to a close. His exertions to secure literary copyright for authorship and his foundation of the National Portrait Gallery were later.

CHAPTER VIII

MORE FRIENDS OF FOX

The *Anti-Jacobin* on Erskine—A flippant conversationalist—
"Trial by jury"—Impromptu verse—Erskine's eloquence—As Lord
Chancellor—A graceless old age—Sheridan and the Whigs—His
mystifications—Carlton House politics—An isolated politician—
Drury Lane—Sheridan's last days—Sheridan in society—Sir Philip
Francis and the Prince—A quarrel with Fox—"Junius Identified"
—Lord Thurlow—An extinguished politician—Lord Macartney—
"Solomon in all his glory"—Sir Gilbert Elliot—The Portland
Whigs—The Grenvilles and the Whigs—Lord Minto in India—
Georgiana, Duchess of Devonshire—The "Passage of the Mountain
of St. Gothard."

ERSKINE was a characteristic member of the Fox
band, brilliant in his abilities, reckless in his wit,
and prodigal with his cash. His ingenuous egotism
has almost passed into a proverb. The *Anti-Jacobin*
parodied his addiction to oratorical autobiography with
inimitable humour in the second part of the " Meeting
of the Friends of Freedom " :

" Mr. Erskine concluded by recapitulating, in a strain of
agonising and impressive eloquence, the several more prominent heads of his Speech. He had been a Soldier and a
Sailor, and had a Son at Winchester School ; he had been
called by Special Retainers, during the Summer, into many
different and distant parts of the Country—travelling chiefly

in Post-chaises. He felt himself called upon to declare that his poor faculties were at the service of his Country—of the free and enlightened part of it, at least. He stood here as a Man—He stood in the Eye, and indeed in the Hand of God—to whom (in the presence of the Company and Waiters) he solemnly appealed. He was of Noble—perhaps Royal Blood—He had a house at Hampstead—was convinced of the necessity of a thorough and radical Reform. His Pamphlets had gone through Thirty Editions—skipping alternately the odd and even numbers—he loved the Constitution, to which he would cling and grapple—And he was cloathed with the infirmities of man's nature."

Vanity, bordering on insanity, was a marked feature in the Erskine family, but, added Sir Walter Scott in his diary, "they all had wit." Of the three brothers, the Earl of Buchan's was "crackbrained, and somewhat caustic ; Henry's was of the very kindest, best-humoured, and gayest sort that ever cheered society ; that of Lord Erskine was moody and muddish. But I never saw him in his best days." The reservation is important. The decline of Erskine was as melancholy as that of Sheridan. But, even when his triumphs at the Bar lay many years behind him, Rogers heard him tell stories of his past life in the navy and army—of a sensational reprieve of a soldier when he was kneeling to receive the fatal shot among them—and of his early struggles in the law, with point and dramatic effect. He ridiculed the sham erudition of the Prince of Wales, calling him, out of " The Vicar of Wakefield," a "cosmogony man," for he had but two classical quotations—one from Homer, and one from Virgil—which he never failed to sport when there was any opportunity of introducing them. Excellent, too, his remark, when he heard that somebody had died worth two hundred thousand pounds, " Well, that's a very pretty sum to begin the next world with." Then there is his famous answer to a begging-letter : " Sir, I feel much honoured by your application to me, and I beg to subscribe "—here the reader had to turn over the leaf—" myself your very obedient servant." [1] His talk was flippant, and sometimes unprintable ; but he wounded no man's feelings, and he never envied the success of others. In his old age Byron met him, and described him as " good, but intolerable."

" He jested, he talked, he did everything admirably, but then he would be applauded for the same thing twice over. He would read his own verses, and tell his own stories again and again—and then Trial by Jury ! I almost wished it abolished, for I sat next him at dinner. As I had read all his published speeches, there was no occasion to repeat them to me."

Lord Campbell, in his " Life of Lord Erskine," gives numerous specimens of puns, mostly legal, and of his impromptu verse. His best lines were taken from his notebook by Lord Holland, who observed him writing diligently while Plumer, a tedious counsel, was keeping him in court when he ought to have been dining with the Lord Mayor :

> " Oh that thy cursed balderdash
> Were swiftly changed to callipash !
> Thy bands so stiff and snug toupee
> Corrected were to callipee ;
> That since I can nor dine nor sup,
> I might arise to eat thee up ! "

[1] Lord Campbell, in his " Lives of the Chancellors," gives a different version of this story, and makes Erskine's letter an answer to Sir John Sinclair, who proposed that a testimonial should be presented to himself by the British nation.

The appearance and phraseology of George III. were thus ridiculed by his Chancellor :

"I may not do right, though I ne'er can do wrong;
I never can die, though I may not live long;
My jowl it is purple, my head it is fat—
Come, riddle my riddle. What is it? What? What?"

"Nostræ eloquentiæ forensis facile princeps" was inscribed on Nollekens's bust of Erskine at Holland House. He was undoubtedly the first of British advocates; pure in style, though he had learnt English "like a foreign language"; gifted with a musical voice, apter, as Brougham thought, to express pathos than indignation; devoted to his client's cause, always on the alert and always courteous. His speeches for the defendants in the State trials of 1794, Horne Tooke, Hardy, and Thelwall, raised him to the height of his renown. Disfigured though they are by appeals to the Creator, they remain masterpieces of passionate pleading and declamatory invective, alike admirable in exposition of the law of treason and exposure of a Government informer. It was hardly the case that, had Erskine failed, Pitt would have proceeded to proscribe those of Liberal opinions, and to institute a White Terror. The acquittals destroyed, nevertheless, the argument for revolution, even when, as in the case of William Stone, the evidence pointed to approval and, perhaps, to actual incitement, of a French invasion.

Erskine failed in the House, and Sheridan bluntly supplied him with the reason. "I'll tell you how it happens; you are afraid of Pitt, and that is the flabby part of your character." Occasionally he tried to hide his want of confidence under abuse, but his frothy

diatribes dashed in vain against the calm scorn of the
Prime Minister.   Erskine ranks, in fact, with the Frenchman, Berryer, as a supreme advocate and nothing more.
" Êtes-vous légiste ? " was the mortifying question of
Napoleon, to whom he was introduced by his official
title as Chancellor to the Prince of Wales.   His acceptance of the Great Seal in the Ministry of Fox and
Grenville was severely judged by the virtuous Romilly,
to whom he confessed his unfitness for the office.   His
shrewdness preserved him, however, from grave mistakes, and he presided with dignified impartiality at
the trial of Lord Melville.   But his innate levity deprived him of any weight in the Cabinet.   A more
incongruous adviser than Erskine when, after the
" Delicate Investigation " of 1806, it fell to him to
admonish the Princess of Wales on her conduct, cannot be conceived, and he appears to have undertaken
the mission in the spirit of Pantagruel.   As the
" Talents " Administration was tottering to its fall,
Erskine tried to pursue a devious course of his own.
Such was his confidence in his powers of persuasion
that he imagined himself, after a long audience, to
have overcome the indomitable will of George III.
" You are an honest man, my lord, and I am very
much obliged to you," was the regal reply to a prolix
harangue.   His embarrassed circumstances explained,
without excusing, his irregular conduct ; and he availed
himself of a delay in resigning the seals, due to various
cases on which he had to deliver judgment, to job his
son-in-law into a mastership in Chancery.   Romilly
considered that, should the Whigs return to office,
Erskine would not be Chancellor, " since his incapacity
for the office was too forcibly and too generally felt."

Erskine's last years, it must be confessed, were
graceless. The £200,000 he laboriously accumulated
at the Bar vanished through the simple process of
buying stock in the dearest and selling it in the
cheapest market. A thriftless Scot, that rare bird, he
gave gay parties at Evergreen Hall, Hampstead, the
guests at what Romilly called a great Opposition dinner
including Lord Holland, and sunk large sums in a
Sussex estate which produced nothing but broom.
He lived the idle life of a man about town, and
haunted the Courts at Westminster, regretting that he
had ever left the Bar. Finally it came to Arabella
Row, Pimlico, a Gretna Green marriage, and indigence.
Yet at times his voice was raised in worthy causes, such
as his own Bill for the Prevention of Cruelty to Animals,
a proposal that lay near the heart of a man who had
pet dogs, a pet goose, a pet macaw, and even pet leeches,
called Horne and Cline, after the celebrated surgeons.
Nor did a long attachment to George IV. deter him
exhausting his enfeebled constitution in chivalrous efforts
to secure a fair trial for Queen Caroline.

Sheridan preceded Erskine to the tomb by some seven
years, having also outlived his reputation. He did not
join the Holland House circle until long after "The
Rivals," "The School for Scandal," and "The Critic"
had been written and the Begum Speeches had been
delivered. The turning-point in his career may be considered to have occurred in 1791, when the rebuilding
of Drury Lane Theatre plunged him into serious financial
embarrassment, followed in the following year by the
death of his beautiful and accomplished first wife, the
St. Cecilia of Reynolds's brush. Nature having denied
method to Sheridan, he lost in his wife the steadying

and stimulating influence of his career. By that time, too, the quarrel between Fox and Burke—a dispute which Sheridan did much to acerbate—had riven the Whig party in twain. It was Sheridan's misfortune to follow the former, while agreeing with the latter in his repudiation of revolutionary excess. He had the sagacity to disapprove of the secession of Fox and his friends from Parliament, and they suspected him of speculating on their leader's retirement into private life, when the much-coveted seat at Westminster would fall vacant.

Sheridan was undoubtedly distrusted, and his descendant, the late Lord Dufferin, did not completely account for the suspicion with which he was regarded by setting it down to his poverty and Irish origin. He carried the habit of mystification, which in private life took the form of practical jokes, into his political negotiations, and loved to create complications, trusting to his mother-wit to extricate him. Fox, who was simplicity itself, was always thrown out by the artificiality of his character. He used without scruple, too, the materials for oratory which his friends were weak enough to show to him, and stole their good things, such as Sir Philip Francis's description of the Treaty of Amiens, "a peace of which everybody is glad, and nobody proud." His tricks behind the scenes stood in strong contrast with his integrity when he faced the footlights. On a general view of his public life, he may be pronounced to have spoken no more than the truth when he said to the Prime Minister of the day, "My visits to you may possibly be misunderstood by my friends, but I hope you know, Mr. Addington, that I have an unpurchasable mind."

It was after the death of Fox that Sheridan's relations

with the Whig leaders became distant to the verge of open enmity. The haughty Grenville disliked him, and, even while he was still holding the post of Treasurer of the Navy—a poor reward surely for all his services !—wished that he might be excluded from their confidences. Now, Sheridan belonged to the class of man that more readily forgives injuries than slights. His resentment became a matter of grave importance when the King's insanity became permanent, and the Prince, to whom he had devoted himself with romantic enthusiasm, assumed the Regency. Sheridan thought he could manage that selfish and astute individual, whom he complimented with the possession of a heart and understanding "beyond all, I believe, that ever stood in rank and high relation to society," adding, with a touch of Joseph Surface, "I am no flatterer, and I never found that to *become* one was the road to your real regard." He greatly overrated his influence ; still, in 1810 Carlton House politics, with Lord Moira as an amusing marplot, acquired an importance which had not belonged to them since the Regency Bill of 1788.

Sheridan's part in the negotiations with the Whigs seems to have been dictated by a mischievous delight in the game of intrigue, a joy in paying off old scores by ridiculing the pompous homilies of the Whig grandees, and fidelity to the Regent's interests as he understood them. He suppressed a good many truths and twisted others into a likeness to falsehood. He had his jest, and possibly his lawful revenge ; but they cost him dearly. Excluded from the Whig councils, he made a speech or two in Parliament in patriotic support of the war in the Peninsula. At the General Election of 1812 he was beaten at Stafford because he had not the wherewithal to bestow the customary five guineas on the electors ; and his exemption from arrest ceasing with his exclusion from the House, he was for a short period an inmate of a sponging-house in Took's Court, off Chancery Lane.

Sheridan's exertions to retrieve the fortunes of Drury Lane after its reopening in 1794 were strenuous ; and both " The Stranger," into which he introduced his well-known song " I have a silent sorrow here," and " Pizarro " brought money into the treasury. But the company had been playing to a loss at the Haymarket while the theatre was closed, and the cost of rebuilding exceeded the estimate by £70,000. To embarrassment succeeded ruin when, on February 24, 1809, Drury Lane was again burnt to the ground. Excluded from the management of the new theatre by the precise Whitbread, he was also prohibited from touching the £12,000 due to him until certain claims, subsequently discovered to be baseless, had been met. When, in 1795, he married his second wife, an extravagant and querulous woman, a level-headed lawyer reckoned his income at £10,000 a year ; after the fire his only certain source of income was the £800 paid him as Receiver of the Duchy of Cornwall, the sole reward for devoted services he ever received from the Regent.

It is no wonder that Sheridan's creditors clamoured round him ; and as they were mostly small tradesmen, the stir they made was prodigious. But his debts at the time of his death only amounted to £5,000, and they were paid by his relations. Report had much exaggerated their amount, and until Mr. Fraser Rae's " Biography " appeared, a pack of lies told by the Regent to Croker had established the legend that

Sheridan's last days were those of a neglected pauper.
As a matter of fact he was attended by the three leading
physicians of the day, and the Bishop of London prayed
by his bedside.   Withal, Moore's well-known lines came
too near the truth to be palatable :

" How proud they can press to the funeral array
    Of him whom they shunn'd in his sickness and
       sorrow—
  How bailiffs may seize his last blanket to-day
  Whose pall shall be held by nobles to-morrow."

Canning and Lord Lauderdale, who cared for Sheridan
in his last illness, cut better figures than those who were
content with attending a magnificent funeral.

In an undated letter, printed by Mr. Rae, Sheridan
describes " the joyous dear manner in which *he* [Lord
Holland] seeing me coming up Berkeley Square yesterday, *ran* like a schoolboy, lame as he was, to catch me
by the hand."   He was, indeed, in great request at
Holland House, where Lady Holland, with a boldness
almost Boadicean, used to instruct him in the niceties
of the English language.   His conversation was irre-
sistible, and in his prime nothing could exceed the
vivacity of his retort.   Moore, who undervalued his
intellectual powers, declared that his *bons mots* in society
were not always to be set down to the credit of the
occasion, but that frequently, " like skilful priests, he
prepared the miracle of the moment beforehand," and
that he remained inert until he could make his point.
Want of spontaneity is a charge often advanced against
professional jesters, and seldom substantiated.   Byron's
praise does not convey the idea of a carefully hoarded

wit : "I have seen him cut up Whitbread, quiz (elsewhere, *iron*) Mme. de Staël, annihilate Colman, and do
little else by some others (whose names as good friends
I set not down) of good fame and address." Byron
proceeded to allude to the failing of his later years :
"Poor fellow ! he got drunk very thoroughly and very
soon." Towards the end, too, his humour became ill-
conditioned, in spite of Moore's saying that his

> "Wit, in the combat as gentle as bright,
> Ne'er carried a heart-stain away on its blade."

"His humour, or rather wit," declared Byron, "was
always saturnine and sometimes savage : he never
laughed (at least that *I* saw, and I watched him)."
But Sheridan was a broken man when Byron came to
know him, and even so he could put down "Monk"
Lewis. "I will bet you, Mr. Sheridan, a very large
sum : I will bet you what you *owe me* as manager for
my 'Castle Spectre.'" "I never make large bets," said
Sheridan, "but I will lay you a very *small one ;* I will
bet you what it is *worth.*"

Sir Philip Francis, the son of Charles Fox's tutor,
Dr. Francis, owed his earliest step in active life, a junior
clerkship in the Secretary of State's office, to the first
Lord Holland. Gratitude, if such a word can be
employed where he is concerned, attached him, therefore to the Whigs, and, in addition, he found them
invaluable instruments for executing his vengeance on
Warren Hastings. The beginning of the nineteenth
century found him excluded for the time being from
Parliament, but he was returned in 1802 for Appleton
through the influence of his friend, Lord Thanet. The

political importance of Francis lay, in any case, outside
rather than inside the House. Members thought his
speeches pompous and pedantic, nor did his "Little
Indian" views carry weight in days when British
armies went forth to conquer. But he was a frequent
guest at the Brighton Pavilion; well regarded by
Mrs. Fitzherbert, and much in the confidence of the
Prince of Wales, but bitterly jealous of Sheridan,
Erskine, and Lord Moira. In the "Francis Letters" an
allusion is to be ιfound to a long conference with the
Prince on public affairs; and as he at that time regarded himself as head of the Whig Party, Francis
must have built up hopes on the intimacy. But when
the Royal affection for the traditional principles of
1688 grew cold his influence declined, and in 1811 the
keen eye of Creevey noted that, though he continued
to frequent the Pavilion, he was "not there on the
Prince's invitation, nor as a member of his suite, and
was evidently slighted." His career as a director of
Carlton House politics was finished.

Five years earlier Francis had quarrelled with Fox
when that statesman, perplexed between multitudinous
claims, decided that the Governor-Generalship of India
must be entrusted to the safer hands of Lord Minto.
His rancorous resentment comes out in a letter written
in 1815 to Perry, the editor of the *Chronicle*: "Do you
think that, if Mr. Fox had found it coincide with his
politics or his partialities to have permitted me to return
to India in 1806, in the office that was as much my right
as was his to be Secretary of State, I would not have put
a stop to such enormities [as the Juggernauth]?" Thus
the malignant satirist of others ended his public activity
in disappointment amply merited, declining the

governorship of the Cape, worth £10,000 a year, and accompanied by the offer of the Bath and a seat on the Privy Council.

In 1812, and again in 1814, Franciss curses came home to roost when John Taylor published, first a pamphlet in which he sought to prove that Dr. Francis and his son were joint authors of the " Junius Letters," and next the remarkable work, " Junius Identified," in which he concentrated his attack on Sir Philip alone. Brougham ably seconded the charge in the *Edinburgh Review*. Francis had just married a second wife, a lady forty years his junior, and she has left an artless but invaluable account of his secretive behaviour under the accusation. He was extremely alarmed ; he refused to read the book for some months ; when he did so he shut himself up in his own room, and emerged thence greatly agitated. At the same time he gave her " Junius " as a wedding present, with the recommendation to keep it quiet and study it attentively, and left her " Junius Identified " as a legacy. " In every word that fell from him in society," wrote Lady Francis, " he seemed, as at chess, to see ten moves before him, and to be on his guard not to lay his game open to any of them. He was ever on his guard against himself." He withdrew his name from Brooks's, though he was a kind of father to the club, and it had been a constant resource. In society his irascibility created dread : "Sir Philip, give me leave to ask one question," said an innocent gentleman. "At your peril, sir !" was the startling and peremptory interruption. It was at Holland House that a familiar and credible incident is supposed to have occurred. Rogers was simple enough to be persuaded by Lord Holland or some other mischievous friend to go and ask

Francis point-blank if he wrote "Junius." He returned discomfited. They questioned him as to his success. " I do not know whether he is in Junius," was the reply, " but I am sure he is Brutus." Rogers always denied the story, but social autocrats do not care to remember early rebuffs, and it is confirmed by Lady Francis. When Lady Holland taxed Francis with the authorship, he resorted, as usual, to an angry evasion : " Now that I am old, people think they may with impunity impute to me such rascality, but they durst not have done so when I was young." [1] At Holland House, anyhow, Sir Philip perpetrated the one magnanimous observation that stands to his credit. " The jackals herd together," said he, speaking of Pitt's isolation ; " the lion walks alone."

Francis feared one man, and that man was Lord Thurlow. Creevey tells us that in the autumn of 1805 he often fixed his time for " making an example of the old ruffian," but that, though the ex-Chancellor was always ready for battle, he never stirred. Even in his decline, Thurlow inspired more dread than any one since Judge Jefferys was wont to " give a lick with the rough side of his tongue." Horne Tooke went down before him at Lady Oxford's despite frequent applications to the bottle ; " it seemed," says Creevey, who witnessed the scene, " as if the very look and voice of Thurlow scared him out of his senses." Curran, readiest of Irish wits, cut no better figure. Though remarkably courteous to ladies, " two or three hours were spent by him at dinner in laying wait for any unfortunate slip or ridiculous observation that might be made by any of his male visitors, whom, when caught, he never left hold of until

---

[1] Mr. C. F. Keary's essay, contributed to " The Francis Letters," summarises the Junius controversy with impartial ability.

I have seen," adds Creevey realistically, "the sweat run down their faces with the scrape they had got into." A full suit of the old fashion, with a great wig and long ruffles, as painted by Phillips in the well-known portrait, huge black eyebrows and a voice of rolling, murmuring thunder added to Thurlow's terrors. Hare alone fairly beat him, so distinguished and daring was his conversation.

Lord Holland, mindful of his uncle's droll remark, "I suppose no man was ever so wise as Thurlow looks," held him a good deal more cheaply than Creevey. He derived some instruction and more amusement from his conversation, but the "Memoirs of the Whig Party" convey that his learning was more singular than accurate, and his wit ponderous, as indeed it was. "With regard to the case of Regulus on which my learned friend has laid such a stress," was his knockdown reply to a classical allusion affectedly advanced by Wedderburn. Lord Thurlow's ascendancy over the House of Lords came from a majestic presence, an oracular manner, and a sincere belief in the excellence of monarchical and patrician institutions. But Pitt took his measure when in 1792 he compelled him to resign because of his intrigues during the Regency Crisis and his factious opposition to the Sinking Fund, much as Lord Melbourne afterwards banished a Chancellor almost as formidable in Lord Brougham. Thenceforward he never met the Government in the open, but became absorbed in the subterranean politics of Carlton House, and shortly before his death in 1806 was believed to have embittered rather than alleviated the domestic differences of the Prince and Princess of Wales by his attempted mediation between them. The public at large invested the surly old dog with attributes almost Satanic ; and it was a matter of general belief that his last utterance took the form of a comprehensive oath hurled at his servants as they were carrying him upstairs to the room in which he died.

Two of Fox's early associates, besides Adair, sought their fortunes abroad. George, afterwards Earl, Macartney, became the early friend of his brother Stephen, and went with Charles himself to the Continent in the capacity half of companion, half of bear-leader. A dashing, handsome Irishman, he married a daughter of Lord Bute, and was a popular member of London society. He acquitted himself with credit in an embassy to the Court of the redoubtable Empress Catherine, and as Governor of Fort St. George, though too much inclined to overrule the military element, he maintained a bold policy against Hyder Ali and his successor, Tippoo Sahib. His objection to the restoration of the Nabob of Arcot, which formed an article of the treaty of peace, was so strong as to persuade him into an injudicious resignation, but he left India with clean hands. Lord Macartney was a bright writer, and the " Journal " of his embassy to China, an enterprise he undertook in 1792, is a classic in its way. The mission failed in its main object, the establishment of a British Resident at Pekin, but its members were much impressed by the Emperor, "a very fine old gentleman, still healthy and vigorous, not having the appearance of a man of more than sixty," though he was eighty-three. "Thus," continued the enthusiastic Irishman—

" have I seen *King Solomon in all his glory.* I use this expression, because the scene recalled to my mind a puppet-show

of that name, which I recollect to have seen in my child-
hood, and which made so strong an impression on my mind
that I thought it a true representation of the highest pitch of
human greatness and felicity."

Lord Macartney's last employment was as the first
Governor of Cape Colony, an appointment he resigned,
owing to ill-health, in 1798. Though much crippled by
the gout, he enjoyed some years of retirement at Corney
House, Chiswick, frequenting the Royal and Antiquarian
Societies and the Literary Club, where, as an original
member, he had, in his younger days, associated with
Burke and Johnson. An agreeable talker, he had a
prodigious memory for dates and genealogies, and it was
said of him at Turin that he knew more about the French
and Italian families than they did themselves.

Sir Gilbert Elliot, first Earl of Minto, was a more considerable man than Lord Macartney. Sprung from a
Lowland stock which gave to the Scottish Bench two
upright judges and to the House of Commons a philo-
sopher-politician whose ability Horace Walpole, no
admirer of those from beyond the border, was forced
to acknowledge, he distinguished himself as a young
barrister by a legal argument on the Poole election, considered by Fox as, perhaps, the best he ever heard.
Elected member for Morpeth, he at first gave general
support to the Administration of Lord North, but before
the close of the American War he became a declared
follower of Fox and Burke. His correspondence, on
which his great-niece, the Countess of Minto, has founded
a fascinating biography, proves him to have been fully
alive to the vagaries of the former, but to have regarded
the latter with an affection not far removed from worship.

At the outbreak of the French Revolution he soon fore-
saw the inevitable schism between Fox and Burke, and
for a time tried to avoid taking a side. But by May, 1792,
he had thoroughly identified himself with the Portland
Whigs, and was the first of that party to accept the
Ministerial overtures. In September they had matured
into his appointment as Civil Commissioner at Toulon.
He spent several years abroad, organising in various
capacities the resistance to Revolutionary France,
notably as Viceroy of Corsica and Envoy Extraordinary
at Vienna. Reduced to be a spectator of events by the
treaty of Lunéville, he resigned his appointment, and
returned home in 1801 to find the Addington Ministry
floundering along.

Lord Minto spent five years at home, attending Dugald
Stewart's lectures in Edinburgh with his son and young
Harry Temple, afterwards Lord Palmerston, and visiting
Nelson at Merton Abbey, where Lady Hamilton
" crammed him with trowelfuls of flattery, which he
went on taking as quietly as a child does pap." He was
also a friend of the Princess of Wales, though scandalised by her indiscretions. Having taken a house in
Kensington, he dined at Holland House in August, 1805.
" I like Lord Holland in private extremely," he wrote.
" Nothing can be more perfectly natural, good-natured,
moderate, or cheerful. She is grown very fat, but otherwise just as she was." Soon afterwards he became
almost domesticated there, and had Frere's room assigned
to him as a regular thing. By that time the Addington
Ministry had collapsed, and Lord Minto's leaders, Lord
Grenville and Windham, by gravitating to the Whigs,
had wrecked Pitt's project of forming a Government on
a broad basis. He joined the coalition, at first, with

great reluctance, but with the honourable feeling that he must "act with those with whom he had been connected all his life in friendship as well as politics"; though he had no liking for Fox. When Pitt died, Lord Holland wrote to him : " Exclusive of that concern that we must all feel for the loss of so remarkable a man, I am one who in a party view do not think this event a fortunate one for the cause or the country." The history of the "Talents" Administration certainly justified that foreboding. On the change of Government Lord Minto was rewarded, however, by the Presidency of the Board of Control, and not long afterwards by the Governor-Generalship of India, a duty seriously undertaken. It is unnecessary to survey a rule which comprised much legal and educational reform and a vigorous foreign policy directed against the French and Dutch. Lord Minto gave his life for India, for in 1814 he returned to England to die, and sank at Stevenage, on the first stage of his journey to his native Scotland.

The Whig Egeria, Georgiana, Duchess of Devonshire, was also a visitor at Holland House before her early death in 1806. In social history she belongs to an earlier world—the world that Dr. Johnson edified, Reynolds and Gainsborough painted, and Horace Walpole quizzed. Her empire over fashion was signalised by her suppression of hoops and adoption of the graceful folds familiar to later generations through Sir Joshua's brush. But she owed her ascendancy not to display, and hardly to good looks, but to charm of manner. ' 'She effaces all without being a beauty," wrote Horace Walpole, " but her youthful figure, flowing good-nature, sense and lively modesty, and modest familiarity make her a phenomenon." She entertained Dr. Johnson at Chatsworth,

though his Toryism was by no means of her way of
thinking. Fox, Sheridan and Hare were, on the contrary,
her favourite associates, and she knew all the moves of
the Whig game. Her partisanship reached its height
during Fox's famous contest for Westminster in 1784,
when she canvassed the slums, and won over a gallant
butcher by a kiss. But she was in the confidence of the
Opposition leaders down to the end of her life. In 1806
Fox consulted her on some business, obscurely indicated
in his letter, in which the Prince of Wales, with whom
scandal connected her name—probably without any
foundation—and Sheridan were concerned. Just before
her death she rejoiced over the advent of her friends to
power, but her patriotism was wide enough to enable her
to lament the death of Fox's great rival. Thus she wrote
to Sir Augustus Foster, the son of her inseparable companion and successor as Duchess of Devonshire, Lady
Elizabeth Foster :

" Mr. Pitt's death was felt by his opponents in a manner that
did equal honour to him and them. They regretted his loss
and talents, and I may venture to say Mr. Fox would be well
pleased indeed could he recall him to life and place him in
his Cabinet. At any other time I should rejoice and exult in
the assemblage of talent and integrity which we now can
boast of, but, alas ! in these times what is to be done ? It is
uphill labour, and it must be to the regret of everyone that
the proposed junction was not suffered to take place when
it might have saved Europe."

According to a story told by Sir Thomas Lawrence,
Hare chaffed her amiable readiness to make promises by
writing a letter in her name which granted an imaginary
interview, and addressing it "Anybody, Anywhere."

The same easy-going disposition caused her to run up many debts, mostly incurred at Martindale's faro-table, but a settlement was effected two years before her death, on which occasion the Duke, though reputed to be an ungracious husband, displayed conduct which, in Lady Elizabeth Foster's opinion, was "angelic." In days when everyone rhymed, the Duchess of Devonshire celebrated her friends and public events in versified effusions. As is well known, her "Passage of the Mountain of St. Gothard" inspired Coleridge with the ode bearing the refrain :

> "O lady, nursed in pomp and pleasure,
> Whence learned you that heroic measure?"

The heroic measure is wedded, unfortunately, to prosaic words ; and poverty of thought accompanies most of the Duchess's verse, such as her tame lines on the death of Hare and on the battle of Trafalgar. She was at her best when prompted by affection, as in the poem addressed, when she was apprehensive of losing her eyesight, to Lady Elizabeth Foster :

> "Ere my sight I was doomed to resign,
> My heart I surrendered to thee ;
> Not a Thought nor an Action was mine,
> But I saw as thou badst me to see."

That is pretty good for a Duchess ; and, in any case, she did not live in vain, since she inspired Reynolds to several portraits, including the delightful and masterly portrait of herself and child, painted in 1786, and Romney to a characteristic head and bust. The famous Gainsborough has undoubtedly been finished by a later hand.

CHAPTER IX

GRENVILLE, GREY, AND WINDHAM

" Our English Cato "—Grenville and Pitt—" Most affectionately yours "—The "Talents" Administration—The Regency Bill—Grenville's rupture with the Whigs—At Dropmore—Lord Grey's beginnings—His quarrel with the Regent—Grey and the Peninsular War—Madame de Lieven and Earl Grey—The Reform Cabinet —Life at Howick—Windham and his diary—His conversation and tastes—" Weathercock Windham "—As Secretary at War—" That excellent statesman "—Windham's death.

THE Administration of "All the Talents" was one of the least efficient in English history ; it was not so much disliked as disregarded. Apart from the incongruous elements of which it was composed, the character of its chief, Lord Grenville, formed the chief source of its weakness. The son of that George Grenville who lost us the American Colonies because he confused pedantry with principle, he inherited most of his father's faults, some of them in double measure, and his one virtue, an intense industry. He was narrow, obstinate, impracticable, and cold ; the title, " Our English Cato," bestowed on him by Sir Augustus Foster in one of his letters to his mother, describes him by no means amiss. He was hopelessly devoid of any quality calculated to strike the popular imagination from afar, and at the same time destitute of the power of managing those with whom he came in immediate contact. "I am not competent," he wrote to his brother, "to the management of men. I never was so naturally, and toil and anxiety more and more unfit me for it." Grenville's reputation bears, besides, the ugly mark of desertion. He owed everything to Pitt, who placed him in the Speaker's chair and gave him the seals of the Foreign Office, yet in the hour of Pitt's necessity he was an active instigator of opposition.

Lord Grenville's conduct during the troubled existence of the Addington Ministry exhibits him at his worst as a parliamentary precisian. He was consistent, no doubt, in his attacks on the Treaty of Amiens, though he ought to have seen that peace had become for the moment a national necessity. He sincerely regarded Pitt as the only possible Prime Minister, and his impatience at the statesman's refusal to concur in assaults on the "Doctor" was shared by many of his friends, notably by Windham and Lord Minto. But, supposing a strong war policy to have been imperative, he was inconsistent in making overtures to Fox, who shut his eyes to the aggressive designs of Napoleon, and affected to look upon France as merely a rival in commerce. Besides, his insistence upon the Whig chief as an indispensable element in a stable administration was largely in the nature of an afterthought. On March 30, 1803, he went to stay with Pitt at Walmer. They discussed affairs earnestly and long, and, wrote Grenville in a narrative of events composed at the time—

"I stated the reasons I had for believing that, with regard to the old Opposition, this [the formation of a Government

to include the representatives of all parties] might be done
by including in his arrangement only Lord Moira and Grey,
and perhaps Tierney (the latter in some office subordinate to
the Cabinet), and that Fox would be contented not to take
any personal share in the Government so formed."

In a little over a year Addington had been frightened
into resignation, and, though they took a roundabout
course, events justified Grenville's predictions. The
King declined to accept Fox as his Minister, Pitt
acquiesced rather than drive his Sovereign mad once
more, and Fox magnanimously accepted the situation.
But a point of form had been raised, and that by one
whose obstinacy had often come into conflict with the
pride of the Grenvilles. In declining to join the Ministry
on behalf of his friends and himself, he wrote, "We rest
our determination solely on our strong sense of the
impropriety of our becoming parties to a system of
government which is to be formed at such a moment
on the principle of exclusion." Fox alone was excluded, and he waived his claims. The letter ends:
"Believe me ever, my dear Pitt, most affectionately
yours." Pitt told Lord Eldon that he would teach
that proud man that, in the service and with the confidence of the King, he could do without him, though he
thought his health such that it might cost him his life.
Grenville's letter found its way to the newspapers, and
thus widened the estrangement. He spent his time
largely among his rhododendrons at Dropmore, ridiculing the idea of a French invasion, until the death
of Pitt caused old feelings to revive, and he mourned
the loss of a friend whom, notwithstanding some
political differences, he had "never ceased to value

and to love." He had dissembled that love with some skill.

Grenville's recourse in forming his Government to the Whigs, in the first instance, rather than to the friends of Addington and the Pittites, stands to his credit, since in so acting he braved the resentment of the Court. But in its final form the "Talents" Administration was a jumble of incongruities. The negotiations for peace failed, and in their conduct of the war the critics of Pitt's expeditions wasted the resources of the country on adventures even more futile. They prepared the way, in addition, to hostilities with the United States. The Act for the Abolition of the Slave Trade was carried, through the resolution of Grenville and Fox, and they risked the existence of the Ministry to attain their object. But the death of Fox deprived Grenville of the one colleague whose popularity tended to counteract his own repellent manners, and nothing could exceed the ineptitude of his treatment of the Catholic question, which brought about the downfall of the Ministry.

Points of form rather than matters of principle dictated Lord Grenville's hesitations, when the Regency Bill seemed to give the Opposition a chance of returning to power. At one time he was pedantically anxious to preserve his reputation for consistency; the arguments of 1788 could not be discarded in 1811. At another he clung to the auditorship of the Exchequer, which he owed to the partiality of Pitt, with its comfortable £4,000 a year. The Regent's overtures to "the two lords," Grey and Grenville, after the death of Perceval, finally broke down over their demand that changes should be made in the composition of the Household, but they merely used it as a plausible

ground for the rupture. Of the pair Grenville was the
more assiduous in blocking his own way to office. He
preferred to lead his own wing of a distracted Opposition, fed by the obsequious gossip of Mr. Fremantle and
Mr. Wynn, and strangely subservient to his disagreeable
brother, the Marquis of Buckingham. The Grenvilles'
correspondence seldom rises above the lowest depths of
politics, except when Francis Horner, who, though he
never belonged to them, sat for St. Mawes, one of their
boroughs, takes up the pen.

As he tended to diverge from the Whigs, Grenville
developed saner views of national policy than Grey. He
was all for a vigorous prosecution of the Peninsular War,
while the Whig leader persisted in regarding Spain as a
fatal charnel-house. A Free Trader of the school of
Pitt, he opposed the oppressive Corn Law of 1815,
whereas Grey was for upholding the landed interest
and preventing a sudden reduction of rents. His last
speech of any moment was an impressive demand for
coercive measures, marking his complete severance from
the Whigs. His followers, therefore, had no hesitation
in joining the Government, though, thanks to the
Marquis of Buckingham's importunity, they exacted
terms which provoked Lord Holland to the sarcasm
that all "articles were to be had at low prices except
Grenvilles."

Lord Grenville in retirement at Dropmore was a more
amiable figure than Lord Grenville lecturing the Regent
or haranguing the peers. Lord Minto visited him in
1804. "There never was a more gallant or attentive
husband," he wrote, "and to all appearance, a better
natured as well as tempered one. We walked after
dinner to his farm, when he patted and poored an old

horse, which they are keeping alive with mashes and care, a full quarter of an hour. This was an old horse he had been used to ride himself in his youth ; but he went half the length of a field out of the way to do the same by an old cart-horse." He wrote Latin epitaphs on his dogs Zephyr and Tippoo, of whom the second swam ashore at Tenby, the sole survivor of a wreck, with his former master's pocket-book in his mouth.

> " Nec pudet invisi nomen gessisse tyranni
>   Si tam dissimili viximus ingenio."

Lord Grenville's " Nugæ Metricæ," renderings into Latin verse of passages from Euripides and the English and Italian poets, justify his claim to be reckoned, with Lord Wellesley as a formidable rival, among the most accomplished scholars of his time. Rogers especially praised his version of Dante's invocation to Virgil. A copy in the British Museum contains corrections and additions by his own hand, and facsimiles of letters from Rogers and Lord Holland, the latter contending, with right scholastic vigour, for his rival imitation of Grenville's favourite, Flaminius :

> " Fame shall say (if of me she should happen to speak)
>   A poor scholar was he, and wrote barbarous Greek,
>   But Grenville, who never would lightly commend,
>   Encouraged his labours and called him his friend."

The other of the " two lords," Earl Grey, was as open and accessible as Grenville was haughty and distant. His maiden speech of 1787 won him a reputation for abilities and character which he never lost. Lord Minto

considered him "extremely ripe indeed for his age," and
capable of drinking more claret than Fox and Sheridan.
More of a genuine democrat than Fox, he joined the
"Society of the Friends of the People," without consulting his leader, and by presenting their petition made
the cause of Parliamentary Reform his own.   In his old
age he regretted having joined a society containing revolutionary elements.   Grey was impulsive and querulous.
When his motion for Reform was rejected in 1797 he
was, as we have seen, one of the chief instigators of the
ill-advised secession of the Opposition, and adhered to
his resolve with a pertinacity as thorough as Fox's.
Inclined throughout his life to regard politics less as a
business than a pursuit proper to a gentleman, he was
far happier at Howick, in the heart of the country,
than in London.   The urgent representations of his
friends often failed to lure him to town for the opening of the session, and he was content with fitful
appearances in debate.   Fox, who understood him,
implored him to bring up his wife.

Grey, become Lord Howick, was Fox's natural
successor in 1806 as Foreign Secretary and leader of
the House of Commons.   In the first capacity he had
little opportunity for distinguishing himself ; his loss of
the second position through his father's death in 1807
was an irreparable misfortune for his party and far from
a gain to himself.   Always in need of a stimulus, he
would have found it in nightly contention with Canning
or Castlereagh, while he would have saved Whiggism
from being identified with the follies of Whitbread and
Brougham.   In the House of Lords the assiduous
oratory of Grenville found an excuse for his own
idleness.   Perceval's overture to him to join the Ministry,

an offer curtly declined, reached him at his beloved Howick; and in January, 1811, Brooks's must have been humming with premature shouts of triumph for days before he made a leisurely arrival on the scene. While the Regent was shaking himself clear of the Whig connection, he rapidly changed from close intimacy with Grey to active dislike. Grey himself completed the rupture by his famous and most injudicious allusion to the "cursed and baneful influence that lurked behind the throne," in the shape of Lady Hertford. He must have known that he was thenceforth impossible as Prime Minister so long as George lived. His attachment to public life continued so weak that in 1812 he actually contemplated surrendering the leadership of the Whig party to Lord Holland. "If I am absent," he sighed, "I hope it will be generally felt that I stand clear of Whitbread's motions."

Grey's most creditable proceedings during the years in which he acted with Grenville consisted in his steady advocacy of the Catholic claims and his equally steady refusal to countenance such Radical extravagances as annual Parliaments and universal suffrage. But the laboured defence of his speeches on the Peninsular War by his son, General Grey, merely amounts to this: that he despaired of the cause in its dark hours and applauded it after it had succeeded. When Napoleon returned from Elba, Grey proposed, too, the impracticable policy that the Powers should treat the change of sovereignty in France as a matter in which they had no concern, and renew the concert on a principle purely defensive—in other words, that they should give the Emperor leisure to strengthen himself. The introduction of Lord Sidmouth's repressive measures in 1817 produced the final rupture between Grenville and himself, the former reverting to the principles of Pitt, the latter remaining faithful to those of Fox.

With his following greatly reduced, Grey continued to play a passive part during the remaining years of the Liverpool Ministry. The strength of the Reform movement had passed from Whigs in Parliament to Radicals on the platform, and he would have nothing to do with the democratic ideals which were actively promoted by his son-in-law, Lambton, afterwards Lord Durham. For the inner workings of his mind after Lord Liverpool's illness had broken up the Government, we have the "Correspondence of Princess Lieven and Earl Grey" to guide us. A leader of Opposition indulges in a somewhat dangerous pursuit when he enters into intimate letter-writing with the wife of a foreign Ambassador, though it is true that the recluse of Howick had far fewer secrets to disclose than the active diplomatist at the Russian Embassy. Madame de Lieven claimed that they both adhered to their native characters, "*lui très Anglais, moi très Russe.*" Of herself that is true enough, but Grey's carping criticism of English statesmen and their measures is not altogether pleasant reading. This was notably the case when Canning formed his unlucky Government out of his own friends and the more moderate Whigs. As the world knows, Grey stood icily aloof, and justified his refusal to support the Ministry in a powerful indictment of Canning's foreign policy. But, though he denied the charge, personal antipathy undoubtedly swayed his decision. When Canning was no more, he contented himself with the cold remark: "The circumstance in his death which I think most to be regretted is, that it took place before his character and conduct were fully developed." The Whig and Tory aristocracies had instinctively closed up their ranks against the man whom they thought fit to style an adventurer. Grey had far more in common with the Duke of Wellington than with Canning, despite the liberal views of the latter on Catholic Emancipation. He toyed with the notion of joining the Duke's Administration in 1829, basing his final rejection of it on his proscription by the King, the Royal hatred having been intensified by Grey's outspoken resistance to the Bill for Queen Caroline's divorce.

As Premier of the Reform Cabinet Lord Grey played a great part ; all the greater because age had blunted his enthusiasm. He was occasionally despondent, and he hardly exercised sufficient control over the fiercer spirits in the Cabinet like Lord Durham. But he perceived that at a time when popular passions were running high the Prime Minister's duty was at once to sustain and to moderate. He managed King William with considerable skill, and set his face resolutely against a premature creation of peers, keeping that weapon in reserve should everything else fail. Firm in essentials, he was conciliatory in detail, while his oratory remained at the level of his best days. When the Bill became law, his course was really finished, and it is a pity that he did not carry out his personal wishes and resign, instead of remaining to fall on a side issue through the treachery of Brougham and the blundering of Littleton, the Irish Secretary. But he cherished no resentment against his overthrowers, and the *mitis sapientia Lælii* remained at the disposal of his successors, until old age divorced him from all interest in affairs.

General Grey has drawn a pleasant picture of his father's life at Howick, with his devoted wife and his

WILLIAM WINDHAM

FROM THE PAINTING BY SIR JOSHUA REYNOLDS, P.R.A., IN THE NATIONAL PORTRAIT GALLERY

THE MARQUIS OF LANSDOWNE

FROM THE PAINTING BY HENRY WALTON IN THE NATIONAL PORTRAIT GALLERY

fifteen children.   Not much of a reader, apparently,
though he admired Spencer, he encouraged them to live
an open air life, wandering at will without tutor or
governess.   They took their daily ride with him through
grounds in which he had planted every tree and planned
every path.   Grey at Howick, in short, was as admirable
as Fox at St. Anne's Hill; the *angulus præter omnes
terrarum* smiled on neither of them in vain.

The junction of the Old and the New Opposition
against Addington brought within the Holland House
circle a remarkable orator and great gentleman in
William Windham.   His diary shows that he was a
fairly frequent visitor there between 1805 and 1810.
From the intimacy then formed Lord Holland was able
to include in the "Memoirs of the Whig Party" an
elaborate and rather baffling sketch of Windham.   But
then Windham was a curious man.   The idols of his
youth and early manhood were Dr. Johnson and Burke,
and he resembled the first in his hypochondria, the
second in his irritability.   At the bedside of the dying
Johnson he acquired maxims of earnest piety which he
never forgot, and no man was less affected by the spirit
of the "Age of Reason" than Mr. Windham of Norfolk.
From the Doctor, too, he received advice of more
dubious utility, namely, that he should keep a diary.
"The great thing to be recorded," he said, "is the state
of your own mind, and you should write down everything you remember and write immediately."   Windham
indulged in mental introspection to excess, while he
imitated his friend by taxing his intellect with long
calculations and laborious conveyances of epigrams
from one language to another.   His diary abounds in
lamentations over hours wasted in idleness or in bed,

and in dissatisfaction with his own speeches. At one time Windham was distressed because he could not suddenly remember a proper name; at another involuntary twitchings of the muscles convinced him that a stroke of paralysis was imminent. These records may have served, to some extent, as a relief to his feelings, as an intellectual escape of steam. But his friends perceived that a tendency to self-depreciation hampered his brilliant gifts.

To the social world, Windham, stalwart and graceful in person, presented an agreeable appearance. His conversation was less that of familiar discourse than of Parliamentary debate, but an undeniable charm of manner did away with the effects of a didacticism which he had probably caught from Johnson. When nearly sixty, Brougham, meeting him for the first time, thought him the youngest of the party. He was a conscientious and attached guardian to his nephews and nieces; and when, after much dubitation, he married rather late in life, he proved a devoted husband. His estate, Felbrigg, was carefully planted and farmed. Devoted to field sports, he was a capital boxer and an assiduous patron of the prize ring, though his records of the prowess of Belcher, Cribb, Gully, and others are meagre. Windham carried his advocacy of manly pursuits, as they were then considered, to limits beyond those tolerated by modern taste. Thus he stood up for bull-baiting, partly on the ground that if it went, hunting would go as well; and his oratory killed Erskine's Cruelty to Animals Bill. His love of ancient Rome may have rendered his essentially chivalrous nature blind to the heartlessness involved in torturing a noble beast.

Fanny Burney, who heard Windham's speech on Faizulla Khan, part of the case against Warren Hastings, founded on it a sagacious prophecy. "I can only suppose," she wrote, "that by nature he is extremely diffident, and by inclination equally ambitious; and if so, the conflict may last through life." "Weathercock Windham," as he was called, was far from a model of political consistency. He brought to debate an eloquence of almost the first rank, never touching the comprehensive philosophy of Burke or the generous ardour of Fox, but remarkable for its fertility of illustration and dexterity, except when his vanity came into play. His famous phrase, "No one would select the hurricane season in which to begin repairing his house," destroyed Flood's Reform Bill of 1790. Eleven years later he used a lively simile by way of commenting on the changes in French politics: "Since the beginnings of the Revolution the Government has been overturned at least a dozen times. They have turned over in the air, as in sport, like tumbler pigeons, but have they ever ceased their flight?" Much influenced by Burke, he took early alarm at the French Revolution, and advocated the extremities of counter-revolution. "Why," he wrote to his political guide, "is all right of interference in the affairs of another country, even without the plea of aggression on the part of that country, to be universally given up?" He identified himself with the extreme war party, which nothing would satisfy but the restoration of the Bourbons and of *ci-devantisme* in its integrity. Yet such was his irresolution that he could not be induced to come up from Felbrigg for the third reading of the Traitorous Correspondence Bill, though his chaise stood ready at the door, consoling himself with the thought that even if he had appeared he might have let the occasion pass without saying a word.

Windham was one of the Old Whigs who, under pressure from Burke, took office under Pitt in July, 1794. The Secretaryship at War, to which he was appointed, must have been congenial to his temper, but on his own admission he failed as an administrator. Alternately over-sanguine and over-despondent, he placed excessive hopes in the French emigrants as a weapon of hostility; and long after the disaster of Quiberon should have opened his eyes, he used to hold mysterious colloquies with Monsieur and other august incompetents. But Windham was a Minister after King George's own heart, on whom he lavished compliments, and whom he would have preferred as Premier to Pitt. Windham actually went down to Weymouth by royal command in 1800 to discuss such a change of men; but, wrote Lord Malmesbury, who was to have been the new Foreign Secretary, his "odd and unacquiescent manner did not encourage his Majesty."

Windham remained ostensibly faithful to Pitt, resigning with him in 1801, until the renewal of peace negotiations which ripened into the Treaty of Amiens brought the pair to a sharp issue, since Pitt supported the Addington Ministry. He was certainly justified in his distrust of Napoleon, but that did not excuse his ill-omened junction with the Grenvilles and Fox in opposition to Pitt's last Government, more especially after hostilities had been resumed. Still less can Windham be forgiven for carrying his resentments beyond the grave, and opposing the resolution that "that excellent statesman" should be interred at the public expense in Westminster Abbey. "Did not execute my task to my own satisfaction," he wrote; "strange that I should miss so many things which are now so obvious and ready." It was, indeed, a lamentable exhibition; a discharge of Old Whig bile against the tactician who had out-manœuvred the party over the Regency Bill, and whom, even as a colleague, they distrusted, because he declined to go to the full lengths of an impracticable anti-Revolutionary policy. It remained for Windham to cut an indifferent figure, on the whole, as Secretary for War and the Colonies in the Grenville-Fox Administration, since, though he shortened military service, he scattered the military resources of the country over ineffective expeditions; and to make some fitful appearances as an eloquent, but indefinite, critic of Perceval and Lord Castlereagh. In June, 1810, he sank under an operation for a tumour, after he had with characteristic piety received the Sacrament in a private room from his friend, the Bishop of Salisbury.

CHAPTER X

WHIGS AND IRISHMEN

The third Marquis of Lansdowne—His junction with Canning—
A typical Whig—Bowood and Lansdowne House—Kindness to
Moore—Lord Moira—The negotiations of 1812—An unadroit
Mascarille—Thomas Grenville—Tierney—His duel with Pitt—
Leader of the House—Whitbread—"The Demosthenes of bad
taste"—An impossible Minister—Whitbread and the Princess of
Wales—The affairs of Drury Lane—Little Creevey—Lord Sefton—
An irresponsible politician—Grattan's maiden speech—Catholic
emancipation—Grattan in society—His attachment to Rogers—
"Longbow and Strongbow"—Curran's appearance—Specimens of
his wit.

LORD HENRY PETTY, the Chancellor of the Exchequer in the "Talents" Administration, stood in
direct contrast to the Secretary for War, Mr. Windham. Whereas the latter retained to the last much of the
indiscretion of youth, the statesman of twenty-five carried
an old head on young shoulders. Nor could two people
well be more unlike than the father, better known as
Lord Shelburne, the subject of universal distrust, and
the son, who as third Marquis of Lansdowne was for
nearly fifty years of public life regarded as a guarantee
for straightforward and moderate policy. In some
respects Lord Lansdowne did not altogether fulfil the
expectations formed of him at the outset. It is diffi-

cult to recognise in the daring financier of 1806 and
1807, whose eloquence seemed almost to have supplied
the loss of Pitt, the quietly sagacious politician who,
whether as Lord President of the Council or member of
the Cabinet without office, was content with frustrating
Reform Bills and acting generally as a Whig breakwater
to the onrush of Radicalism. The presumption must be
that his removal to the House of Lords in November,
1809, on the death of his half-brother, helped to extin-
guish Lord Lansdowne's ambition. For the next
eighteen years he steadily supported such Liberal
measures as Catholic Emancipation, the removal of
Nonconformist disabilities, and the suppression of the
slave-trade. Lansdowne House and Bowood acted, too,
as rallying points to the Opposition of much the same
importance as Holland House. None the less, their
owner by no means filled the place in the public eye
that would have been his if he had stood up as leader
of the Opposition against Canning and Castlereagh.

In 1827 Lord Lansdowne closed with Canning's overtures, on the advice of Lord Grenville, and brought about
the coalition between a section of the Whigs and the
friends of the Prime Minister. The step was distinctly
reasonable, since in it lay the only hope of keeping out
a Government of " Ultras," such as was subsequently
formed under the Duke of Wellington. But Lord Grey
and Lord Althorp held aloof; Brooks's revolted, and
Lord Lansdowne's position became highly invidious.
The Duke of Bedford considered that "he had been
the dupe and victim of the two greatest rogues (politically
speaking) in the kingdom"—George IV., that is, and
Canning. Lord Lansdowne, however, abided by the
arrangement, and, on the sudden death of the Prime

Minister, he amiably consented to serve under Lord Goderich, though his friends thought he ought to be at the head of the Government. "Whilst honest as the purest virgin," wrote Lord John Russell, "Lansdowne was too yielding, too mild, and most unfit to deal with men in important political transactions." That, of course, is the opinion of a zealous politician, but Lord Lansdowne had reason to regret that he had not pressed his claims. The introduction of an incongruous element in Mr. Herries rent the rickety Administration in twain; and when in January, 1828, it finally collapsed, he went quietly back to the Whigs.

Though Lord Lansdowne did not retire from public life until 1861, the rest of his career does not invite much comment. He might have been Foreign Secretary in the Grey Ministry of 1830, or even First Lord of the Treasury, but he preferred the greater leisure of the Presidency of the Council. The Premiership came within his grasp in 1852, but, crippled with gout, he declined the responsibility. To him the Court turned for advice on the collapse of Lord Aberdeen's Government in 1855, and by a process of elimination, Palmerston became Prime Minister. Without Lord Lansdowne neither the coalition of 1852 would have been possible nor the short-lived coalition of three years later. But it would be futile to claim for him any profound zeal for popular measures. He accepted the Act of Reform of 1832 as a final settlement, and thereafter he, in conjunction with Palmerston, resisted further instalments far more determinedly than Peelites like Lord Aberdeen or Sidney Herbert. His sympathies with Free Trade in corn never carried him much further than a low fixed duty, and in that again he was in agreement with

Palmerston. But he perceived the danger of bringing
up the masses in ignorance, and his speeches in favour
of State grants for educational purposes are characteristic
specimens of that cautious Whiggism which prefers to
avert Revolution from without by Reform from within.
Greville, essentially a Tory, though he associated mainly
with Whigs, regarded Lord Lansdowne as his ideal
statesman, particularly after he had succeeded in making
Lord John Russell withdraw the Reform Bill of 1851.
"You may be sure," Lord Lansdowne told his admirer,
"that if any strong measure was to be contemplated by
the Cabinet, I should walk out of it."   Seven years earlier,
when invited to express his opinion on the expediency
of admitting Cobden to office, he replied that "the risk of
inviting him would be greater than the gain," a phrase
that appropriately sums up the attitude of the aristocratic
Whigs towards the Radicals.

After a visit to Bowood in 1841, where Mrs. Butler
(Fanny Kemble) had recited, Moore had sung some of
his own "Melodies," and Macaulay had poured forth a
perpetual stream of conversation, Greville wrote, "I never
passed a week with so much good talk, almost all literary
and miscellaneous, very little political, no scandal and
gossip."   Numerous entries in Moore's journals bear out
the truthfulness of this description.   Both at Bowood and
at Lansdowne House the traditions of Lord Shelburne's
time, when their hospitable doors opened to Bentham,
Mirabeau, and other illustrious men, were carried on ;
the libraries were replenished and the picture galleries
recruited from the easels of Wilkie and Lawrence.   Guizot, oppressed by its statuary, regarded the splendours of
the mansion in Berkeley Square as frigid, but a foreigner
who enters English society for the first time is hardly a

fair judge. In his Wiltshire home, at any rate, Lord Lansdowne was the most unaffected of hosts, importing ease into all his relations, and caring for the poor on the estate. After he had induced Moore to make Sloperton Cottage his home in 1824, his kindnesses to the man of letters went on unabatingly. It was Lord Lansdowne who deposited £1,000 with Longman when Moore became involved through the defalcation of his deputy in Bermuda, with injunctions to secrecy which the amiable publisher promptly broke. Lord Lansdowne, too, urged Moore, in 1835, to accept a literary pension of £300 in terms which, out of regard for the poet's susceptibilities as an Irish patriot, almost amounted to entreaty. After one delicate offer of assistance, Moore feelingly observed: " Lord Lansdowne is a man who measures every step he takes, and therefore means all he professes."

Carlton House politics were represented in the Fox and Grenville Ministry by Lord Moira, who became Master of the Ordnance, with an understanding that attention should be paid to his recommendations for peerages and honours. The arrangement was well calculated to tickle the vanity of that expansive Irishman, though he appears to have used it without much regard to his own or Whig interests. By the year 1806, the military reputation which he had won, as Lord Rawdon, during the American Rebellion, notably at the battle of Hobkirk's Hill, had been impaired by his failure to effect anything as commander of the expedition of 1793 to the Breton coast, and, with less justice, by the poor results derived from the capable support he lent to the Duke of York in Flanders. Still, he impressed the public as a voluble exponent of Irish grievances in the House of Lords— where, as Curran put it, he " aired his vocabulary"—as a

Commander-in-Chief in Scotland given to lavish hospitality, and, above all, as the confidential adviser of the Prince of Wales.

The ways of Carlton House were generally mysterious, and the darkest of them all was that trodden by Lord Moira as the Prince's political go-between. Sanguine and unsuspecting, he had few qualifications as a manager of cabals, beyond a staunch fidelity to the interests of his patron, as he understood them. After the murder of Perceval by the madman Bellingham in 1812, Lord Moira, when Lord Wellesley had failed to form a Government, came rather near being Prime Minister of England. He was troubled with no doubts either as to his own fitness or the willingness of others to act with him. He scoured the town in search of colleagues and scattered promises about broadcast. On the strength of a list of names suggested by Canning, he even arranged an hour for kissing hands at Carlton House. Canning, it is said, appeared not in Court, but in morning dress, to show that he had merely come to see what was going on. Meanwhile the Regent had prudently decided on keeping on the existing Government under Lord Liverpool, and blandly informed Lord Moira that the Premier and Chancellor designate were actually in waiting. Soon afterwards his factotum and victim departed for India as Governor-General. There his memorable nine years' rule resulted in the destruction of the Mahratta power and the freebooting Pindaries, but Royal recognition exhausted itself in his elevation to a Marquisate, and Lord Hastings was driven during the last years of his life to eke out his broken fortunes with the salary of Governor of Malta.

In political annals the Marquis of Hastings is destined

to be remembered not as an able soldier and administrator but as the Regent's unadroit Mascarille. Stately
in presence and magnificent in manner, he affected an
exuberance of whisker and costume which the *Anti-
Jacobin* turned to pointed ridicule. He was apter at
promises than performances, and though he does not
appear to have behaved shabbily to his *protégé* Moore,
the needy bard built up hopes on his patronage which
were but meagrely fulfilled. His extravagance assumed
strange forms, as when, before his departure for India,
he bought fifty black dolls to accustom his numerous
progeny to the complexion of the natives.

Among the less conspicuous members of the "Talents"
Government was Thomas Grenville, an elder brother of
Lord Grenville. He had played, however, an active part
in negotiating the junction between the Grenvilles and
the Whigs, thanks to his early friendship with Fox. But
political life was probably but little to Grenville's tastes.
As President of the Board of Control, and afterwards First
Lord of the Admiralty, he took but little part in debate,
and with the fall of his brother's Administration he practically renounced politics. Becoming a reactionary in
his old age—for he nearly completed his ninety-first year
—he never set foot in Holland House after the Act of
Reform had been carried, and used fiercely to denounce
Cobden, O'Connell, and all their works. Charles Greville
has given us a delightful portrait of "the most amiable
and engaging specimen of an old man" he ever beheld,
"abounding in anecdotes of Lord Chatham and Lord
North, doing the honours of his table with all the energy,
gaiety, and gallantry of a man in the prime of life." He
never married, for, having been desperately in love when
young with the Duchess of Devonshire, he remained

faithful to her image. Unlike his brother, "the Bogey," in most respects, Tom Grenville resembled him in his love of literature, and was an assiduous collector of books. His name is perpetuated in the Grenville Library at the British Museum, his bequest to the nation, with its 20,000 volumes, valued at over £50,000, and including editions of Homer, Ariosto, and Italian and Spanish works which, once lost or destroyed, could never be replaced.

Tierney, who replaced Thomas Grenville in September, 1806, as President of the Board of Control, was one of the numerous politicians of middle-class origin whom the aristocratic Whigs used, but never regarded as one of themselves. Inclination as well as accident seems to have made him something of a hack. The son of an Irish prize-agent and merchant, his wealth carried him into Parliament as member for Southwark, after several failures. His cosmopolitan ideas gained for him an unenviable immortality from Canning and Frere as the "Friend of Humanity" in the "Needy Knife-grinder." But Tierney was essentially a Parliament man rather than an advocate of emotional causes. He became a fluent debater, though he never rose without a feeling of nervousness, with some knowledge of finance, and more powers of sarcasm and repartee.

Alive to all the moves of the game, Tierney tried to prevent the Whig secession of 1798, and by refusing to join it earned the resentment of his party and the compliments of Pitt. Lord Holland, in his "Memoirs of the Whig Party," asserts that Tierney, though lavish of insincere expressions of attachment to Fox, endeavoured to separate Grey from that statesman and thus create a new party. It may have been so, but definite evidence is wanting. Tierney's famous duel with Pitt, in which

the two combatants were so ignorant of their weapons
that the Prime Minister, for one, was surprised to find no
hair on his hair-trigger, arose out of the heat of debate,
and left no rancorous memories behind it. Pitt, on the
contrary, persuaded Addington to secure his services as
Treasurer of the Navy, and when he came to the desperate
attempt of forming his own last Ministry he tried to
persuade Tierney to remain. George Rose, no believer
in elevated motives, noted in his diary: " He certainly
thought Carlton House the better speculation."

Tierney soon discovered that Sheridan, not himself,
was the chosen bearer of the Prince's communications.
He slipped back into the Whig fold, and became President of the Board of Control in the " Talents " Administration, but had to reckon with the hostility of the
Grenvilles. That faction did not easily forget or forgive,
and they lent no support to the arrangement of 1818,
which, on the death of George Ponsonby, made Tierney,
by a process of exhaustion, leader of the Opposition in
the Commons. For some four years he held that thankless position, raked in the flank by the extreme " Mountain," and dubbed " Old Cole " by Creevey, after a
disreputable character in one of Foote's farces. In
Palmerstonian times he might have made a reputation,
since he was personally popular, experienced in affairs,
and expert in that familiar oratory of which M. Thiers
has been perhaps the most finished exponent. But, with
faction rampant, he exercised little authority, and chafed
under the divisions of his party. Never deficient in
political courage, he risked in 1819 a trial of strength
with the Government and was routed by the stolid good
sense of Lord Castlereagh. The Tory wits exultingly
parodied Byron, and jibed at " Old Tierney " who " came

down like a wolf on the fold." Two years later he abdicated the leadership, and though in 1827 he was one of the Whigs who joined Canning, entering the Cabinet as Master of the Mint, he was little more than a cipher. When he died, on the eve of the return of the Whigs to power, Grenville dismissed him in a single sentence as a loss to his friends.

Tierney only held office for a few years of a long political life ; Whitbread never became Minister at all. He would not have made a disciplined or even a passably loyal colleague, being essentially a politician to catch the popular ear when in Opposition and to wreck any Government that had been unfortunate enough to enlist him. Whitbread advanced from his brewery within the Whig pale through his marriage with the sister of his schoolfellow, Lord Grey. He retained to the last middle-class feelings and prejudices, and Byron aptly described him as the Demosthenes of bad taste and vulgar vehemence, but strong and English. The French Revolution had already infected English politics when he made his mark as an indefatigable follower of Fox, sparing no labour in getting up a case ; a sincere advocate of causes like the abolition of the slave-trade and the improvement of the condition of the poor, but unscrupulous in his attacks on Pitt's foreign policy. "Sam is all for Boney," remarked his admirer Creevey in 1814 ; and except for a brief period when the rising in Spain aroused his admiration, Whitbread's sympathies were with his country's enemies. They assumed the vexatious form of denouncing Governments for wantonly continuing war when peace was attainable.

By slow degrees the Whig chiefs seem to have made up their minds that Whitbread was impossible as an

official colleague.   He was to have been excluded, to
the interested anger of Creevey, if they had come to their
own in 1812.   His omission in 1807, however, appears to
have been due to Grey's misapprehension that he did not
want an appointment.   Whitbread was profuse in expressions of disinterestedness, combined with refusals to
serve under any leader in the Commons, were he Lord
Henry Petty or Lord George Cavendish or Mr. Ponsonby.
After an awkward interview with Grey, he wrote to
Creevey : " I have no object but the public good ; I want
nothing ; I seek nothing."   Yet Whitbread resembled
other people of exalted professions in getting angry when
taken at his word.   His sincerity was questioned, even by
his own friends, when he entered upon the most important
task of his public life, the impeachment of Lord Melville.   " Mr. Whitbread," we find in the " Memoirs of the
Whig Party," " though he had pursued the subject with
prodigious diligence, and understood the whole transaction thoroughly, was so occupied in displaying his wit
and eloquence, or, as the lively Duchess of Gordon expressed it, with teaching his ' dray horse to caper,' that
his speeches convinced nobody " ; and Lord Melville
was acquitted.   His egotism inspired Canning to the
well-known jest upon the annual dinner of the Whitbread
family on the day of their father's death :

"So that day still I hail with a smile and a sigh,
    For his " beer " with an *e* and his "bier" with an *i*."

Whitbread had easier game in the Duke of York, when
victimised by Mrs. Clarke, and in Lord Chatham, when
he returned in disgrace from the Walcheren expedition ;
in each case he brought down his man.   But he did

small service to his country or to the Whigs when in
1813 and onwards he came forward as the intemperate
advocate of the Princess of Wales. In so doing he threw
a slur on the Cabinet of 1806, which had been concerned
in the " Delicate Investigation," while the looseness of
his allegations stung one of its members, Lord Ellenborough, into the exclamation that they were " as false as
hell in every part." From the candid pages of Creevey
we learn the inner history of that demonstration, namely,
that he, Brougham, and Whitbread wished to strike at the
Government through the Regent. Of the trio Whitbread
was, probably, the only one who took any concern in the
merits of the case.

Whitbread, the man, was upright and considerate, but
disputatious. When Tierney lent him a pew at St. James's,
Piccadilly, he added the warning that no reply was permitted in that church. As chairman of the committee
formed in 1810 to rebuild Drury Lane Theatre, he came
into collision with Sheridan, but his action merely
amounted to the strict interpretation of the not unfair
bargain that the late manager and his family should be
bought out at a price. The austere man of business
was naturally antipathetic to the irresponsible man of
letters, who, though he resented the earmarking of money
to meet pressing claims, had no scruple about appealing
to the just steward to rescue him from the sponging
house. Sheridan avenged himself by an elaborate sarcasm
on Whitbread's address, written, after the open competition had failed, in case Byron did not produce the
prologue he had undertaken at Lord Holland's request.
All the bards, he said, had introduced the Phœnix, but
" Whitbread made more of this bird than any of them;
he entered into particulars, and described its wings,

beak, tail, &c. ; in short, it was a *poulterer's* description
of a Phœnix." The late Mr. Fraser Rae, by an excess
of ingenuity, discovered in Whitbread's dealing with
Sheridan traces of that insanity which caused him to
take his own life three years later. In sober fact,
politics, not Drury Lane Theatre, killed the unfortunate
man. Sir Philip Francis, however, supplies a most
Franciscan detail of character. Whitbread had " an
habitual laugh, a laugh without merriment. It was
a trick he had got ; he laughed whenever he spoke.
He was labouring to conceal the state of his mind ; he
wished to be gay, to believe that he was happy."

During the first thirty-five years or so of the nineteenth century Creevey and his crony, Lord Sefton,
were industrious *claqueurs* and busybodies in Whig
interests. The former is so undisguisedly portrayed
in his racy correspondence that it is unnecessary to
say much about him. Sir Herbert Maxwell, his admirable editor, compares Creevey with Croker ; other
parallels suggest themselves in " Bear " Ellice and
Bernal Osborne. Brimming over with animal spirits,
officious, and devoured by curiosity, he knew everything that was going on, and sometimes a good deal
more. Mr. Tadpole would have rejoiced to compare
notes with him, for he was no respecter of secrets,
and would cheerfully malign the hostess with whom
he had just been dining, or Brougham, the confederate
in his political plots. Creevey's sense of honour was
not nice, but it existed ; and though the violent Whitbread was the man for his stake, he kept a warm corner
in his heart, almost amounting to reverence, for Earl Grey.
In his descriptions of that statesman in retirement, left
alone by his friends, he touches eloquence. The Whigs

did their best for Creevey ; and it was not their fault that his poverty was only relieved by the salary of Secretary to the Board of Control in the " Talents " Ministry and, in his old age, when they returned to power again, by the treasuryships, first of the Ordnance and then of Greenwich Hospital. Though he entertained ardent hopes during the various crises that they would " do something " for him, the laughing philosopher bore disappointment with equanimity. In the clubs and society he was in great request, through his ingenuity in borrowing or inventing nicknames and in putting an impish construction on public events and the conduct of public men. Greville tells how he spent his life in easy vagabondage, visiting friends who were delighted to have him, and staying here and there until his meagre funds—he had less than £200 a year—were exhausted. " I think," he adds, " he is the only man I know in society, who possesses nothing." It is much to the credit of that society which, with all its faults, was not servile to wealth, that Creevey should have held his own there. He would be extinguished nowadays by gratuities to servants.

Lord Sefton was a typical figure of the Regency. An accomplished whip to a four-in-hand with a team of fine bays, and a capital horseman, he is at one time admiringly chronicled by Creevey as breaking the bank at Crockford's two nights following, and carrying off £7,000, at another as winning £600 at whist. In the end, however, Crockford's relieved him of £200,000. He was a pronounced epicure, and secured Ude, the famous *chef* of Louis XVIII., for his table. Though he was devoid of knowledge and ungainly of figure—Captain Gronow calls him a gigantic hunchback—Lord Sefton was one of the most delightful men of his time. " Never was there," writes Greville, "such a master of what is called *persiflage*," adding that he graduated in that brilliant society of which Hatfield and Cassiobury were the temples, and Lady Salisbury, Lady Essex, and Mrs. St. John the presiding divinities.

Lord Sefton took to politics, much as he had taken to cards and the turf, from love of excitement. His friendship with Brougham furnished the cause, and in 1830 he was employed by Lord Grey to settle the conditions of that wayward politician's accession to office. His letters to Creevey are not conspicuous for any depth of conviction: " You and I don't care a damn for the Catholics," is a confession which would have horrified a Liberal historian like Harriet Martineau, had she lived to read it. But he was a shrewd judge of affairs, though given to downright condemnations, such as that of Lord Lansdowne to be "the damnedest idiot that ever lived, not even excepting the domestic Goderich ; " and he appears to have composed quarrels of greater moment than one between Creevey and himself and another between Creevey and Lady Holland. He was a close friend of Lord Grey, and Creevey, comparing the two, went so far as to state that Sefton, though ruined by want of early cultivation, was not inferior to the other in natural talent, and should have been a most powerful, though not as eloquent a speaker. As it is, he lives in his prophecy that "some damnable thing" must come from the invention of the railway locomotive.

Two great Irishmen, Grattan and Curran, had practically played their parts when they joined the Holland House circle. After the consummation of the Union, Grattan entered the Imperial Parliament in April, 1805, as member for Melton, in Yorkshire, a seat he exchanged six years later for the more appropriate representation of Dublin. The " Memoirs of the Whig Party " describe in an often-quoted passage how he gained the ear of an assembly prepared to laugh at him, in spite of " the brevity and antithesis of his sentences, his grotesque gesticulations, peculiar and almost foreign accent, and arch articulation and countenance." As he proceeded, " Mr. Pitt beat time to the artificial but harmonious cadence of his periods, and Mr. Canning's countenance kindled at the brightness of a fancy which in glitter fully equalled and in real warmth far exceeded his own."

In his conduct of the agitation for Emancipation, however, Grattan never succeeded in reconciling the scruples of Whig politicians in England and their aristo-cratic Irish allies like Lord Fingal, and the exaggerated anticipations of the priesthood and peasantry. He accepted, too, rather than led the incipient movement for the repeal of the Union. The cause of Emancipation came nearest success, during his lifetime, in 1812, when Canning carried by 235 votes to 106 a resolution that the House should, early in the next session, take into consideration the laws affecting the Catholics. Victory seemed in sight when, in the new Parliament of the following year, Grattan's proposal that the civil and religious disabilities of the Catholics should cease was accepted, and a Bill based on that proposal was intro-duced. But Grattan acquiesced in its being weighted by the " securities," designed chiefly to secure the allegiance of the priesthood, which were scouted in Ireland, and the highly irregular intervention of the Speaker, Mr. Abbot, resulted in a fatal defeat. The Emancipation movement passed under the stronger and more unscru-pulous guidance of O'Connell, and Grattan died soon after the accession of George IV., having exhausted his enfeebled health in coming over from Ireland to make, as he hoped, one last brilliant effort on behalf of his Catholic countrymen.

Grattan's appearances at Holland House do not seem to have been numerous. In a letter to Miss Fox, written on the day of his funeral, Lord Holland alluded to him as one for whom he had "really more affection and regard than the few opportunities I had of cultivating his friendship would seem to justify me in expressing." Mackintosh found him there in October, 1818, when he kept the party up to two o'clock giving interesting and spirited sketches of the great men he had seen in his youth, notably Lord Chatham. "There is nobody so odd, so gentle and so admirable," was Mackintosh's verdict; "his sayings are not to be separated from his manner." Byron, too, was much struck "with the simplicity of Grattan's manners in private life; they were odd, but they were natural." He formed a strong attachment for Rogers, so much so that Mrs. Grattan once angrily exclaimed, "You'll be taken for Mr. Rogers's shadow." The poet addressed to him the lines in "Human Life":

"A walk in spring—Grattan, like those with thee
By the heath-side (who has not envied me?)
When the sweet limes, so full of bees in June,
Led us to meet beneath their boughs at noon;
And thou wouldst say which of the great and wise,
Could they but hear and at thy bidding rise,
Thou wouldst call up and question."

The lime-trees were near Tunbridge Wells, and

Grattan used to imagine the bees as holding parliamentary debates in them and going into committee. The ancients he would have liked to converse with were Scipio Africanus, Julius Cæsar, whom he would have questioned as to his part during Catiline's conspiracy, though without pressing the question ; but not Cleopatra, who would have told him nothing but lies, and whose beauty would have made him sad. At Tunbridge Wells, too, Grattan originated the ideal of spending his whole life in a small neat cottage, content with cold meat, and bread, and beer—and plenty of claret ! He would enter Kentish homesteads, hat in hand, and question their inmates about their wages and food ; he would return the bow of a child.

Curran's career at the Irish bar ended in 1807 when the Whigs, sorely exercised to find him an appointment, persuaded him to accept the Mastership of the Rolls in Ireland. Thenceforth he was reduced, as he said, "to be stuck up in a window, the spectator of the procession," living on the fame he had gained as an Opposition orator in the Parliament on St. Stephen's Green and as counsel for the defence in the State trials of Hamilton Rowan, the "Drogheda defenders," and the rebels of '98. A failure on the Bench, and tired of Dublin society, which had lost much of its charm through the migration across the Channel consequent on the Union, he spent as much time as he could in England. He lived, somewhat squalidly, in various lodgings ; the last of which was at No. 7, Amelia Place, Brompton. Curran inevitably challenged comparison with Erskine, through the similarity of their fortunes and of their talents. Byron drew in "Don Juan" the playful yet discriminating parallel between them :

" There also were two wits by acclamation,
    Longbow from Ireland, Strongbow from the Tweed,
Both lawyers, and both men of education ;
    But Strongbow's wit was of more polished breed ;
Longbow was rich in an imagination
    As beautiful and bounding as a steed,
But sometimes stumbling over a potato,
While Strongbow's best things might have come from
        Cato.

Strongbow was like a new-tuned harpsichord ;
    But Longbow, wild as an Eolian harp,
With which the winds of heaven can claim accord,
    And make the music either flat or sharp.
Of Strongbow's talk you would not change a word ;
    At Longbow's phrases you might sometimes carp :
Both wits—one born so and the other bred—
This by the heart—his rival by the head."

When Longbow and Strongbow came into friendly collision, the former had the advantage. Thus, when
Erskine was trying to force from Curran an acknowledgment that Grattan had felt intimidated at the idea of a
first appearance before the British Parliament, the egoist
was silenced by, " Mr. Grattan is a very modest man ; *he
never speaks of himself.*" Byron, indeed, implicitly con-
ceded the palm to Curran when he wrote to Moore : " I
have met Curran at Holland House—he beats everybody ;
his imagination is beyond human, and his humour (it
is difficult to define what is wit) perfect. Then he has
fifty faces and twice as many voices when he mimics—I
never met his equal." Elsewhere Byron represented him
as taking off Grattan, bowing to the very ground, and
thanking God that he had no peculiarities of gesture or
appearance. Curran himself reminded Croker of the
devil with his tail cut off ; he had jet black eyes and

hair, a face like a monkey, with a protruding underlip ; his hands were dirty and his dress slovenly.

Rogers lamented that more specimens of his wit had not been preserved, and blamed Moore for his remissness in that respect. It was at Moore's expense, by the way, that Curran made the joke : "So—I hear—you have married a pretty woman—and a very good creature too—an excellent creature—pray—um—*how do you pass your evenings ?*"   Most of the authenticated Curran stories are redolent of the Dublin law-courts, and are therefore, it must be confessed, rather esoteric. Nothing, however, could well be more to the point than his censure of Byron's histrionic "farewell" to Lady Byron : "I protest I do not understand this kind of whimpering ; here is a man who first weeps over his wife, and then wipes his eyes with the public." He could be most offensive when provoked, as in his smashing retort to the Englishman who was laughing at him on the top of a coach : "May God Almighty never humanise your countenance, you odious baboon." Curran's wild wit, in fact, kept company with a profound melancholy, which seldom left him in his later years, and which drove him into retirement in 1814, to die in intense gloom three years later. "I have never painted your portrait at all," exclaimed Lawrence, after he had seen him in a rare moment of animation ; "I never saw your proper character before." The result was a sugary idealisation, dashed off at a single sitting.

CHAPTER XI

SOME MEN OF LETTERS

Dr. Parr—His correspondence with Lord Holland—The doctor's retorts—His friends and his pets—"Monk" Lewis—A guest of the great—His plays and ballads—Lewis and Scott—Hookham Frere—His talk and his habits—Frere as a diplomatist—The *Anti-Jacobin* and "The Monks and the Giants"—Frere as a translator.

OF the many men of letters associated with Holland House, Dr. Parr dated back to the first half of the eighteenth century. After he had been a Master at Harrow School, he settled in 1783 at Hatton, near Warwick, where he held a perpetual curacy, which, with a plurality or two, after the comfortable Whig tradition, enabled him to collect a library of 10,000 volumes, and, in his old age, to set up a coach and four. But his visits to the "capital," as he called it, were great events. The Regent humoured Dr. Parr by joining him in a pipe at Carlton House, and the Whig aristocracy were glad to have him at their tables, where he plied his knife and fork to excellent purpose.

An established oracle, Dr. Parr imitated the Delphic utterances in his obscurity. His voice was so thick that, when he spoke, no one unaccustomed to him could make out what he said, and when he wrote nobody could read his handwriting.   The second defect he remedied through the help of a neighbouring parson with £1,000 a year called "Jack," otherwise his "male auxiliary," who acted as his secretary.   But no calligraphy could redeem Dr. Parr's correspondence from a verbosity which makes it a weariness to read.   Yet the Whigs set store by his opinion, and it was not without reason that he cherished hopes of a bishopric in 1806.   The death of Fox, over whom he was anxious to perform the last offices of religion, wrecked his chance.   The Grenvilles provided for their own, and Lord Holland in vain urged upon the Prime Minister "the situation in which his uncle and his political friends stood in respect to Dr. Parr."   Time did not lessen the regard of Dr. Parr for the Fox family.   In his chaotic correspondence are included numerous letters to Lord Holland discussing points of scholarship, condemning the banishment of Napoleon to St. Helena, and exulting in his own letter of retort to the Archdeacon of Worcester when requested to sign a petition against Catholic Emancipation.   A prolix epistle, adjuring Lord Holland to "employ his sound judgment and ingenuous spirit on the subject of toleration" can only be described as calculated to overwhelm its recipient with discursive learning.   Dr. Parr's last public exploit was hardly to the taste of Holland House.   In 1820, on the return of Queen Caroline to England, he constituted himself her chaplain, inspired the answers to addresses, and prompted Denman, one of her counsel, to an infelicitous classical allusion.

Few men stood out more distinctly from their age than this affectionate, vain and hot-headed old pedant, with his huge wig, velvet coat, pipe, and shaggy eyebrows.   It was Dr. Parr's good fortune to have won the esteem of a large number of pupils, Sheridan among them, and they propagated his renown.   Even Dr. Johnson allowed that he was a "fair man," and, as his conceit was adamantine, he was generally master of his company.   His retorts, as a rule, were Johnsonian in vigour, though less compact than those of his Tory prototype.   "Sir," he said to a well-known lawyer, "you are incapable of doing justice to your own argument ; you weaken it by diffusion and perplex it by reiteration."   To a would-be scholar : " You have read a good deal, you have thought very little, and you know nothing."   His quarrel with Mackintosh, according to Rogers, was over the justice of the sentence passed on Gerrald, the Scots political agitator and Parr's old pupil.   It inspired his description of Mackintosh as one who had come up from his native land with "a metaphysical head, a cold heart, and open hands," and winged the famous reply when Sir James was denouncing O'Coigley, the Irish conspirator.   "Yes, Jamie," said the doctor, "he was a bad man, but he might have been worse ; he was an Irishman, but he might have been a Scotsman ; he was a priest, but he might have been a lawyer ; he was a Republican [*v.l.* traitor], but he might have been an apostate."   But though Dr. Parr quarrelled freely with High and Low Churchmen, being himself an eighteenth-century Latitudinarian, and with men of letters who were not of his way of thinking, the warmth of his friendships excelled the heat of his disputes. Bentham, Romilly, Rogers, Moore, Bishop Copleston, Bishop Maltby, and Dr. Butler of Shrewsbury were all held in high regard by him, and he made an excellent parish priest. His kindness embraced criminals and animals, and the story is told of him that he cut the throat of the picture of his first wife—a dame with a tongue—when she irritated him by destroying a favourite cat. Of his likes, a pronounced one was a May-day dinner to his parishioners with a dance round the maypole ; he detested the east wind. By fixing the weathercock in that direction Sheridan's son, Tom, is said to have kept the doctor a prisoner in his house for a fortnight.

A touch of absurdity is also associated with the memory of Matthew Gregory Lewis, known from his most popular romance as "Monk" Lewis. Few writers who have held such a high reputation in their day have been so completely forgotten as this facile inventor of horrors. Rogers questioned his taste, but admitted that he had genius. Byron addressed him in "English Bards and Scotch Reviewers" :

> "Oh, wonder-working Lewis ! Monk or Bard,
> Who fain would make Parnassus a churchyard."

The stupendousness of Lewis's works was by no means realised in his person. He was very small, though well-proportioned ; with eyes projecting, according to Sir Walter Scott, like those of some insects, and flattish at the orbit ; and, it may be added, on the evidence of his portrait, a round, mild face, not unlike that of the Mock-turtle in "Alice in Wonderland." Though he dealt freely in the gruesomely indecent, he was an honourable and kindly soul. He played with discretion the part of mediator between parents who had separated, and when he came into his West Indian estates he established his mother in a cottage near Leatherhead. Lewis himself lived in a villa at Barnes, with bronze statues of Cupid and Fortune on the lawn, where he collected knick-knacks, entertained the Duchess of York, and paraded, *sous les réserves*, a hopeless passion for Lady Charlotte Campbell, a daughter of the Duke of Argyll. While walking with the object of his adoration Lewis met the lunatic who inspired his once admired ballad, " Crazy Jane," which in turn gave its name to a fashionable hat, the "Crazy Jane" hat.

Lewis was a frequent guest at country houses both in England and Scotland, since he exuded ballads at will, and even produced at Inverary Castle, in conjunction with William Lamb, the future Lord Melbourne, a weekly paper entitled *The Bugle*. But both Scott and Byron voted him a bore—"a damned bore" added the latter, though in another place he calls him a " jewel of a man." He was also inordinately vain. Lewis was once observed at Oatlands looking very sentimental ; his explanation was that the Duchess of York had just said something so kind to him. " Never mind, Lewis," broke in Colonel Armstrong, " don't cry. She didn't really mean it." He was, besides, a kind master to his West Indian slaves, and it was on the return from a voyage to Jamaica to see that they were properly used that he died at sea from yellow fever.

Monk Lewis knew exactly what his public wanted, and gave it to them. Horace Walpole's " Castle of Otranto" set the fashion : it had been sedulously cultivated by " Perdita" Robinson and Mrs. Radcliffe. Castles and dungeons, spectres and shackles were the mode ; people relished what in modern literary slang is called "a direct appeal." They got it, with a flavour of indecency super-added. Lewis's prehensile hands made free use of the ample quarry provided by the Romantic movement in Germany. Not without cause were his " Tales of Wonder," to which Scott was induced to contribute,

re-christened "Tales of Plunder." But Lewis's instinctive
skill in the manipulation of the supernatural made the
"Castle Spectre" a prodigious success, and his judgment
as to stage effect proved wiser than Sheridan's, who
advised him to keep the ghost out of the last scene. His
monodrama, "The Captive," had to be withdrawn from
the boards, for so startling was Mrs. Lichfield's representation of a maniac that it sent the ladies amongst the
audience into hysterics. As printed, it consists chiefly of
notes of exclamation and stage directions. But Lewis's
chief claim to remembrance is that by his ballads "Alonzo
the Brave and the Fair Imogene" and "Durandarta"
he rekindled, as Lockhart says, the poetic ambition in
Scott's breast. "He had," wrote Sir Walter, "the finest
ear for rhythm I ever met with—finer than Byron's."
The praise is strangely exaggerated, but Scott was grateful to Lewis for some encouragement; and thirty years
afterwards he told Allan Cunningham that he never felt
such elation as when the Monk first invited him to dine
at an hotel. On formal occasions the Monk failed to
shine. His "Lines Written on Returning from the
Funeral of the Right Hon. C. J. Fox, Addressed to Lord
Holland" are affectionate but tedious.

Christ Church brought Lord Holland and Lewis
together; but his acquaintance with Hookham Frere was
of even earlier date, since it began at Eton. That fine
and delicate flower of Eton and Cambridge culture was a
constant guest at Holland House, where his own room
was reserved for him, until in 1818 the health of his wife,
Lady Erroll, banished him to Malta, whence, as Sir
George Cornewall Lewis said, in allusion to his absent-
mindedness, he forgot to come back, except for a single
brief visit. An early entry in Greville's journal records

what must have been one of his last appearances, in June, 1818, when he repeated a great deal of the unpublished part of "Whistlecraft," somewhat to the boredom of the diarist. Greville kept no record of Frere's conversation, the charm of which has for the most part to be taken on trust.   To Moore we owe his saying, " Next to an old friend, the best thing is an old enemy," and the story that Madame de [Staël ?] having said, in her intense style, " I should like to be married in English, in a language in which vows are so faithfully kept," some one asked Frere, "What language, I wonder, was she married in ? " " Broken English, I suppose," answered Frere. His admiration for Spain as a country "where God Almighty kept large portions of land in His own hands" has been perpetuated by many pens.

Frere's chroniclers confessed that his repartees, when set down on paper, failed to preserve the peculiar character of his humour.   His airily discursive correspondence with his family brings out this quality to some extent, but he by no means puts his best self into his letters.   Slovenly in dress, dreamy, and apt to be wrapped up in the book of the moment, time and place went unregarded by him.   On the day of his wedding he became so absorbed in a literary discussion with Murray, the publisher, that he overstayed the time when he promised Lady Erroll to be ready for their journey into the country.

Frere's failure as a diplomatist is commonly overstated. Procrastinating and absent, he was naturally ill-fitted to cope with the situation in Spain when a raw Junta and mobs of armies were struggling to make head against the flower of Napoleon's military system.   At the same time his case, as stated by his nephew, the late Sir

Bartle Frere, in the memoir introductory to the collected edition of his works, is by no means one of absolute incompetence. If Frere overestimated the striking power of Sir John Moore's expedition, it is equally certain that the General erred on the opposite side, and that accident played its part in bringing about the retreat to Corunna as well as miscalculations. "But," wrote Sir Bartle, in words strikingly applicable to his own fate, "a victim was required to appease popular discontent." Frere was recalled under conditions wounding to a sensitive spirit; he renounced a public career and twice declined a peerage. He lived thenceforth the life of a literary aristocrat, dreaming the days away, first in London and on his estate at Roydon and afterwards at Malta, serene in his retirement, and philosophically interested in the world beyond the Mediterranean waters.

Over-fastidiousness and a certain indolence of intellect prevented Hookham Frere from attaining the place in literature that was his due. In his contributions to the *Microcosm* at Eton and to the *Anti-Jacobin* in Piccadilly, his humour, in so far as their separate shares can be distinguished, barely yields precedence to that of Canning. If the latter was more daring, Frere excelled him in happiness of allusion and unexpected flights of fancy. He is at his best in "The Loves of the Triangles," the parody of Erasmus Darwin's "Loves of the Plants":

> "Lo! where the chimney's sooty tube extends
> The fair Trochais from the corner bends!
> Her coal-black eyes, upturn'd, incessant mark
> The eddying smoke, quick flame, and violent spark"—

Trochais being the nymph of the wheel, in love with the smoke-jack. But Frere's peculiar gift, the mimicry of

bygone literature, which first found expression in his
extraordinarily clever "Ode on Athelstan's Victory,"
written when he was a boy at Eton, reached its high-
water mark, perhaps, in the "Monks and the Giants,"
purporting to be written by William and Robert Whistlecraft, of Stowmarket, harness and collar-makers.   Byron,
of course, imitated his use of the octave stanza of Pulci
in "Beppo," and "Beppo" was the forerunner of "Don
Juan."   When it appeared, "The Monks and the Giants"
failed to acquire popularity, chiefly because people persisted in searching it for political satire.   "Well, indeed,"
said Mackintosh with due solemnity, "I could not make
out the allegory."   For pure fun, however, the adventures
of Sir Tristram and Sir Gawain, and the strategy of Friar
John against their monstrous enemy, the giants, are
hard to beat, and Frere alone could have written the
dog-Latin of the monkish chronicle :

> "Erant rumores et timores varii ;
> Dies horroris et confusionis
> Evenit in calendis Januarii."

Frere's capacity for thinking in two languages and for
extracting the spirit out of his author's text made him
supreme as a translator, whether his subject was "The
Cid" or Aristophanes or Theognis.   The more recondite
the original, the more triumphant were his efforts to
wrest its meaning from it.   "A poetical translation of
Aristophanes," to quote from Sir George Cornewall
Lewis's friendly criticism in the "Classical Museum," "is
peculiarly difficult.   Comedy is harder of translation than
tragedy ; it is easier to copy the lofty and serious than
the ridiculous and familiar."   But Frere as a critic was

inferior to Frere as a renderer of Greek comedy into English. Through excess of ingenuity he attributed to Aristophanes an intensity of purpose that never was his, and erected an unauthentic if graceful biography on the fragments of Theognis.

CHAPTER XII

ROGERS AND "CONVERSATION" SHARP

Samuel Rogers's good fortune—His house in St. James's Place—
"A liberal host"—Rogers's intercourse with Fox—As brother and
friend—Rogers's jealousy—His caustic comments—His cadaverous
appearance—Built of a piece—"Columbus"—Lord Dudley's review
—"Human Life"—"Italy"—"Conversation" Sharp—As host and
politician—Sharp's "Letters and Essays."

ROGERS, Luttrell and Sydney Smith formed what
may be termed the inner triad of Holland House.
The first of them is still commemorated by his
seat in the Dutch garden, with the inscription by Lord
Holland which commended itself by its happy terseness
to Macaulay :

> " Here Rogers sate, and here for ever dwell
> With me those Pleasures that he sang so well,"

together with another, erring in diffuseness, by Luttrell.
Rogers, if he is to be summed up in a phrase, must be
counted among the most fortunate of men, though he
complained that he had never enjoyed two consecutive
days' good health before he was fifty. He was fortunate
in the appearance of "The Pleasures of Memory" at
a moment (1792) when poetry, except for Cowper, was

SAMUEL ROGERS

FROM THE PAINTING BY THOMAS PHILLIPS, R.A., IN THE NATIONAL PORTRAIT GALLERY

GOING TO WHITE'S

FROM THE CARICATURE OF LORD ALVANLEY BY DIGHTON IN THE POSSESSION OF
WHITE'S CLUB

practically dead in England from inanition and imitative-
ness.   He was fortunate in the Whig beliefs of his family,
which gained for him the acquaintance of Fox and
Sheridan ; he was fortunate in his circumstances, which
enabled him to entertain freely at an age when most
bachelors have to subject their ideas of hospitality to
a rigid revision.   It was on the advice of his friend
"Conversation" Sharp that he left Stoke Newington,
after his father's death, and established himself first in
Paper Buildings, the Temple, and finally in the well-
known house, 22, St. James's Place.

Rogers narrowly escaped matrimony, and that, when
his fastidiousness is remembered, must be accounted
another piece of good luck for him.   A slipshod or Mala-
propian wife would soon have despatched him to the
tomb ; and against the possibility of a wise choice there
stands his favourite saying that it mattered little whom a
man married, for he was sure to find next morning that
he had married somebody else.   He lavished instead his
affections on his house in St. James's Place, with the
bow windows looking over the Green Park, in which
the drawing-room was decorated by Flaxman, who also
designed the mantelpiece, while Stothard executed the
cabinet for antiquities.   Rogers was a sage bibliophile
and a sound judge of prints ; he had a genuine feeling
for Italian art.   Among his curios was Milton's receipt
to the publisher for the five pounds paid him for
" Paradise Lost."   Another treasure, Addison's table, was
acquired by him from Sir Thomas Lawrence and found
its way to Holland House after the sale of his effects.
In one of his best essays Hayward contrasted the purity
of Rogers's taste with the floridity of Horace Walpole's,
and pointed out that his collections simply supplied the

place of the ordinary furniture of a gentleman's house.
" There was nothing beyond their intrinsic excellence to
remind the visitor that almost every object his eye fell
upon was a priceless gem, a coveted rarity, or an acknowledged masterpiece."

Having cut himself free from the paternal banking
business, Rogers set himself to live a life of literary and
intellectual ease, with rare and painful periods of literary
parturition.   He entertained much and with discrimination, and dined out but rarely, and was no club man.
His famous breakfasts were not, as was jokingly said,
probationary to dinner, but really less of formalities than
the later meal.   Visits to country houses, such as
Bowood, Dropmore, and Longleat, made up Rogers's
autumn, with a tour abroad as a rare variant ; and winter
generally saw him at home again.   Thus, with the constant drawback of feeble health, the easy years passed
with Rogers, until extreme old age brought with it loss of
memory and a longing for death.   He won, and he held
for fifty years, a position without a rival, maintaining
friendship on equal terms with Lord Lansdowne, Lord
Holland, and the Duke of Wellington, yet keeping in
touch with necessitous authorship, as in the instances
of Cumberland in one generation and Campbell in the
next, and holding out the hand of encouragement to the
aspiring genius of Dickens.   Yet, as Hayward reminds
us, successful authorship was not regarded as a recommendation to the best society at the time when Rogers
was ambitious to enter it.   " His first cautious advances
were made rather in the character of a liberal host than
of a popular poet."   His intercourse with Fox, recorded
with minuteness in the " Recollections " and with much
feeling in the well-known apostrophe in " Human Life,"

made him free of Holland House, and membership of
the King of Clubs was a parallel road to the inner
circle of Whiggism. As the years went on his political
enthusiasms declined and his cosmopolitan sympathies
widened. He had a strong liking for Americans, partly
because his family had taken the extreme Whig side at
the time of the War of Independence, partly because
they saved him the trouble of talking French.

Byron remarked of Rogers that he had good qualities
to counterbalance the littleness of his character. Over-
balance would have been a correcter word to use. Of
Rogers's virtues the strongest was only revealed when the
late Mr. P. W. Clayden published the " Early Life " and
" Rogers and his Contemporaries," namely, the steadfast-
ness of his home affections. His sister Sarah, a remarkable woman, was his special companion ; she died only
a year before him, and her home at Hampstead was a
reduced copy, as a storehouse of art, of his own in St.
James's Place. Despite his long intercourse with fashionable society, Rogers remained a pattern of middle-class
domesticity. Nor was he backward in kindness, whether
the claimants on his good offices were intimate friends or
unknown literary aspirants. He reconciled Moore with
Jeffrey and Byron with Moore. His draft of £150 saved
the person of the dying Sheridan from arrest ; he was
one of the many who tried to extricate Lawrence from
his difficulties ; Moore and Campbell were under obligations to him. " Borrow five hundred pounds of him,"
said the last, "and he will never say a word against you
until you come to repay him." Lord John Russell added
a footnote to Moore's acknowledgment of his generosity
to the effect that Rogers's charity was not only abundant
but discriminating. His income, however, amounted to

but £5,000 a year, so that it would be an exaggeration to call him wealthy. He delighted besides in giving Twelfth Night parties to children, and his kindness to his servants approached weakness. The conversation at his table was that of high thinking; idle gossip was excluded, but letters and the arts were habitually discussed.

Rogers's faults were jealousness of rival attainments in society and an inveterate propensity to say disagreeable things. He could not endure being eclipsed by a copious talker like Mackintosh or Macaulay, and Sir Henry Holland declares that on such occasions he infused additional acid into his remarks. His familiar excuse to Sir Henry Taylor was that he had a very weak voice, and that if he did not say ill-natured things no one would hear what he said. But at one time of his life his habitual severity of comment had become so formidable that, as Hayward tells us, his guests might be seen manœuvring which should leave the room last, so as not to undergo the dreaded ordeal. Rogers envied Luttrell his social distinction, and his annoyance took the characteristic form of regret that the wit devoted his time entirely to fashion. At the same time, Greville used too strong an expression when he declared that the two inseparables hated one another, since Luttrell was amiability itself, and there is no reason to doubt the sincerity of Rogers's accurate compliment, "Luttrell is indeed a pleasant companion. None of the talkers whom I meet in London society can slide in a brilliant thing with such readiness as he does."

Much of Rogers's acerbity came, no doubt, from an intolerance of assumption and intellectual emptiness, as witness his retort to the pretentious gentleman who tried to make a third to Rogers and Hayward on their way back from an evening party. The intruder protested that he hated walking alone. "I should have thought, sir," said Rogers, "that no one was so well satisfied with your company as yourself." But he appears in a less praiseworthy light in Lady Granville's correspondence, as gratuitously snubbing two young men at Bowood. Were they coming for a walk with Lord Lansdowne and himself? They said, "No." "There is a Providence," murmured Rogers. One of his female favourites, possibly Mrs. Norton, made up a little dinner for him, in which, as she hoped, all his tastes had been consulted. After a glance round the table, he remarked that the fish was out of season. Sometimes the smartness of his humour amply excused its tartness. "Is it the contents you are looking at?" asked an anxious author about a presentation copy of a book. "No, the discontents," answered Rogers, pointing to the list of subscribers. But there was reason in Moore's complaint when Rogers commented on the dining-room at Sloperton, hung round with the portraits of Lord Grey, Lord Lansdowne, and other Whig notables, "Why, you have all your patrons about you!" "A good-natured man," observed Moore, when he told the story, "would have said *friends*."

Yet Rogers could pay the most graceful of compliments when he chose, and in his happier hour overflowed with kindliness and good sense. He had, besides, to live up to his reputation, while his cadaverous appearance made him the butt of innumerable jokes, the most classical of which is Lord Dudley's inquiry why, since he could afford it, he did not set up his hearse. They seldom went unavenged. Lady Eastlake told in the *Quarterly Review* the story of a dinner-party being suddenly interrupted by a tremendous knock at the front door. "What's that?" said the host, starting. A man of free speech, looking straight at Rogers, interposed, "It's the devil come to carry off *you*." "Perhaps," replied Rogers in his blandest tones, "he may have the discrimination" (the word of six syllables being pronounced with special clearness, and with a slightly nasal pause on the fourth syllable) "to prefer another member of the company."

Few literary men have been built more completely of a piece in habits and character. Rogers's handwriting was neat, clear, and regular, corresponding with the preciseness of his habits. He kept himself in good health by walking. Thanks to that habit, he was able, shortly before the accident—he was knocked down by a carriage—which crippled him at the age of eighty-eight, to have a breakfast party at home, go to a wedding breakfast, where he returned thanks for the bridesmaids, then to Chiswick, where he was presented to an Imperial Highness, dine out, go to the Opera and look in at a ball—all within the space of forty-eight hours. If his fancy for keeping nightingales in cages to sing to him was an affectation, and rather a cruel one, he could be perfectly natural when drinking tea with Wordsworth at Grasmere or listening in admitted bewilderment to the monologues of Coleridge.

The labour Rogers bestowed on his poems, happily quizzed by Sydney Smith, was characteristic of the man. Anxious consultations with Wharton and Gilpin, with Sharp, Moore, and Mackintosh, on meticulous variations, and the weighing of here a line and there a line, here a little and there a little, preceded publication. The gestation of "Columbus," in particular, was elephantine in its slowness, and the result was a fragmentary production,

disfigured by a straining of language and held together by
supernatural machinery that might have been borrowed
from pantomime. The versification, too, was careless,
despite the labours of the committee, and Lord Dudley
pounced in the *Quarterly* on lines like :

"There silent sate many an unbidden guest."

If Rogers touched absurdity in "Columbus," he descended to feebleness in "Jacqueline," the "highly
refined but somewhat insipid pastoral," as George Ellis
called it, also in the *Quarterly*, which he was misguided
enough to publish in the same volume with Byron's
"Lara." But "The Pleasures of Memory," the "Epistle
to a Friend," "Human Life," and "Italy" display Rogers
as a genuine poet; though Byron's famous triangle, in
which Scott is placed above the apex, Rogers just under
it, in the division below Moore and Campbell, and under
them Southey, Wordsworth, and Coleridge, has been
repudiated by modern critical taste. Lord Dudley, in a
review which pushed the candour of friendship to its
extreme limits, and perhaps beyond them, and which
Rogers avenged by the often-quoted epigram about
Ward and his heart, defined the position of "The
Pleasures of Memory" with a much nearer approach
to exactitude :

"Not that the "Pleasures of Memory" entitles its
author to a place in the higher class of English poets.
But it was published at a moment of great political
dearth, when the old school (if we may so express
ourselves) was drawn almost to the lees, and before the
new one had appeared. The subject was very fortunate
and it was not too long ; it abounded in pleasing though
detached pictures, and everywhere it afforded evidence
of a highly cultivated and elegant mind."

This criticism holds good, so far as praise goes, of Rogers's other pieces, and more particularly of " Human Life," where the pictures are essentially pleasing, and the evidence of elegant cultivation conspicuous on every page. Hayward justly praises the closing scene, the deathbed of the good man :

> " Come and stand round—the widow and the child,
> As when she first forgot her tears and smiled.
> They who watch by him see not, but he sees,
> Sees and exults—were ever dreams like these ?
> Those who watch by him, hear not ; but he hears,
> And Earth recedes, and Heaven itself appears ! "

Rogers, unfortunately, is remembered less through this elevated production than through " Italy," partly from its inevitable fate, to be transcribed into guide-books, partly from the charm of the illustrations. It must be confessed that the admirable prose of the notes sometimes finds its way into the text, and that invention is overlaid by historic allusion. Still, the revelation of the author's self is in Rogers's best manner :

> " Nature denied him much,
> But gave him at his birth what most he values ;
> A passionate love for music, sculpture, painting,
> For poetry, the language of the gods,
> For all things here, or grand or beautiful :
> A setting sun, a lake among the mountains,
> The light of an ingenuous countenance,
> And what transcends them all, a noble action."

An ideal fireside companion on a winter afternoon, Rogers rescued the school of Pope from an undignified end, though it was time that that end arrived.

Richard or "Conversation" Sharp is as inseparable from Rogers as Dundas from Pitt or Farrington from Lawrence. The two were much of an age, Sharp, who was born in 1759, being by about four years Rogers's senior ; and, except for an occasional tiff over metaphysics, their friendship continued without a break until the death of the first of them in 1835 brought it to a close. "Conversation" Sharp's name inevitably provokes a smile, but he was a man of some attainments and the object of universal esteem. The son of a British officer, he was born in Newfoundland, and made a large fortune in the City of London, first as a member of a West India firm, and secondly as a hat manufacturer. His complexion and his occupation were combined by Luttrell in the excellent joke, when some one said that he had transferred the dye of his hats to his face, that it was " darkness that might be felt." Sharp made his way in society by much the same means as Rogers, partly by advocating strong Whig principles, partly by making his town house in Park Lane and his " cottage home " at Fredley, near Dorking, literary and political centres. He corresponded with all the Whigs, from Dr. Parr to Horner, was the friend of men of letters like Hallam and Moore, and behaved with great kindness to Macaulay when he made his start in the world.

This wealthy and travelled bachelor had many interests in life. Active behind the scenes, he was a member of political clubs like the Society for Obtaining Constitutional Information and the Friends of the People, though he failed to make much of a figure in Parliament. He was prominent at the literary clubs, the King of Clubs among them. It was in preparation for one of those appearances that his partner, Boddington, was discovered noting down the topics that Sharp wished to have introduced—a truly remarkable instance of business methods carried out of business hours.   But prompted or unprompted, the conversationalist could hold his own with the best of them at Holland House or anywhere else.   The records of his prowess are scanty, and it may be inferred that he conveyed information rather than coined epigrams, and abounded in illustrative anecdote.

The slim volume of "Letters and Essays in Prose and Verse" which Sharp left behind him scarcely substantiates Mackintosh's eulogy that he was the best critic he had ever known ; wide reading and a retentive memory are there, but they merely help out the superior commonplace, as in some sententious letters to a young friend, probably one of his numerous wards.   In an "Epistle to Lord Holland," written at Windermere, the sight of some school-buildings erected by his friend inspired the fine rapture :

> "Yet can there still remain one generous doubt
> Whether a People with sense, or without,
> Is happier, better, less disposed to err,
> Or which an honest statesman must prefer ?"

Miss Berry, who understood men, thus summed up "Conversation" Sharp : "He is clever, but I should suspect of little real depth of intellect."   The supposition is tenable.   None the less Sharp was an influence.

CHAPTER XIII

HENRY LUTTRELL

The premiership of wit—Luttrell's social position—"A philosopher in all things"—London and Paris—Luttrell's epigrams—"Letters to Julia"—Gifford's review—Almack's—The Park and Kensington Gardens—The Argyll Rooms and Brooks's—An apostrophe to London—The dead season—Hunting and the House—"Crockford House"—Luttrell's last years.

THE premiership of wit had many claimants under the Regency. Lady Granville assigned it to Frere, and placed Lord Dudley above Luttrell, on the score of his greater *abandon*, precisely the quality that other observers denied him. Sir Henry Holland thus differentiates :

"The wit of Lord Dudley, Lord Alvanley, and Rogers was poignant, personal sarcasm—in Luttrell it was perpetual fun, of lighter and more various kind, and whimsically expressed in his features as well as his words. *Natio comœda est* was the maxim of his mind, and expressed the whole field of his humour."

Charles Greville, in the second of the two characters he drew from Luttrell, also contrasted him with Rogers :

185

"Rogers and Luttrell were always bracketed together. . . . Luttrell's *bons mots* and repartees were excellent, but he was less caustic, more good-natured, but in some respects less striking in conversation than his companion, who had more knowledge, more imagination, and, though in a different way, as much wit."

Byron described Luttrell as "the most epigrammatic conversationalist" he ever met; Rogers's tribute has been already given. Altogether Greville paid him no more than his due when he wrote that, though Luttrell never attained any but a social position, it was one of great eminence and success. It was won, too, in the face of many obstacles. He was believed to be the natural son of the second Lord Carhampton, a brave, witty, and disreputable Irish peer, more familiar as the Colonel Luttrell who contested Middlesex against Wilkes, and Greville seems to imply that he had the manliness not to be ashamed of his mother's family. His father did little for him, beyond obtaining for him a seat in the last Irish Parliament and an appointment in the Irish Government, which he commuted for a pension—it seems to have been his only source of income.

Luttrell triumphed over narrow means and mystery of origin on entering London society, shortly after the Union, under the wing of the Duchess of Devonshire. Greville, on first meeting him, thought him extremely sensitive and easily disconcerted, though tolerant of everything except boredom. He inevitably occupied an isolated and defensive position, keeping his secret to himself. Both Greville and Lady Granville were struck by his contempt for mere riches and rank. "He has that *don du ciel*," wrote the latter, "of never being *de trop*, and I never met with so independent a person." He declined any further invitations to Holland House until Lady Holland had suppressed an aggressive cat which mauled Rogers and which Brougham only kept at bay with pinches of snuff. Taken as a whole, Luttrell seems to have been a singularly engaging and high-minded man, "a philosopher in all things," says Greville, "and especially in religion," too idle to cultivate his literary powers, fond of his ease and dinner, and perhaps disappointed that his abilities had not been tried in public affairs. But the presumption is that the slights of fortune affected him but little.

It was a great thing, after all, to be in universal request. Mr. Clayden printed a letter from Luttrell to Rogers in which he planned out his autumn campaign with the certainty of a skilled tactician. "I cannot, upon my soul I do not think I can"—go to Trentham, he lamented to Lady Granville. As became a thorough man of the world, he admired sportsmanship in others, if not a sportsman himself, and his "Letters to Julia" contain some capital descriptions of shooting parties and the hunting field. But London was his favourite haunt, because there, as Greville puts it, "genius and ability always maintain an ascendancy over pomp, vanity, and the adventitious circumstances of birth or position." A striking passage in the "Letters to Julia" dwells upon another of London's gifts, immunity from being overlooked by one's neighbours—a freedom that a man like Luttrell would particularly appreciate. He knew his Paris, too, with an extensive and peculiar knowledge, though in 1815 he purposely lingered at Brighton on his return to avoid being pestered as "the last well-informed gentleman" from the French capital.

A considerable crop of his detached sayings could be extracted from Moore's diary, but most of them read like things of the moment. He did not disdain the pun, and took great delight in Hood's achievements in that line. The true Luttrell is to be found, however, in his familiar definition of the English climate—"On a fine day, like looking up a chimney; on a rainy day, like looking down it." His illustrations of current events were happy. "A king broken loose" was his summary of the antics of George IV. in Ireland; and he said of a slim lady's figure that it was just enough to keep the muslin together. The two most disgusting things in the world, because you could not deny them, were Sir George Warrender's wealth and Croker's talents.

Luttrell's epigrams had an extraordinary vogue in their day, quite equal to Fitzpatrick's. Through Moore's agency they sometimes appeared in the *Times*. The happiest of them by far was the epitaph he wrote at Rogers's house in an album belonging to Wordsworth's daughter :

> " Killed by an omnibus—why not ?
>   So quick a death a boon is.
>   Let not his friends lament his lot—
>   *Mors omnibus communis.*"

Luttrell, as well as Rogers, was provoked to epigram by Lord Dudley's habit of learning his speeches by heart, and his verse, if less pointed, is better-natured than his friend's :

" In vain my affections the ladies are seeking,
  If I give up my heart there's an end of my speaking."

Contributions to albums were more to Luttrell's taste than his appearances in print, which were generally anonymous. His "Lines written at Ampthill Park in the Autumn of 1818," and dedicated to Lord Holland, are pretty but vapid :

"Holland and Ampthill—be the names combined
   Through unborn ages : o'er this hallowed ground
Ne'er may the spoiler tread, nor wasting wind
   Nor axe among those storied woods resound."

Luttrell's "Advice to Julia" or, as it was finally called, "Letters to Julia" stands far higher than this mild effusion. Moore, who suggested the subject, thought it "full of well-bred facetiousness and sparkle of the very first water. It was just what I advised him to do, and what few could have done half so well." Byron wrote to Lady Blessington that it was "pointed, witty and full of observation, showing in every line a knowledge of society and a tact rarely met with." Those were the opinions of friends, and they were echoed by Greville and Macaulay. Not so Gifford, who castigated the poem in the *Quarterly*, with severity but without malice. "While it had merits, it failed in interest and "—here the reviewer was evidently drawing his bow by no means at a venture—"the accumulated pleasantries of years had apparently been lavished in an incautious fortnight on the extravagant Julia." Lady Granville sketches Rogers for us, carrying the *Quarterly* about under his arm, as other people their cocked hats, and ejaculating "Poor Luttrell ! it's all over with him ; he can never look up again. He never can stand it, not being blest with a particularly good temper." Luttrell did look up, and

most sensibly took the reviewer's advice. He reformed
Julia from a lady of battered reputation into a fashionable widow ; he divided the poem into four letters ; he
transposed, polished, and made additions.

The " Letters to Julia" have been unduly neglected,
since nowhere else is the London of the Regency and
reign of George IV. more faithfully drawn. Captain
Gronow is quoted again and again as an authority on
Almack's ; but his opportunities of observing that select
assembly must have been much fewer than Luttrell's.
In easy though unambitious rhyme the whole social
world of the day is passed under review. The heartlessness of Julia has driven Charles to give up his winter
ride in Rotten Row, or his walks there in the summer to
pick up all the gossip about balls and marriages, and
about the proceedings of the committee at Almack's :

> " Of passports just obtained, or missed
> For Almack's on each Lady's list ;
> What names of all the young and fair,
> High-born and rich, are blazoned there ;
> Who are returned as sick, and who dead,
> Among the luckless girls excluded."

Julia is next invited to mount her barouche or dappled
grey and watch the whole town thronging into the Park
on a Sunday afternoon in May :

> "Th' enfranchised tradesman, when he stirs,
> Here jostles half his customers.
> Here, in a rage, the Bond-street spark
> Is bearded by his father's clerk ;
> While yon proud dame (O sad event) is
> Out-elbowed by her own apprentice ! "

The scattering of the "unumbrella'd" crowd by a shower
receives lively treatment ; and the scene shifts to Kensington Gardens and its alcoved seats, the survivor of
which still stands near Lancaster Gate.   Luttrell hits off
the solemnity of a well-behaved London crowd in an
amusing manner.   He then passes under rapid review
the pastimes Charles has forsaken, the gloves and fives,
skating on the Serpentine, the charms of which are
minutely described—fallow-deer on the banks among
them.   Charles has also given up the art of dressing,
the Cossack trousers, wasp-like waist, buckram-wadded
shoulders, and more especially the cravat.

> "' Have you, my friend,' I've heard him say,
> ' Been lucky in your turns to-day ? ' "

In the second letter Luttrell gives a minute description
of Almack's, with Willis sternly refusing admission to
those who had left their tickets behind, or who arrived
after the stroke of twelve—a ukase under which Lord
Castlereagh, Lady Worcester and the Duke of Wellington suffered.   Tea, it appears, was the only refreshment,
and the company much debated the point—champagne
or hyson.   Some cynical reflections on the wearisome-
ness of a honeymoon spent at a country seat act as a
digression, but Luttrell soon returns to the French plays
in the Argyll Rooms, Brooks's, and the Opera.   He is at
his best in a faithful account of the horrors of a London
fog, followed by an appeal to chemistry to

> " Make all our chimneys chew the cud,
> Like hungry cows, as chimneys should."

Incidentally Luttrell shows a thorough understanding of Paris, its fêtes and its gaming-tables, and is inspired by the openness of vice in France to a Hudibrastic denunciation of Government lotteries, in which

> " Ye, pious statesmen, share the plunder,
> And thus extracting good from evil,
> Compound with God and cheat the Devil ! "

Some apt satire also attacks the London spark who has to go shooting because it is the fashion, though he would much sooner remain in town. There follows a fine apostrophe to London, a word " whose sound breathes independence," and

> "To a tittle
> The place for those who have but little ;
> Here I endure no throbs, no twitches
> Of envy at another's riches,
> But, smiling, from my window see
> A dozen twice as rich as he."

All admirably felt and put. London in the dead season comes under rather prolix observation, partly actual, partly retrospective. Sadler's Wells has put on " a melodrame of slaughter" with " real water" from the New River. But criticism no longer descends from the bow-window at White's

> " On some unconscious passer-by
> Whose cape's an inch too low or high,
> Whose doctrines are unsound in hat,
> In boots, in trowsers, or cravat."

The current amusements were water-parties in eight-oar funnies, or in barges, to the " Ship " at Greenwich or the " Star and Garter " at Richmond ; excursions by steam-boat to Margate, when the start was made from the Tower at eight and the destination reached at four, or expeditions by coach to Brighton.   The country-side, no longer haunted by Charles, supplied Luttrell with his most ingenious couplet :

> " For, like a shrimp, a fox-chase fails ;
>   Both have but sorry heads and tails."

That is, the ride to cover in the cold early morning, and the ride back in the dark.   The threat that Charles may take to politics gives Luttrell an excuse for poking fun at the House of Commons of his time, which, but for the intervention of the bustling agent, the lordly patron, and the jobber, bore a close resemblance to the House of Commons of to-day ; and the " Letters to Julia " con-clude with some sage advice on the retribution awaiting a flirt after she has once married.

" Crockford House" came as an indifferent sequel to the " Letters to Julia."   The prolix satire was occasioned by the rise of the notorious gambling-club in St. James's Street in the year 1827, with all its luxury of appoint-ment.   Luttrell showed the poem in manuscript to Lord Sefton, Henry de Roos, and Charles Greville before publishing, an act of deference to society for which, Moore prognosticated, society would little thank him. The best thing in the book is the account of the gambler's downward progress from the selling of his consols to exile on the pier at Calais.   But Luttrell's threats and admonitions, courageous though they were, went unregarded by Crockford, who in a few years amassed a fortune of something like £1,200,000. " Crockford House " was the last of Luttrell's appearances in print, but he lived an amiably epicurean existence, until seized by a painful illness two years before his death, in Brompton Square, at the end of 1851. Rogers was in constant communication with his old friend in his retirement.

CHAPTER XIV

SYDNEY AND ROBERT SMITH

Sydney Smith on Luttrell—Foston—Combe Florey—As a social reformer—The timidity of the Whigs—"Peter Plymley's Letters"—"Persecuting Bishops"—"Letters to Archdeacon Singleton"—A licensed jester—His letters to Lady Holland—A parody of Mackintosh—A sermon on temperance—Sydney Smith's wit—Bobus Smith—A suppressed individuality.

L UTTRELL had no warmer admirer than Sydney Smith, who used him as a screen for strokes at Rogers. Lord John Russell, for instance, reported to Moore in 1827 : "Sydney Smith says Rogers was in very bad humour at Ampthill House. Luttrell was helped to bread sauce before him." The acquaintance must have begun soon after the young clergyman had established himself at No. 8, Doughty Street, in the autumn of 1803, with his contributions to the newly-founded *Edinburgh Review* as his main source of income, to which were added the proceeds of his audacious lectures on moral philosophy delivered at the Royal Institution. Sydney Smith's departure to the rectory of Foston-le-Clay, in Yorkshire, on the peremptory summons of Archbishop Vernon Harcourt, in the autumn of 1808, did not break off his friendship with the man about town whom he accused of believing that muffins grew on trees. Luttrell soon paid him a visit, and we are told that "Mrs. Sydney was dreadfully alarmed about her side dishes, and grew pale as the covers were lifted; but they stood the test. Luttrell tasted and praised." The same theme was elaborated in 1829 after Sydney Smith had migrated to Combe Florey, in Somerset, having become Prebendary of Bristol.

"Luttrell came over for the day, from whence I know not, but I thought not from good pastures; at least, he had not his usual soup-and-pattie look. There was a forced smile upon his countenance, which seemed to indicate plain roast and boiled; and a sort of apple-pudding depression, as if he had been staying with a clergyman. . . . He was very agreeable, but spoke too lightly, I thought, of veal soup. I took him aside and reasoned the matter with him; but to speak the truth, Luttrell is not steady in his judgments on dishes. Individual failures with him soon degenerate into generic objections, till, by some fortunate accident, he eats himself into better opinions."

Sydney Smith's correspondence is frequently that of a Londoner in exile, writing to Londoners in possession of their own sacred city. At Combe Florey, as he told Macaulay at their first meeting, he was "in a delightful parsonage about which I care a great deal; and a delightful country, about which I do not care a straw." "You may depend upon it," he wrote, "all lives lived out of London are mistakes, more or less grievous—but mistakes." Yet he was buried in the country during the greater part of his active career, except for the five blissful years in its prime, the period of "Peter Plymley's Letters," and the thirteen

SYDNEY SMITH
FROM THE PAINTING BY HENRY PERRONET BRIGGS, R.A., IN THE NATIONAL PORTRAIT GALLERY

THOMAS MOORE

FROM THE PAINTING BY JOHN JACKSON, R.A., IN THE NATIONAL PORTRAIT GALLERY

serene years at its close, the period of the canonry at
St. Paul's and the " Letters to Archdeacon Singleton."
But, as he wisely wrote, he had not much time left
on his hands to regret London.   At Foston he was
" village   parson,   village   doctor,   village   comforter,
village   magistrate,   and   *Edinburgh*   reviewer."   He
turned schoolmaster, since he could not afford to
educate his son ; he turned farmer, since he could not
let his land.   A village carpenter, who came to him
for local relief, furnished the house which Sydney
Smith   designed   and   built.   Everybody   knows,   or
should know, Bunch, otherwise Annie Kay, the little
garden-girl, made like a milestone, who became the
best butter-maker in the county and attended Sydney
Smith in his last illness ; Molly Mills, who presided
out of doors ; the ancient green chariot, called the
Immortal ;   the   horse   Calamity,   and   Bitty,   the   pet
donkey.   It is sometimes forgotten that Sydney Smith
was one of the first clergymen to establish allotment
gardens, and to teach his parishioners to live on sensible
diet.

Among the more amenable surroundings of Combe
Florey, there was more building and more physicking.
Hayward doubts if the health of the village was
improved by the blue pills Sydney Smith delighted in
" darting into its vitals."   But healing is largely a matter
of faith, and the rustic mind believes in medicines nasty
to the taste and potent in their operation.   According to
a familiar story Sydney Smith furnished his house with
pictures, and gravely consulted two Royal Academicians
as to their purchase, adding, by way of afterthought,
" Oh, I ought to mention that my outside price is
thirty-five shillings."   To his garden he gave adventitious

charms for the benefit of his London visitors by tying oranges to the shrubs, while he improved his two donkeys into deer by fitting them with antlers, and then placed them in front of the windows.

In an essay written on the appearance of the Memoir of Sydney Smith by his daughter, Lady Holland, Hayward claimed for him that he was a social, moral, and political reformer, second only to Brougham, and that his character of wit was incidental and subordinate. Time has inevitably reversed the importance of these two aspects of the man. All the causes he advocated have been won, and most of them are forgotten. His jokes, whether correctly reported or distorted, make inevitable reappearances in every book dealing with the first half of the nineteenth century. Yet there have been few more vigorous controversialists, and certainly no more loyal party servant, though it is clear that he would have accepted promotion at the hands of Lord Eldon. He risked much to remove abuses, and, as he was not slow to remind his aristocratic Whig friends, got next to nothing by way of reward. The living of Foston was with difficulty wrung from Lord Erskine by the exertions of Lord and Lady Holland; the stall at Bristol came from a Tory Chancellor, Lord Lyndhurst; Lord Grey, who is supposed to have said on entering Downing Street, " Now we shall be able to do something for Sydney Smith," exhausted his benevolence with the canonry at St. Paul's. When the "Plymley Letters" appeared Lord Holland reminded him that Swift " had lost a bishopric for his wittiest performance." The jest turned to earnest in 1830. Sydney Smith's flippancies at the expense of his ecclesiastical superiors had been confused with irreverence for things sacred. Observa-

tions about the Thirty-nine Articles and heaven were
attributed to him which he always indignantly repudiated, and the result was that the Whigs shrank from
the clamour that his promotion would have created.
Two years before his death he summed up the situation with his invariable good sense : " They showed a
want of moral courage in not making me a bishop,
but I must own that it required a good deal."

Supreme common-sense under the guise of fun
constitutes Sydney Smith's chief merit as a contro-
versialist. He excelled in rendering ignorance and
prejudice absurd, in riddling them with jocular similes,
and knocking them down with apologues. But, if he
is to be compared with Swift, it must be, as Hayward
points out, to Swift without the " Tale of a Tub " or
" Gulliver." For the irony of the Dean of St. Patrick's
he substituted chaff, excellent chaff, but still chaff.
Apart from errors in taste, " Peter Plymley's Letters "
suffer from repetition of argument ; they rely too
much on appeals to fear of a French invasion—a line
of reasoning more calculated to strengthen the country
in its stubbornness than to convert it—and they never
treat political opponents like Canning, who, after all,
was as sincere an Emancipationalist as Sydney Smith
himself, with decent civility. Their practical effect was
momentary. The pamphlet ran through many editions
in 1808, and frightened the Government of the day ;
the Catholic Relief Act was not passed until twenty-one
years later, and then it came like a thief in the night.
The fact is that Sydney Smith addressed his satire not to
the general public but to the coterie of Holland House,
who may possibly have appreciated such appalling
classicisms as " political acupuncturation " and *sudarium*

for handkerchief. He had easier game with a narrow
divine like Dr. Marsh, and no more righteous appeal
for toleration has ever been penned than " Persecuting
Bishops." The speech into which he introduced the
immortal Mrs. Partington may almost be said to have
lent the Reform Bill the breeze that brought it into
port.

In the " Letters to Archdeacon Singleton" Sydney
Smith appears as a Liberal whose enthusiasms had
become exhausted, and as the chivalrous defender of
ecclesiastical institutions which, in his own way, he was
zealously strengthening from within. He poked legitimate fun at Lord Melbourne in the disguise of a reformer,
and photographed Lord John Russell for ever in the
famous phrase about his assuming command of the
Channel Fleet, with or without ten minutes' notice.
Still, when the Bishops of the Church of England
are discovered in an innovating mood, they deserve
encouragement, not ridicule. Sydney Smith the
defender of ecclesiastical things as they were is a less
admirable person than Sydney Smith denouncing the
inequalities of the penal code or the severity of the game
laws. His charity stopped at Methodists.

Sydney Smith talked, as he wrote, out of the abundance
of his heart. He had little of Luttrell's epigrammatic
neatness, and the charm of his humour lay mainly in its
unexpectedness and in the heaping of one grotesque
image on another. He seldom abused his position of
licensed jester ; his talk was not for display, and he
enjoyed drawing out the talents of silent and shy people.
At the same time, he undeniably took aback by certain
of his sallies those who were far from stupid or strait-
laced, and he once drew upon himself a deserved and

historic snub. They were discussing at Holland House, with the Regent present, who was the wickedest man that had ever lived. Sydney Smith said, "The Regent Orleans, and he was a priest." The Prince's retort was smashing : "I should give the honour to his tutor, the Abbé Dubois, and he was a priest, Mr. Sydney." Moore hesitated before surrendering to him, and he struck Macaulay as being less clerical than might have been desired. Lady Granville preferred him in the pulpit to society ; Fanny Kemble was sometimes a little disturbed by his free and easy wearing of the cloth. But he never deliberately wounded. "You have been laughing at me for the last seven years," said Lord Dudley at their final parting, "and you have never said anything which I wished unsaid." To Byron he was

"that o'erwhelming son of Heaven,
The very powerful parson, Peter Pith,
The loudest wit I e'er was deafened with."

His daughter, however, assures us that he was shy when he first entered Holland House, at the age of thirty-three. Those were the days when he could not afford a hackney-coach, and used to carry a pair of dress shoes in his pocket and change them in the hall.

Anyhow, Sydney Smith soon acquired an acknowledged position at Holland House; he paid Lady Holland in her own coin—though the repartee, "Yes, and shall I sweep the room ?" is probably apocryphal—with the result that they became the warmest of friends. His letters to her, which begin with the whimsical conjecture that the "Plymley Letters" were written by Romilly, Sir Arthur Pigott, or Horner, three solemn lawyers, are, on the whole, the liveliest in the collection edited by Mrs. Austen. In one of them he perpetrated a specimen of his numerous jokes against the Scotch :

"I take the liberty of sending you two brace of grouse— curious, because killed by a Scotch metaphysician ; in other or better language, they are mere ideas, shot by other ideas, out of a pure intellectual notion called a gun."

Presents of provender, the annual tribute of a cheese among them, figure frequently in his letters, for he was fond of good cheer. But he also discussed his prospects in a spirit of manly independence, and lectured Lady Holland on the merits of water-drinking. To Lord Holland he sent the capital parody of Mackintosh's style :

"Pepper may philosophically be described as the dusty and highly pulverised seed of an oriental fruit ; an article rather of condiment than of diet, which, dispersed lightly over the surface of food with no other rule than the caprice of the consumer, communicates pleasure, rather than affords nutri- tion ; and, by adding a tropical flavour to the gross and succulent viands of the North, approximates the different regions of the earth, explains the objects of commerce, and justifies the industry of man."

A drive with Lady Holland after he had become Canon of St. Paul's inspired him with a mock sermon on temperance. " Lay aside pepper and brandy and water and *baume de vie*. A single mutton chop, a glass of toast and water"—here she cried and he stopped ; but she began sobbing, and he was weak enough to allow two glasses of sherry, on which she recovered. When Lord Holland died, he consoled himself with the reflection,

" I have learnt to live as a soldier does in war, expect-
ing that, in any one moment, the best and dearest may
be killed before his eyes."

The wit of Sydney Smith is more easily recoverable
from his letters than from the various catalogues of his
jokes. Many of them have become tedious from constant repetition; others have been mangled out of all
knowledge. As with most professed humourists, he has
standing against him specimens of his weakest nonsense
and his most outrageous puns. It would have been
different if they had all reached the level of his compliment to Mrs. Tighe and Mrs. Cuffe : "Ah ! there you are ;
the cuff that every one would wear and the tie that no
one would loose." The honour of having been Sydney
Smith's most discriminating recorder may be fairly divided
between Moore and Lord Houghton. The former gives
a vivid idea of his enjoyment of his own jokes, his transi-
tions from gay to grave, and comedy to farce, but he is
too often content to dispose of Sydney Smith's humorous illustrations with an "&c." To Moore, however, we
owe the classical reply to Leslie, the Scots philosopher,
when he complained that Jeffrey, being in a hurry, had
disposed of his explanations on the North Pole with
"Oh ! damn the North Pole." Sydney Smith gravely
informed him, in confidence, that he had " once heard
Jeffrey speak disrespectfully of the Equator." Lord
Houghton has chiefly preserved personalities ; Macaulay
"not only overflowed with learning, but stood in the
slop"; Croker would " dispute with the recording angel
on the date of his sins."

Sydney Smith once expatiated on India as a glorious
possession for England. " My brother Bobus comes to
me one morning when I am in bed, and says he is going

there and wishes me good-bye. I turn round, go to sleep
for some time, and when I wake, there he is again, standing by me, hardly at all altered, and with a large fortune."
In sober fact, Robert Smith lived in Bombay as Advocate-
General for the best part of seven years.   His connection
with Holland House was close, since he formed an
intimate friendship with Lord Holland at Eton, and
married Miss Vernon, the half-sister of Lord Holland's
mother and daughter of the Whig member for Tavistock.
His affection for his younger brother, whom he helped in
the days of straitened means, went deep, and they were
divided in death by little more than a fortnight.   Sir
Henry Holland was present at "the very touching scene
of their last meeting with the event in view of both."

There must have been something very attractive about
a man who was known through life by his school nickname. People of taste, Lord Lansdowne among them,
preferred Bobus Smith to his brother for the very
conversational qualities in which Sydney excelled.   A
fine classical scholar, he produced some remarkable verse
in the manner of Lucretius.   Lord Dudley was once
asked his opinion of the relative merits of certain Roman
poets. He began with Lucretius, Catullus and Bobus and
went on without a stop to Virgil, Horace, and Juvenal.
Bobus Smith could also hold his own in metaphysical
discussion against Mackintosh, and he was noted for his
happy turns of phrase.   But Bobus was a suppressed individuality ; he was to be seen now and then at Holland
House, but rarely in any other society.   Whether in town
or in his house at Cheam—built, said Sydney Smith, by
Chemosh, the Abomination of the Moabites—he shut
himself up with his classics, and was happiest in the
company of children. An anxious letter from Sydney

Smith, after Robert had failed to catch the ear of the
House of Commons as member for Grantham, confirms
the idea that he was the sort of man to sit down under a
rebuff.   But he deserves to be remembered for other
reasons than as the butt of Talleyrand's wit.   When he
incautiously boasted of his mother's beauty, he was
effectually silenced by the remark, "C'était donc votre
père, monsieur, qui n'était pas si bien."

CHAPTER XV

MOORE, BYRON, AND SCOTT

Moore and Lady Holland—The " Twopenny Post Bag "—Moore
and Sheridan—Byron's " Memoirs "—" Tommy dearly loves a lord "
—Moore's independence of mind—" Lalla Rookh " and the " Irish
Melodies "—" English Bards and Scotch Reviewers "—The Drury
Lane Committee—Lady Caroline Lamb—" Glenarvon "—Byron at
Holland House—His marriage—Lord Holland's intervention—" Such
a lovable person "—Scott's quarrel with Lord Holland—His descrip-
tion of Holland House—" Tales of my Landlord."

MOORE'S patrons, as Rogers called them, his
friends, as he would have preferred them to be
called, lived not so much at Holland House as
at Donington, Lord Moira's seat, and at Bowood, Lord
Lansdowne's. Still, he was an intimate member of the
circle, and Lord Holland's advice had from time to time
important bearings on his career. The first entry in his
journal relating to Holland House is dated January, 1812,
when he was taken to dinner by Lord Moira and brought
back again. Moore must have met the Hollands before,
since he had played and sung his way into English
society a dozen years previously, when his presentation
to the Prince of Wales, whom he was subsequently to
attack with much vehemence, opened every Whig door to

the son of the Dublin grocer.   Thenceforward he was a
frequent diner and sleeper at Holland House; he met
his host and hostess on their visits to Bowood, and his
exile in Paris, owing to his financial difficulties, partly
coincided with one of their prolonged stays in the French
capital.   He appears to have regarded Lady Holland with
a mixture of esteem and awe, duly chronicling her exceedingly frank remarks on his poetry and her praise of
Mrs. Moore's good looks.   A compliment to his Bessy
went straight to his heart.   His self-complaisance was
also touched by Lady Holland's remark, when he expressed his gratitude for Lord Lansdowne's kindness—
this was after he had established himself at Sloperton in
the autumn of 1817 : "For those who know you and have
the means, it is no more than is due to you."   Still, there
were occasions when he quailed ; in 1821 he arrived at
the Hollands' hotel in Paris with the intention of break-
fasting, but she looked so much out of temper that he
dissembled his hunger and went off to a restaurant.

Moore's relations with Lord Holland were of a much
easier kind.   They discussed the classics and poetry
together, and polished each other's translations.   Lord
Holland it was who suggested that Moore should parody
the Regent's letter to the Duke of York.   When the
Regent had become King, however, he recurred to the
subject in a manner that puzzled Moore, confessing that
the conduct of the Whigs in 1812 had been anything but
prudent, as they must have known that George would
never forgive the personalities directed at him.   That was
true enough, but though the great family connections
may have lamented the indiscretion of their ally, the rest
of us should thank him for the best light satire in the
language.   "By the by," wrote Byron, "what humour

what—everything in the Post Bag!" Humour there is
and to spare in the passage describing

> " That awful hour or two
>   Of grave tonsorial preparation
>   Which, to a fond, admiring nation
>   Sends forth, announced by trump and drum,
>   The best-wigg'd Prince in Christendom!"

Moore had frequent recourse to Lord Holland while
labouring at his Life of Sheridan, and the anecdotes as
they appear in his journal are frequently livelier than
when re-trimmed for publication. He deserves credit for
adhering to his own view of Sheridan's conduct at the
beginning of the Regency, though that view was far from
acceptable to the Whig hierarchy, and for speaking out
on their neglect of the dramatist as he lay dying. His
failure to appreciate Sheridan's powers arose partly,
no doubt, from their superiority to his own, partly
because a man of his fatal facility would be naturally
inclined to undervalue another who was understood to
elaborate both his dramas and his conversation with
infinite care. Rogers relates how once at his house,
when Sheridan was talking at his best, Moore, who could
never keep still, broke up the party by proposing an
adjournment to Miss Lydia White's.

Lord Holland's scruples were in part responsible for a
much and idly discussed proceeding on Moore's part, the
destruction of Byron's " Memoirs." As Moore loosely
reports the conversation, he wished that Murray's 2,000
guineas could have been got in any other way, and
seemed to think that "it was in cold blood depositing a
sort of quiver of poisoned arrows for a future warfare

upon private character," though he could only remember
a passage or two that came under that description. The
objection eventually carried weight with the chivalrous
poet, and after taking, as was his wont, numerous friends
into his confidence, he arrived at the high-minded, if
irrational, conclusion that the "Memoirs" should be
suppressed and Murray repaid. The wishes of Hobhouse, Byron's most intimate friend, and Mrs. Leigh,
Byron's sister, were strongly for immediate destruction.
Luttrell, who, if Rogers can be trusted, was indifferent to
the whole thing, also voted for committal to the flames.
Accordingly, at a meeting held in Murray's house, on
May 17, 1824, he repaid the publisher with interest by
means of an advance from the Longmans: the manuscript
was returned to him, and burnt by Mr. Wilmot Horton
and Colonel Doyle as the representatives of Mrs. Leigh.
Lord John Russell, one of the many who saw the
"Memoirs," declared that they contained little traces of
Byron's genius and no interesting details of Byron's life.
The loss to posterity, therefore, was presumably small;
none the less, the precipitate act made a loophole for
much calumny. Moore's refusal of remuneration from
the family, in spite of abundant advice to the contrary, is
much to his honour, though it provoked Rogers to the
bantering comment, "Well, your life may be a good
poem, but it is a damned bad matter-of-fact."

Byron, in a familiar passage, asserted that "Tommy
dearly loved a lord." As his most recent biographer,
Mr. Stephen Gwynn, has pointed out, it would be more
correct to say that he dearly loved some lords, and those
of the best type. His enjoyment of the society of the
highly born was too artless for toadyism. They sought
him, besides, as much as he sought them. It was an

emotional age, and Moore tugged at its sensibilities. His singing—or rather his recitation to music—of "Poor Broken Heart" so affected the beautiful Lady Tullamore that she left the room, sobbing violently. In conversation he does not seem to have played a conspicuous part, except as a teller of Irish stories, but he brought good-humour with him wherever he went. He rose from under his crowning financial disaster, the loss of £6,000, through the defalcation of his deputy at Bermuda, with an Irishman's happy buoyancy; and, until he broke down over his luckless "History of Ireland," he cheerfully bore the burden of much literary drudgery. His independence of mind found expression in his refusal to listen to Lord Holland and postpone the publication of his biography of Lord Edward Fitzgerald until Ireland had quieted down, arguing with justice that if he did he would find himself in the position of Horace's rustic. That feeling was also conspicuous when his literary pension of £300 a year came under discussion. Rogers, who reserved for himself the luxury of blaming Moore, which he refused to others, asserted that he used to leave Mrs. Moore at Sloperton to carry on the household on a guinea a week, while he spent that amount on hackney-coaches and gloves. Money did not remain long in Moore's pockets, it is true, but, on the other hand, it was important for him to keep in touch with the fashionable world for which he wrote. So far from neglecting his wife, it was to shield her from social slights that he settled in the country, and as Lord John Russell ornately put it, the penniless actress "received from him the homage of a lover from the hour of their nuptials to that of his dissolution."

Though Moore luxuriated in adulation, especially when

it assumed the form of quasi-regal receptions in Dublin, his native city, he made a fairly just estimate of his proper place on Parnassus. He admitted the superiority of Scott and Byron, whom the age regarded as no more than his equals; his attitude towards his "noble friend," as revealed in the biography, was one of unqualified admiration for the poet, combined with sententious abhorrence of feminine influences. He never placed "Lalla Rookh" and its gushing narrative among the immortal creations, as contemporary criticism was disposed to do. Twenty years after it was written, he told Longman that "in a race to future times (if *any* thing of mine could pretend to such a run) those little ponies, the 'Melodies,' will beat the mare *Lalla* hollow." Such sage self-prophecies are rare in literature. Though the "Melodies" may have fallen into temporary neglect, they are bound to live, at any rate on Irish soil, in spite of their lack of concentration and floridity of taste. At his best, as in "The young May moon is beaming, love," or "Dear Harp of my Country, in darkness I found thee," he is worthy to be the poet of a nation. The "Melodies" were written to be sung, therefore they were lucid and appealed widely rather than deeply. Moore never reached genuine inspiration, but he did many things exceedingly well. The "History of Captain Rock" is a brilliant piece of prose satire, and much quiet fun lurks in the pages of "The Fudge Family in Paris."

Lord Holland's acquaintance with two illustrious men of letters, Byron and Scott, opened ominously. The former imagined that the famous criticism of his "Hours of Idleness" in the *Edinburgh Review* for January, 1808, was inspired by Holland House, and that George Lamb, Lord Melbourne's youngest brother, was its author.

Brougham really wrote it, in his usual style of heavy and malignant facetiousness. Byron, as is well known, drank three bottles of claret, and set to work on the reply, "English Bards and Scotch Reviewers." In it he satirised Holland House, where "Scotchmen dine, and duns are kept aloof." "Bad enough and on mistaken grounds besides" was his subsequent annotation at Geneva, and on Rogers's suggestion he suppressed the fifth edition, and told Murray that the poem must never be republished.

Before this handsome atonement Byron had been introduced to Lord Holland by Rogers. Anxious, no doubt, to secure recruits for the Whig Party, Lord Holland supplied Byron with hints for his first and most successful speech in the House of Lords, on the Bill for suppressing the riotous propensities of the Nottingham frame-workers, and they became fast friends. He received, in return for his kindness, a copy of a "thing," accompanied by a witty letter, the "thing" being no less than the volume containing the two first cantos of "Childe Harold." In the following year came the invitation of the Drury Lane committee, at the instance of Lord Holland, to write the opening address. Byron's letters show the amicability with which he accepted the commission, and the good temper in which he took the suggestions as to amendments pressed on him by Lord Holland and Whitbread. Combe the brewer, the third member of the committee, appears to have been more interested in vats than in verses. The end of it all was that Elliston murdered the address, and that the mighty Perry of the *Morning Chronicle* censured it as unmusical in parts, and in general tame ; not altogether, it must be confessed, without reason.

"Holland's society is very good," wrote Byron in 1813; "you always see some one or other in it worth knowing." Though he rebelled against the "damned screen" placed before the fire by Lady Holland, he held her in high regard, and was careful to keep in her good graces by means of presentation copies. But they laboured in vain to reconcile him to Lord Carlisle, his guardian.

Holland House was destined to set its mark on Byron's life ; for it was there, according to her most coherent version of the event, that he first had speech of Lady Caroline Lamb, after she had turned from him, on her introduction by Lady Westmorland, on the ground that he was "mad, bad, and dangerous to know."[1] Lady Elizabeth Foster, afterwards Duchess of Devonshire, described Lady Caroline as a "wild, delicate, odd, delightful person, unlike everything." Neither her parents, Lord and Lady Bessborough, nor her easy-going husband, subsequently Lord Melbourne and Prime Minister, appear to have regarded her as a responsible being. None of them seems to have interfered when she threw herself at Byron's head, as the saying is, and paraded her passion throughout a London season. Rogers has told the unhappy story of her private assignations and public displays of jealousy, of their driving off together from parties, and of her waylaying him in the street after receptions to which she was not invited. The affair culminated in the supposed attempt to stab herself at Lady Heathcote's ball—" Ye Dagger Scene of

[1] Thus Lady Caroline to Lady Morgan. She gave a totally different account of her first meeting with Byron in a letter to Medwin (Byron's "Letters and Journals," edited by Mr. R. E. Prothero, vol. ii., Appendix), but it was written some years after the event, and when her mind had become affected.

indifferent memory," as Byron called it. In that strange human document, the letter she wrote to Medwin on the appearance of his scandalous " Recollections of Lord Byron," Lady Caroline denies that she tried to stab herself ; she ran out of the room with the knife in her hand, and was cut as they snatched it from her. The correction is credible but unimportant.

As to their loves, enough of the correspondence has been preserved to show that the adoration was all on Lady Caroline's side, though she, poor creature, believed the contrary. Byron was first attracted by " the cleverest, most agreeable, absurd, amiable, perplexing, dangerous, fascinating little being that lives now, or ought to have lived two thousand years ago." But he soon felt that she was making him ridiculous, and judiciously tried to divert her from declarations of the grand passion to criticism of the poems of Miss Milbanke, his future wife, to whom in an evil hour she introduced him. His letter, written when Lady Bessborough determined to take her off to Ireland, contains an offer of elopement, but it is evidently perfunctory. Unfortunately, Lady Caroline continued the siege from over-seas, and so drew down upon herself the cutting dismissal, composed on Lady Oxford's notepaper, which she published, in part at least, in " Glenarvon." There followed the burning of him in effigy at Brocket Hall, and, though not until after further meetings, the novel. Lady Holland's reception of " Glenarvon " has already been mentioned ; Byron's was brutal. " As for the likeness," he wrote to Moore, " the picture can't be good ; I did not sit long enough." Yet, despite " Glenarvon," Lady Caroline wrote Byron an affectionate, though none too lucid, epistle when he was about to separate from his wife, and, with more wisdom, urged him to suppress " Fare thee well." From the letter to Medwin it may be gathered that the story of her losing her reason from the shock of meeting Lord Byron's funeral on its way to Newstead, while she was out driving near Brocket, has been improved in the telling. Her husband, who was riding ahead, met the funeral, but did not inform her of it at the time ; and it was the news of his death rather than the sight of his hearse that overthrew her ill-regulated but by no means ignoble intellect.

The Lady Caroline episode made no difference, it would seem, to Byron's position in tolerant Holland House. We find him dining the following year in the town house in St. James's Square, and meeting Sir Samuel and Lady Romilly, Sir Samuel Bentham, Jeremy Bentham's brother and a naval architect, Horner, "Conversation" Sharp, Sir George Philips, a Lancashire manufacturer and friend of Sydney Smith, and Lord John Russell, "all good men and true." Shortly afterwards he met Thomas Campbell, when Lord Holland, who was carrying a censer, exclaimed to them, " Here is some incense for you." " Take it to Lord Byron," answered the sensitive poet; " he is used to it "—a remark justly rebuked by Byron in his journal as uncharitable. This was in December, 1813.

In January, 1815, Byron married, and with matrimony his financial difficulties accumulated. Shortly before his separation from Lady Byron he sent Lady Holland a set of drawings by Stothard, on the subjects of his poems. She told Macaulay, on one of his earliest visits to Holland House, that she returned them with the injunction that if Byron gave them away, he ought to give them to Lady Byron. " But he said he would not, and that, if I

did not take them the bailiffs would, and that they would
be lost in the general wreck." The proceeding was rather
cavalier, since the drawings appear to have been a present
to Lady Byron from Murray.

About that time Lady Byron asked Lord Holland to
bring about a private and amicable arrangement between
her husband and herself. He evidently accepted the
mission, since on March 3, 1816, he forwarded to Byron
the terms drawn up by Dr. Lushington, her legal adviser,
with an appeal to him to save both parties from the
" trouble, inconvenience, vexation, and expense of a
suit." The conditions were that Byron should claim
immediately a pecuniary profit of £500 a year in consequence of his marriage with Lady Byron, and that at the
death of his mother, Lady Noel, he would be benefited
to from £3,500 to £4,000 per annum. Byron ultimately
signed the deed of separation, and on April 16th left
England for ever. He generously refused to benefit
from his wife's fortune, but when death carried off his
detested mother-in-law he had no scruples about taking
half her property on the decision of two arbitrators, Sir
Francis Burdett and Lord Dacre. Lord Holland's intervention, therefore, had been of service to him.

It remained for Lady Holland to make a feminine but
hardly vital contribution to the Byronic controversy.
When Moore asked her if Lady Byron really loved
Byron, the reply was that she must have done so. "He
was such a lovable person. I remember him," said she,
" sitting there with that light upon him, looking so
beautiful ! " Byron, for his part, kept the Hollands in
affectionate recollection, and rejoiced in his exile when
he heard that a windfall had come to them. He also
asked Lord Holland to use his influence to prevent

Elliston from putting "Marino Faliero" on the boards
at Drury Lane, but the actor carried his point by forcing
Lord Eldon to hold a court on his doorstep, and Byron
took refuge in the epigram :

> "Behold the blessings of a lucky lot !
> My play is *damned* and Lady Noel *not.*"

Lord Holland's quarrel with Sir Walter Scott arose out
of a speech in the House of Lords. The author of
"Waverley" had dined at Holland House during a visit
to London in 1806, after refusing to go there before, to
avoid suspicion of changing his Tory principles. He
thought himself justified three years later in making it a
personal as well as a fraternal matter when Lord Holland
joined Lord Lauderdale in condemning the pension which
was to be bestowed on Scott's brother Thomas on the
abolition of his extractorship to the Court of Session.
Lord Melville had defended what looked uncommonly
like a job on the ground that it was a reward of literary
merit. He was twitted by Lord Holland with Scotland's
neglect of Burns, and reminded that Thomas Scott had
been appointed to a post which he had good reason to
believe was about to be suppressed. The opposition
failed, but Scott was bitterly offended. A few weeks
later Lord Holland met him at the Friday Club in
Edinburgh, a society formed on the model of Dr.
Johnson's club at the "Turk's Head," and there Scott,
as he wrote triumphantly to his brother, "cut him with
as little remorse as an old pen." Jeffrey, who was
present, remembered the scene as most unpleasant, and
one for which he had been wholly unprepared ; it was

the only instance of rudeness he ever witnessed in Scott during a lifelong familiarity.

Time, however, cooled Scott's resentment, and eighteen years afterwards—that is, in 1828—he dined and slept at Holland House after an afternoon at the Duke of Devonshire's at Chiswick. He contrived to make a demi-toilette on his arrival rather than drive all the way to London—a detail illustrative both of easy-going manners and difficulties of locomotion. He found the dinner most agreeable, and next morning wandered about the grounds with Rogers. " It will be a great pity," he commented in his diary,

" when this ancient house must come down and give way to rows and crescents. It is not that Holland House is fine, as a building—on the contrary, it has a tumbledown look ; and, though decorated with the bastard Gothic of James I.'s time, the front is heavy. But it resembles many respectable matrons who, having been absolutely ugly during youth, acquire by age an air of dignity. But one is chiefly affected by the air of deep seclusion which is spread around the domain."

It was a source of regret to Scott that he could not go to Holland House when he passed through London on his last journey abroad. But when he reached Rome he told a friend that Lord Holland was the most agreeable man he had ever met, remarkable for his critical faculties, his knowledge of English authors, and his power of language, which adorned his thoughts "as light streaming through coloured glass heightens the brilliancy of the objects it falls upon." Holland House, on its side, received the " Waverley " novels in a far less captious spirit than that which animated a prominent member of the circle, Sydney Smith. When the first part of "Tales of my Landlord" appeared, Lord Holland was asked his opinion. "Opinion ?" he replied to Murray ; "we did not one of us go to bed all night, and nothing slept but my gout."

CHAPTER XVI

AUTHORS AND WITS

Campbell and the King of Clubs—A present from Lady Holland
—"A somewhat awful meeting"—An estrangement and reconciliation—Southey and Whig principles—From the *Edinburgh* to the
Quarterly—Hallam, the "bore contradictor"—His correspondence
with Lord Webb Seymour—A domestic martinet—Jekyll and his
puns—A *protégé* of George IV.—Jekyll on Holland House—Lord
Alvanley and Talleyrand—Chief of the *ton*—Alvanley's money
affairs—His jokes and appearance—Alvanley as a politician.

THOMAS CAMPBELL, minor poet, made the
acquaintance of Lord Holland through Perry,
the editor of the *Morning Chronicle*, in 1801,
when he paid his first visit to London, after the
"Pleasures of Hope" had established his reputation.
An invitation to the King of Clubs followed, and the
poet enthusiastically hailed it as an era in his life. He
never met a man who so reconciled him to an hereditary
aristocracy as Lord Holland, or one who gave him a
higher idea of human nature than Mackintosh. Later
impressions of the club were not so favourable; you
could have too much of brilliant talk when all talked for
effect. Campbell had caught, however, the infection of
London; he brought his bride to Sydenham, and the rest

of his life was practically spent within sound of Bow
bells.

In the days of Campbell's early indigence he received
a present from Lady Holland, to which, full thirty years
afterwards, he referred with deep feeling. " Everything
that is false in my pride gives way to the gratitude which
I owe to those friends who rallied round me at that
period ; and it would be black ingratitude if I could
forget that, in one of those days, I was saved from taking
a debtor's lodgings in the King's Bench by a magnificent
present which the Rev. Sydney Smith conveyed to me
from Lady Holland." The amount of the gift is
unknown, but from Sydney Smith's correspondence it
may be gathered that Campbell, from motives of honourable delicacy, hesitated before he accepted it. In 1805,
through the influence of Fox, Lord Holland, and Lord
Minto, he received a Crown pension of £200 a year, and
was able to add an exultant postscript, ending " God save
the King ! " to a despondent letter to Scott.

The first decade of the Holland House circle is
amusingly etched in Beattie's " Life of Campbell." The
poet arrived to dinner in the spring of 1806 arrayed in
a yellow waistcoat which he had stolen from his friend
Richardson. He was introduced to Fox, walked arm-in-
arm with him round the room, and discussed Virgil with
him. Campbell hardly knew, if his correspondent would
excuse the phrase, whether he was standing on his head
or his feet. Fox invited the poet to St. Anne's Hill, and
told Lord Holland that he liked Campbell; he was so
right about Virgil—their point of agreement being that
the charge of monotony was unjustly brought against
the characters in the " Æneid." Campbell was struck by
the electric quickness and wideness of Fox's attention in

conversation ; at a table of eighteen persons nothing that was said escaped him. Two years afterwards he spent half the day at Holland House, "a somewhat awful meeting. Lady Holland is a formidable woman. She is cleverer by several degrees than Buonaparte." Camp- bell, however, walked about for an hour with her, almost alone, and never did he feel " such self-possession, such a rattle of tongue, and springtide of conversation so per- fectly joyous." A curious colloquy, more especially as Campbell, by his own confession, was dressed like a barber's clerk, with a cravat resembling a halter. The bard's taste in costume inclined to floridity. Byron describes him at Holland House in 1811 as " dressed to sprucery. A blue coat becomes him—so does his new wig. He really looked as if Apollo had sent him a birth- day suit, or wedding garment, and was witty and lively." An instance of his humour that night was his allusion to Madame de Staël's new lover, Rocca, as " the only proof *he* had seen of her good taste." On the next page we get his onslaught on Byron in the matter of incense. Campbell had, in 1809, paid Lord Holland the graceful if insipid compliment of dedicating to him " Gertrude of Wyoming." But he took the huff on the same occasion, because " —— had shown him a face of snow and ice," and absented himself from Holland House. For " —— " we shall probably be not far from the mark if we read " John Allen." Both were Scots, both irascible.

Friendly relations continued with Lord Holland, how- ever, and when in 1837 Campbell's nephew received a situation of £300 a year in the Customs, Campbell, imagining that the interest of Holland House had been at work with the Whig leaders, poured forth his gratitude. The reply undeceived him, but its amiability appears to have persuaded him to renew his visits during the remainder of Lord Holland's life. He excused himself from subscribing to his patron's monument because the step would entail a corresponding withholding of money from the Mendicity Society. Certain it is that five-pound notes were never too plentiful with Campbell, particularly in the years of his decline, when he had sunk into a bookseller's hack and the fire which had animated his war-lyrics had long since flickered out.

Southey, whose complacent confidence in his own immortality was in complete contrast to Campbell's self-mistrust, came in for bitter denunciation as a renegade from Whig principles. Lord Holland assailed him in the passable epigram:

> " Our Laureate Bob defrauds the King,
> He takes his cash and does not sing ;
> Yet on he goes, I know not why,
> Singing for us who do not buy."

But Southey's abandonment of those principles of the French Revolution which brought him in his youth under the lash of the *Anti-Jacobin* was really one of gradual conviction. His Whiggism lasted, no doubt, beyond the death of Pitt. He had the run of the library at Holland House, much to his advantage when he was writing about the Spanish Peninsula, and it was to Holland House he looked when the Whigs had office and place to give away. Lady Holland told him that the rule at St. Anne's Hill was to read aloud till eleven, but that when "Madoc" was on hand they often read till the clock struck twelve. The author accepted this somewhat incredible anecdote without demur. Southey considered that he had a promise from Fox, and looked upon his death as a personal loss, adding, however, significantly, that he had lived a year too long. However, while the Grenville Ministry was tottering to its fall, Southey's friend Charles Wynn "picked something out of the fire for him" in the shape of a Crown pension of £200, reduced by fees to £144. In a letter to Wynn, acknowledging his kindness, Southey frankly avowed his strong aversion to the emancipation of the Catholics on the ground that toleration was unknown to them.

Southey's opinions, like those of Coleridge and Wordsworth, were evidently on the turn, and before the end of 1807 he wrote to Scott that he had scarcely one opinion in common with the *Edinburgh Review* on any subject. It needed only the invitation of two years later to become a contributor to the *Quarterly* to confirm and strengthen Southey in his Toryism. He appeared at Holland House so late as 1813, where Byron found him to be "a person of very *epic* appearance, and has a fine head—as far as outside goes, and wants nothing but taste to make the inside equally attractive." Established at Keswick, and with every hour of the day devoted to literary labour, Southey had but few opportunities of visiting London, and the presumption must be that on those rare occasions he did not feel much at home in Liberal society.

Of all the *habitués* of Holland House, Hallam the historian is the most elusive. The anecdotes about him are concerned chiefly with his disputatiousness. The parentage of his nickname, the "bore contradictor," lies in dispute. But Sydney Smith originated the definition of the electric telegraph as a device that would enable Hallam to contradict somebody at Liverpool; and Sydney Smith, too, facetiously described the historian as jumping out of bed and wrangling with the watchman about the hour of the night. But the terms of respect in which most of his contemporaries allude to Hallam forbid a strict application of these pleasantries, and we learn from Guizot that his character mellowed with age. Moore evidently set high store by his opinions, though the journal is frequently content with the brief entry, "Met Hallam," or the mention of his name among the diners at some celebrated house. Hallam does not seem to have shone in conversation, though he could produce apt stories from a retentive memory. When his own subject was started he was hard to hold, and a party which met in honour of one of Sir Walter Scott's rare visits to London saw the Wizard of the North sitting silently by while Hallam descanted on some topic that Mackintosh had put forth. Still, he seems to have been much appreciated by Whig and literary society, and Bowood knew him as intimately as Holland House.

Hallam lived mainly in and for his books. He took interest in current politics, his views being essentially those of moderate commonsense, and when the Grey Ministry came into power, he astonished his friends by declaring against Reform. But his real world was his study in Wimpole Street, "the long unlovely street" of "In Memoriam," where his three great works were produced. Hallam's correspondents among the frequenters of Holland House were, as might be expected, serious men like Horner, Wishaw, and Lord Webb Seymour, the learned brother of the equally studious Duke of Somerset, a man of high thinking but small achievement, who dwelt chiefly near Edinburgh, in close intellectual companionship with Professor Playfair. Hallam contributed a character of that laborious inquirer after truth, whose sole literary accomplishment was a few pages on geology, to Horner's "Memoirs and Correspondence," and it is a graceful monument to the friendship of the three. Lady Guendolen Ramsden's "Correspondence of Two Brothers," Lord Webb and the Duke of Somerset, proves how much the historian relied on the judgment of Lord Webb, not only as to matters literary, but also on the whole conduct of life. He wrote fully to Lord Webb on the progress of the "Middle Ages," complaining at first that the scheme was indefinitely extensive, and in many of its details little adapted to his inclination, but in 1818, on the eve of its publication, serenely confident of its success. When it did appear he received a budget of criticism, including, it would seem from his reply, the grave charge that the perusal of the book was a heavy task, with supreme good-humour. Sydney Smith's saying that Hallam had less modesty than any man he had ever seen is unintelligible except on the score of personal animosity.

Hallam laid down his pen after publishing his "Introduction to the Literature of Europe during the Fifteenth, Sixteenth, and Seventeenth Centuries" in 1837-39. He lived twenty years longer, and a pleasing picture of the historian in his retirement is given in "Mrs. Brookfield and her Circle." Hallam seems to have been something of a domestic martinet, inclined to be fussy over the cooking of whitebait, and of such fixed habits that when he travelled with his family they had to take surreptitious lunches by turns in the rumble of the coach. But he was essentially a generous, high-minded man, and bore with Roman fortitude the going before him to the grave of child after child.

The wits of the Regency were mostly men of letters or

politicians in the first place and jesters in the second. To Joseph Jekyll it was reserved to hold his place in society, and that in the highest flight, almost entirely as a professional maker and utterer of jokes. As a rule they assumed the form of puns, and those of a crack-jaw kind. That form of humour has come to be regarded as positively criminal, but if Jekyll sinned, he sinned bravely. His most shameless pun is given in many versions. The best of them sets forth that his sister-in-law, Lady Gertrude Sloane Stanley, was deploring the fact that Sir Hans Sloane's house had passed into the hands of a tailor; she could not sleep for thinking of it. "Ah," said Jekyll, "I see what it is: Snip has snapped your snorum"—the allusion being, of course, to "snip, snap, snorum," the cry at the game of forfeits. Moore has preserved his pun when he escaped dining at Lansdowne House, on a night when the ceiling fell down, by an engagement to meet the judges: "I had been asked to *Ruat Cœlum*, but dined instead with *Fiat Justitia*." When Scarlett became Lord Abinger, Jekyll saluted him with "I say, Scarlett, how came you to get hold of your new name? I have heard of Porringer before and Scavenger, but never of Abinger." To those in very robust health Jekyll may have been tolerable enough, but Sir Walter Scott complained that his jokes were "fired like minute guns, and with an effect not much less melancholy." Still, every diarist thought it necessary to harvest a large crop of them, such as his description of the supposed Russian habit of eating tallow candles—"bad for the liver and good for the lights."

Jekyll talked himself into popularity and position at the Bar, where his jokes must have been to the taste of

the junior members. When an old lady was brought
forward as a witness on a tender made, he scribbled :

> "Garrow, forbear ! that tough old jade
> Will never prove a tender maid."

His jokes, besides earning welcome guineas for him in
the *Morning Chronicle,* when he was a rising barrister,
induced Lord Shelburne to nominate him M.P. for
Calne, to the exclusion and fury of Jeremy Bentham ; but
he failed dismally and frequently in the House.   They
gained him the appreciation of the Prince of Wales, who
made Jekyll his Solicitor-General, and in 1815 forced
Lord Eldon to appoint him to a mastership in Chancery,
by closeting himself, so the story goes, with the
Chancellor in Bedford Square and declining to go until
the deed was done.   The business was undoubtedly a
job, but Jekyll always remained grateful to his Royal
patron.   In the last year of the life of George IV. he
visited him at Virginia Water, and brought back strange
stories about afternoon meals of tea and broiled bones,
and lacing postponed to a late hour to avoid the pain.
He was one of the very few who regretted that selfish King.

His letters to his sister-in-law represent Jekyll at sixty
as a happy, good-natured man, who resolutely declined
to grow old and scoffed at his valetudinarian contemporaries as Methusalems.   When he was eighty-two or
three, Denman called on him and found him extremely
deaf and entirely helpless, but as lively as ever.   He
termed the Attorney-General's reconciliation with the
Government the camel (Campbell) going through the
eye of the needle.   An insatiable, but not a malignant
gossip, he placed Holland House under persistent obser-

JOSEPH JEKYLL
FROM THE DRAWING BY GEORGE DANCE, R.A., IN THE NATIONAL PORTRAIT GALLERY

SIR DAVID WILKIE, R.A.

FROM THE PAINTING BY HIMSELF IN THE NATIONAL PORTRAIT GALLERY

vation. " The *fricandeaux* tell," was a concise comment
on *Miladi's* state of health.   Mackintosh, writing in the
Foreign Quarterly Review, declared of Holland House
that " No such assemblage can ever again be found until
another house can find such a master."   Jekyll gleefully
queried, " Will *Miladi* be pleased to hear that Holland
is master there ?"   It is a pity that more of his correspondence has not been preserved, since he was an
intimate friend of Erskine during his early struggles,
and was the accepted guest of the great and the talented
for over forty years.

Jekyll seems to have been rather jealous of a brother-
wit, Lord Alvanley.   The epilogue to Lord Glengal's
comedy, "The Irish Tutor," was written " to manifest
that the best joker of White's bow window could not
string two lines together."   But Lord Alvanley could
afford to miss the mark occasionally, since his fame as a
sayer of good things was European.   He stayed frequently with Talleyrand both in Paris and at Valençay,
and was allowed to see those memoirs from which the
world expected so much and gained so little by way of
revelation.   From one visit he brought back the Prince's
definition of the doctrine of non-intervention : "C'est un
mot metaphysique et politique, qui signifie à peu près la
même chose qu'intervention."   On two occasions Alvanley saw Talleyrand in tears, the first after the death of his
friend the Princess de Vaudemont, the second after the
Duke of Wellington's chivalrous defence of the Prince
when he was attacked in debate by Lord Londonderry.
His social gifts took Alvanley as far as the Crimea, where
he used to spend the winter with Count Woronzoff, the
Governor of Odessa.

Lord Alvanley, after a short career in the army, became

a prominent member of the dandy set led by Brummell until, in 1816, his debts and princely displeasure drove the beau abroad, and consisting of Lord Sidney Osborne, Lord Allen, commonly known as "King" Allen, Lord Foley, Sir Henry Mildmay, Byron's friend Scrope Davies, and many more. When Brummell went into exile, Alvanley took his place as chief of the *ton* and reputed author of its happiest sayings. Most of his friends went to ruin, but he kept above water, thanks to his exemption from arrest as a peer, and the forethought of an uncle who had carefully tied up his property. Alvanley was a thriftless soul, and Greville accuses him of having left in the lurch without remorse the friends who assisted him. Animus probably lurks in the charge, since Gronow relates that the "Gruncher" once took upon himself to set Alvanley's affairs in order and, having gone through them with more cheerful results than had been expected, was much disconcerted to receive a note from that reprobate next morning to say that he had quite forgotten a debt of fifty-five thousand pounds. Tradesmen fared ill with the mercurial peer. "I have no credit with either butcher or poulterer, but if you can put up with turtle and turbot I shall be happy to see you," was his invitation to a friend. His dinners in Park Street, St. James's, and at Melton were excellent, and he insisted on having an apricot tart on the sideboard the whole year round. If Gronow is correct in estimating Alvanley's income at no more than £8,000 a year, he must have met very few of his obligations, since in addition to being a great traveller he was a hard rider to hounds. "Ice him, Gunter, ice him," was his consoling advice when that pastrycook complained that he could not hold in a hard-mouthed horse.

Pointed but good-natured "chaff" seems to have been Alvanley's chief stock-in-trade as a humourist. He often met his match—sometimes it was Lord Yarmouth, at others Lord Deerhurst—but take him day by day, he had no equal, while a slight lisp only heightened his drollery. Lord Alvanley was a great favourite at Oatlands, the happy-go-lucky establishment of the Duke and Duchess of York, where "week-ends" were instituted a century ago, but he made himself at home everywhere. His request for "more carving and less gilding," when he was given a poor dinner among gorgeous surroundings, has been localised in the house of a *parvenu* named Nield. At the same time, his habit of putting out his bedroom candle by throwing it on the floor and taking a shot at it with a bolster, or thrusting it, while still alight, under his pillow, must have been disconcerting to most hostesses. His appearance, says Gronow, resembled that of a jolly Italian friar, and, after deep potations, his copious pinches of snuff had some difficulty in finding their way to an unusually small nose. Yet, after the Dandies had persuaded Madame de Staël that Alvanley had £100,000 a year, she found it in her to praise his beauty to his face.

The Reform Bill aroused such political convictions as Lord Alvanley possessed, and it was during the existence of the Grey Ministry that he frequented Holland House. His challenge to O'Connell for calling him a "bloated buffoon" and his duel with the Liberator's son, Morgan, are matters that have grown stale by repetition, as also have the jokes with which he decorated the occasion. But it is less well known that Lord Alvanley continued to regard politics with a serious eye, and after 1841 took upon himself to instruct the Duke of Wellington and Peel in statesmanship. He gravely reported his colloquies to Tom Raikes, who while his money lasted was one of the Dandies, and Tom committed them with equal gravity to his journal. Alvanley's recipe for the governance of the Empire appears to have been the "squaring" of the Irish priesthood, an idea which has possessed politicians of more substantial pretensions than his, but which none, somehow, has been able to realise.

CHAPTER XVII

AMATEURS, ARTISTS, AND ACTORS

Lord Egremont—Life at Petworth—Payne Knight—The Elgin marbles—Lawrence and Lord Holland—Leslie and Holland House —Hoppner—"Bilious from hard work"—Wilkie's preciseness—At Holland House—Wilkie's friends—Some sculptors and Canova— Kean—Jack Bannister—John Kemble—The Kemble banquet.

AMONG the patrons of art who visited Holland House the third and last Earl of Egremont was perhaps the most discerning. If he had so chosen, he would have made a considerable figure in politics, since his rare speeches in the House of Lords were effective, and he took a keen interest in the moves of the game. But his unconventional habits would have unfitted him for office ; besides, as the years went on, his zeal for Whig principles abated, and he revolted altogether from the Catholic Emancipation movement. Lord Egremont is best remembered as a singularly successful owner of race-horses, a promoter of agricultural experiments, and above all, as an amateur of art who enriched the collection at Petworth, be- queathed to him by his father, with carefully selected specimens of Renaissance and contemporary painting. He early discerned the genius of Turner, who had a studio at the house ; he helped Benjamin Robert Haydon in his necessities ; he employed Flaxman in preference to the more fashionable Chantrey, and the results were the " Michael and Satan" and " Pastoral Apollo," exhibited at the Royal Academy in 1824.

Having passed under the sway of a great lady, Egremont remained a bachelor all his life, and was the father of numerous illegitimate children, acknowledged and unacknowledged. In the autobiographies of Haydon and Leslie, his yearly guest, and in the Greville "Memoirs," his dislike of ceremony, eccentric habits, and unconventional manners are entertainingly described. Petworth, where the Allied Sovereigns were entertained in 1814, was like a great inn, entered and left by all as they pleased without any formal leave-taking. Those, however, who abused its hospitality were, in more than one instance, ordered to make themselves scarce. The host himself was perpetually on the move, shy in his address, and after conferring a favour he had left the room before there was time to thank him. A lady's-maid was known to mistake him for one of his own servants, whereupon he politely escorted her to the servants' hall. About the year 1825 he abandoned London society, and living entirely at Petworth, set himself to use his great wealth for the benefit of the people about him. Greville describes an open-air fête given by him in 1834 to the poor of the neighbourhood, some six thousand in number, which he declared was one of the gayest and most beautiful spectacles he had ever seen. When Lord Egremont died, three years later, the diarist said that the whole county of Sussex would feel the event more keenly than the loss of an individual had ever been felt before.

Unlike Lord Egremont, Payne Knight, a rival virtuoso, particularly in bronzes, was a selfish epicurean. Shropshire ironworks gave him the wealth he spent partly in building Dounton Castle in Herefordshire— a gimcrack castle and bad house, Greville calls it—only to go and live in a cottage in the park, partly on the museum in his house in Soho Square. He lived royally, and always had a dish of lampreys on his table. As a collector Payne Knight had many merits; he appreciated the beauty of Greek coinage, and had a fairly sound judgment in gems. Besides, he had the good sense to leave his treasures to the British Museum. "The collection," writes Mr. Warwick Wroth, "was valued at the time at sums varying from £30,000 to £60,000. The acquisition of the coins and bronzes immensely strengthened the national collection," and the bequest included as well 273 works by Claude. But as an author he acquired a reputation among his contemporaries, of whom Dr. Parr allowed him to be a scholar and Byron wrote of him with reverence, which cannot be said to have endured. His dully didactic poem "The Progress of Civil Society" is now remembered solely through the admirable banter in the *Anti-Jacobin*:

"The same of Plants—Potatoes 'Tatoes breed,
Uncostly Cabbage springs from Cabbage seed;
Lettuce to Lettuce, Leeks to Leeks succeed;
Nor e'er did cooling Cucumbers presume
To flow'r like Myrtle, or like Violets bloom.
Man only—rash, refin'd, presumptuous Man,
Starts from his rank, and mars Creation's plan."

Payne Knight's "Analytical Inquiry into the Principles

of Taste" is completely forgotten, and even in its day
it was severely trounced by the *Edinburgh Review*.
Though a man of some learning, and undeniable taste,
he is destined to go down the ages chiefly through
his egregious blunder over the Elgin marbles. "You
have lost your labour, my Lord Elgin. Your marbles
are overrated; they are not Greek, they are Roman of
the time of Hadrian." B. R. Haydon tells the story,
and as he hated Knight and worshipped the sculptures,
we may be sure that he has recorded all there was to
record, and perhaps a little more. Be that as it may,
the evidence of the "eminent scholar whose *ipse dixit*
no one dared dispute" before the Select Committee of
the House of Commons was against the acquisition of
the marbles by the nation, nor did he mend matters by
a quibbling "Explanation" put forth in reply to a
searching onslaught by the *Quarterly*. He saw, declared
that genial periodical, "that they would eclipse his
collection of small bronzes and shake the supremacy
with which he reigned over *drawing-room literature*
and *saloon* taste." Payne Knight seems to have
carried his autocracy into private life, and to have
preferred his own to others' conversation. When, in
1822, he had grown very deaf, Rogers's comment was,
"'Tis from want of practice."

C. R. Leslie, Hoppner, and Wilkie appear to have
been the artists in most general request at Holland
House. Sir Thomas Lawrence, the handsome and
sentimental, does not figure as one of its frequenters;
he was, for one thing, an almost insatiable worker, and
in his rare moments of leisure he preferred, no doubt,
the tender adoration of Mrs. Wolff. Leslie records,
however, a conversation between him and Lord Holland,

in which the latter had the advantage.   When Stuart
the American painter died, Lawrence asserted that he
had returned to the United States—not, as some said,
out of admiration for their institutions, but because he
had become tired of the insides of various British
prisons to which his debts had consigned him.   "Well,
then," said Lord Holland, "after all it was his love of
liberty that took him to America."

Leslie himself, that amiable executant of the literary
anecdote, was introduced to Lord Holland in 1825,
apparently by Lord Egremont.   He painted the portraits
of Lady Affleck, Lady Holland's mother, of Lord
Holland and his daughter Mary, afterwards Lady
Lilford, and the group, familiar through engravings, of
Lord and Lady Holland, Allen and the page-librarian.
Though his price was only thirty guineas for each
painting, his host sent a cheque for a hundred guineas
for the pictures of himself and his girl, explaining that
the price "even in its amended shape, bears no pro-
portion to the value I annex to the works; but it
unfortunately does bear a more correct one to the
sum I can with any prudence devote to such objects."
Later on Lady Holland managed that the artist should
be presented to Queen Victoria, and his paintings
"The Queen receiving the Sacrament at her Coronation" and "The Christening of the Princess Royal"
were the result.   Leslie's "Autobiographical Recollections" contain several characteristic stories about her.
When she heard of a gentleman and his wife being
murdered in their bed by a servant, who entered the
room through a back window, she had the window
communicating with her own bedroom covered with an
iron grating. Sydney Smith gave another account of

the precaution. "Allen," he said, "keeps a clergyman in confinement there, upon bread and water."

Lawrence failed with his portrait of Fox; Lord Holland reckoned it an unprecedented instance of a distinguished painter falling short of his distinguished subject. The commissions of Holland House went, therefore, by preference to Hoppner, who painted several of the circle, including Bobus Smith. He has been called "the most daring plagiarist of Reynolds, and the boldest rival of Lawrence." Hoppner lacked the grand manner of the other two, but he was a good straight-forward painter of nearly the first class, free from Lawrence's effeminacy and affectations. To him are due, after all, the best likenesses extant of Nelson and Pitt. "Ah," said Hoppner's patron, the Prince of Wales, who employed him rather than his father's favourite, the deplorable West, "there Pitt is with his damned obstinate face!"

Naturally, the artist was a man of fine mind; but said Haydon, and Lawrence agreed with him, he became "bilious from hard work at portraits and the harass of high life." He hated Northcote, and Northcote returned the compliment to the "poor man-milliner of a painter" with interest; he was also unworthily jealous of Lawrence. Rogers used to assert that Hoppner had an awful temper, and was the most spiteful person he ever knew. "Is not a man to be pitied," Hoppner would say, "with such a wife as mine and such a friend?"—the friend being Gifford, the editor of the *Quarterly*, whom Mrs. Hoppner tried to dissuade from attacking Keats. Yet his bitter tongue was compatible with much genuine consideration for his family. As the son of one of the German attendants at Windsor, he

was allowed the run of the Royal kitchen.   That favour
was withdrawn, soon after his marriage, as Hoppner
suspected through the machinations of West.   Whereupon he would sometimes put a roll in his pocket and go
out for the day, pretending on his return that he had
dined at the Palace.

The manners of Wilkie, humble to the edge of
obsequiousness, differed *toto cœlo* from the bluntness
of Hoppner.   That precise Scot is represented by Leslie
as laboriously learning the figures of the quadrille, and
then executing them with minute formality, never
omitting a bow at the prescribed moment.   Wilkie
could not quite forget that he was the son of the
minister of Cults and that his mother came of a
farming stock.   Even the tutelage of the boisterous and
thriftless Haydon failed to convert him from the habit
of making his own bargains with print-sellers and
exacting the uttermost farthing of his change in Paris
restaurants.   Lord Mulgrave, Sir George Beaumont, and
Whitbread were among his earliest patrons, and by 1800,
two years after "The Village Politicians" had made
his reputation, he had entered Lansdowne House.   But
" The Blind Fiddler," " The Village Festival," and " The
Rent Day " had all been exhibited and he had become
a full Academician, before Alan Cunningham's minute
biography records any visit to Lord and Lady Holland.

It was in 1815 that Holland House witnessed Wilkie's
introduction to Canova, as commemorated by Macaulay,
but the artist's disappointing letter to his friend, John
Anderson, conveys little more than the characteristic
reflection that the acquaintance might be of importance
at a future time.   Wilkie was now established in
Phillimore Place, Kensington, and was therefore a

neighbour. He had painted "The Waterloo Gazette" and passed into his Spanish style when, in 1835, he is found meeting King William, the ex-Premier Earl Grey, and many of the Cabinet at an evening reception. " I felt myself," he wrote to his sister, "a very inconsiderable person. Her ladyship contrived, however, in the kindest manner to get me spoken to by the great star ; and the others, who were scarcely less than Ministers of State, were very obliging and civil." Lord Holland was, of course, introduced into Wilkie's well-known picture of Queen Victoria's first Council, and the artist saw him just before starting on the journey to the East whence he was never to return. The news of Lord Holland's death reached Wilkie at Constantinople, and he wrote to his brother, "I lose in him a most kind, steady, and powerful friend." To Rogers he sent a more extended tribute, dwelling on—

"the interruption of an acquaintance, since I was first introduced to his lordship and his esteemed and noble lady, of twenty-five years. The last time I saw his lordship I was proud to be at the same table with those he most loved : you were present with Mr. Moore ; never was he in better spirits, nor his conversation (always most delightful and instructive) more brilliant."

The effusiveness of this reminiscence was natural to Wilkie. Though an eloquent speaker in public, he was slow of words in society, and never conveyed the appearance of ease, though he laboured to be like other people. " I am glad I went to Windsor to-day, for it will *inure* me to the King " was his confidence to Chantrey, after the pair had had an interview with George IV. lasting for several hours. There was, on the other hand, no guile in the painter of " The Waterloo Gazette." The true Wilkie was revealed at Lawrence's funeral, when, walking next Constable, he caught sight of the City Marshal's headgear. Looking down with every semblance of woe, he whispered, "Just look at that cocked hat. It's grand !" In an age when artistic cabals raged with a fury unknown to the larger times of Reynolds and Gains- borough, Wilkie's goodness of heart kept him on friendly terms with the touchy Hoppner and the sensitive Lawrence. He had, it is true, a quarrel with Haydon, but backing a bond was the cause, and there the national prudence told. Otherwise his affectionate relations with that unhappy man were unbroken, though Collins, in Wilkie's later years, was a closer associate.

Nollekens, puny of body and large of head, who encouraged young Wilkie by the prophecy that he would soon be a member of the Academy " among the best on 'em " ; Chantrey, the hospitable and piscatorial ; and the uninspired Westmacott, whose replica of the statue of Fox in Bloomsbury Square, stands in the grounds, were among the sculptors who are represented at Holland House. They all paled their ineffectual fires before Canova, when he arrived in London, shortly after Waterloo had been fought and won, partly to pronounce judgment on the Elgin marbles, partly to inform the Pope on the state of the fine arts in England. Enter- tained at a banquet given by the Royal Academy and organised by Flaxman, he was received everywhere as the personage that he undoubtedly was. His verdicts were eagerly circulated, such as his admiration for Rennie's work, Waterloo Bridge, and his failure to appreciate Westminster Abbey, though he allowed that bits of it were fine. Haydon felt about Canova as if he were a descendant of the great. But then the sculptor was diplomatist enough to pass a compliment on the painter's " Jairus's Daughter," while his taste led him to pronounce aright on the Elgin marbles. " La verité est telle, les accidents de la chair et les formes sont si vraies et si belles, que ces statues produiront un grand charge-ment dans les arts "—notably in that of Canova himself. Canova also placed Sir Benjamin West, P.R.A., in his proper place ; he did not compose, he grouped models together.

Sir Martin Archer Shee, who was preferred to Wilkie as President of the Royal Academy, an uninspired portrait painter, but a dignified head of a society of painters, was met by John Cam Hobhouse at Holland House, apparently in the year 1815. Fluent talker though Shee was, Edmund Kean, who made that night one of his rare and unwilling appearances in society, outshone him after they had joined the ladies. Hob-house gives us the portrait of "a very handsome little man, with a mild but marked countenance, and eyes as brilliant as on the stage. He knitted his brows, I observed, when he could not exactly make out what was said. Kean ate most pertinaciously with his knife, and was a little too frequent with ladyships and lordships, as was natural to him." Under the examination of Lady Holland, he disavowed the pronunciation of " they " as " the "—one of the mannerisms probably with which Kemble had infected the stage—and denied that he could play comedy, except when it touched farce, as the character of Tyke in the " School of Reform." The great tragic actor was then at the height of his renown. In the previous year his Shylock, though first performed

at Drury Lane with a poor company to a house more
than half empty, had conquered the town ; Whitbread
was heaping salary on him, and all seemed well.

Fashionable company, which Kean, after a brief trial,
avoided altogether, was a congenial element to handsome
Jack Bannister, the finest comedian of the day, and,
probably, as acceptable a Bob Acres and Dr. Pangloss in
"The Heir at Law" as have ever occupied the boards.
To his friendship with the painters of the time was due
his suggestion of "Reading the Will" as a subject to
Wilkie. From his generosity as a man came his reply
to the depreciator who sneered at Kean as an admirable
harlequin, "That I am certain of, for he has jumped over
all our heads."

Princess Liechtenstein, who passes over Kean, mentions Bannister and John Kemble as two actors who
visited Holland House. Our English Roscius we should
expect to find there, because he filled the place in his
profession occupied before him by Garrick, and after
him by Macready and Sir Henry Irving. Though
mummer-worship had not then become the craze, an
accomplished actor of good sense and gentlemanlike
feeling, such as we know Kemble to have been, on
Sir Walter Scott's evidence, had the entry of London
drawing-rooms ; nor was his habit of swallowing wine
"by pailfuls," to which Scott also bears witness, taken
amiss in London dining-rooms.

"The great" (exclaims his mellifluous biographer, Boaden)
"who sought the society of Mr. Kemble, sought it on the
only terms that could be honourable to themselves or him.
So it was at Wroxton Abbey that he was welcomed by Lord
Guildford—thus it was that, in the lifetime of the late Marquis

of Abercorn, he was the happy and honoured guest at the Priory. It was thus that Lord Holland knew and loved Mr. Kemble ; thus that the accomplished Earl of Aberdeen, Lord Egremont, Lord Blessington, and a long list of his noble admirers bestowed a lasting and a most cordial *friendship* with their notice."

Kemble played at Covent Garden from September, 1803, to June, 1817, a period which witnessed the burning of the theatre and consequent migration to the Haymarket, the O.P., or old prices, riots on its re-opening, much interpretation of Shakespeare in the grand, sonorous manner, but the discovery of no new dramatist. When the curtain had fallen for the last time on his Coriolanus, Lord Holland took the chair at a dinner given in his honour at the Freemasons' Tavern. The ceremony was as tremendous as the guest of the evening. The dinner lasted from seven to midnight ; the band played selections from Handel, " and, on the removal of the cloth, the matchless *Non nobis* was rendered in all its thrilling awe," by the best singers of it that Boaden had ever heard. Young, the actor, recited an ode by Campbell. Talma, Kemble's most illustrious contemporary, acknowledged with emotion the toast of his health, in excellent English, but, adds a conscientious reporter, with an occasional mixture of the French accent. A piece of plate was to have been presented to Kemble, but it was not ready, and so the cast and drawing had to serve instead. The inscription duly eulogised Kemble's " labours and perseverance in the advancement of the legitimate Drama, and more particularly of Shakespeare, whose Muse his performances had aided and embellished." The chairman's speech touched a similar note, and Lord Holland further remarked with much force that Kemble united in himself the claims of the actor, the scholar, and the critic. Did not Lamb write that no man could deliver brilliant dialogue, the dialogue of Congreve or of Wycherley, because none understood it, half so well as John Kemble? The actor departed from what Boaden calls a scene of perfectly rational and ennobling hospitality to end his days at Lausanne, jealous, said Rogers, of the homage paid to Mont Blanc.

CHAPTER XVIII

MEN OF SCIENCE

Count Rumford—"Useful" and "practical"—The arrival of
Davy—His marriage and knighthood—Lady Davy—Sir Humphry's
carriage and four—Davy and Wollaston—"A sporting Archbishop"
—Faraday—William and Alexander von Humboldt—Alexander in
society—His reminiscences of England—Charles Waterton—Sir
Benjamin Brodie at Holland House—Sir Henry Holland.

THE eighteenth century, until it drew towards ·its
close, had been content with the pseudo-science
of Lavater and the impostures of Cagliostro.
The beginning of the nineteenth witnessed the creation
of a genuine interest in the researches of Volta and his
contemporaries. With the hour came the man in Benjamin Thompson, Count Rumford, who, in 1799, gave
Science a home by founding the Royal Institution of
Great Britain in Albemarle Street. That extraordinary
American inevitably calls up to mind his greater com-
patriot, Benjamin Franklin. Born in Massachusetts, he
developed Loyalist sympathies during the War of Independence, and smelt powder outside Charleston, after an
unfortunate experience in England as Under-Secretary
for the Colonies to an incompetent chief in Lord
George Germaine. Though he remained a British subject, Thompson entered the service of the Elector of

Bavaria, for whom he reformed the army, policed the capital, and beautified it with a public park. On his return to England he took up his abode at Kensington Gore. The man of action was all the while a man of scientific investigation. Rumford destroyed the material theory of heat by establishing that it was nothing else than motion. He applied his discoveries to such eminently practical objects as the curing of smoky chimneys and the economy of fuel for purposes of cooking. The liberality of the Elector of Bavaria was applied by him to presenting the Royal Society with the gold and silver medals, and the Society had no other choice than to make him their first recipient. "Useful" and "practical" were favourite words with this precursor of Morse and Edison. To realise them, he persuaded the world of science to support his Royal Institution, designed its lecture-room, and obtained its charter. Being at a loss for a lecturer, he entered into negotiations in 1801 with young Humphry Davy, who had made a name for himself as assistant to Dr. Beddoes in the Pneumatic Institute at Bristol. Davy was Count Rumford's most important and final discovery before his desire to improve yet another country prompted him, in the following year, to migrate to France, where in 1814 he ended his energetic days.

During the twelve years he lectured at the Royal Institution, Davy had fashionable London at his feet. The simple man from Penzance, of twenty-two, with a smirk on his face and pert of manner, succeeded in packing the hall with audiences of the first rank and talent—the literary and the scientific, the practical and the theoretic, blue-stockings and women of fashion, the old and the young. They were charmed by the

Corinthian abundance of his style. " I attend Davy's lectures," said Coleridge, " to increase the stock of my metaphors." They were fascinated by the daring of his experiments, strongly contrasted as they were with the attention to microscopic accuracy by which Wollaston attained his results. The Duchess of Gordon and other leaders of fashion asked out to their receptions the young professor who, a few months earlier, had been gravelled by his attempts to answer a letter of invitation. They were right ; for Davy in his laboratory was making science before talking about it in familiar terms to his well-born audiences. In November, 1807, he delivered the momentous Bakerian Lecture before the Royal Society, summarising his discoveries in electricity, which carried his name over the civilised world ; and Napoleon, then First Consul, founded a prize for experiments on the galvanic fluid, which in due course was awarded to him. The farming interest, much occupied in the application of chemicals to the land, also made a hero of Davy. He became chemical professor to the Board of Agriculture ; he was invited to the annual sheep-shearing of Mr. Coke, of Holkham, and a print of the day represents him engaged at that solemn function in conversation with his host, Sir John Sinclair, Sir Joseph Banks, and Arthur Young.

According to the generally accepted story, knighthood and matrimony, two events which befell him in 1812, turned Sir Humphry Davy's head. But quite early in his career Coleridge had noticed dissipation and flattery as " the two serpents at the cradle of his genius." He went everywhere, dashing from his laboratory to dinner-parties and from dinner-parties to his laboratory, economising time by putting on fresh linen over that which was underneath. His biographer, Dr. Paris, gravely relates that he was known to have on as many as five shirts and as many pairs of socks at the same time. Davy's devotion to science had lost, therefore, its first fine ardour when he led to the altar Mrs. Apreece, a West Indian heiress, whose vivacity had won the approval of Madame de Staël and made her the toast of Edinburgh. Accustomed to flattery, she was not calculated to make the best of wives for the unsophisticated man of science. She vented her temper on him during the foreign tour they took in the year following their marriage, by the special permission of Napoleon, with Faraday as their companion, so that, as Davy's illustrious successor bitterly recorded, she "made it oftentimes go wrong with me, with herself, and with Sir Humphry." "Lady Davy," said Rogers, in reply to a challenge across the table, "I pass my life in defending you." Still, she numbered many distinguished men—Sir Walter Scott, Moore, and Sydney Smith, for instance— among her friends, and could be, when she chose, both interesting and agreeable.

Davy himself is said to have annoyed the French *savants* by the flippancy of his manner, and his outspoken biographer declares that after marriage "his feelings became more aristocratic, he discovered charms in rank which had before escaped him, and he no longer viewed patrician distinction with philosophic indifference." Yet easy circumstances and social ambitions, though they may have diminished his devotion to science, failed to destroy it. The Felling Colliery accident roused him to invent the safety lamp with which his name is inseparably connected, and for which he denied himself any reward. "More wealth," he remarked, with

ingenuous vanity, " might enable me to put four horses to
my carriage, but what would it avail me to have it said
that Sir Humphry drives his carriage and four ? " To
the last he was ready with advice and assistance to rising
investigators; and though declining powers ruined his
plan for sheathing vessels of war, the devotion with
which he placed his talents at the public disposal was
none the less conspicuous. As his health failed he tried
to resuscitate it by fishing and shooting. Poole, of
Nether Stowey, the friend of Davy and the Lake poets,
related that in 1827, two years before his death, he rode
to the covers on his pony, with his dogs around him,
and his servant carrying the gun, which he never
fired.

Their contemporaries frequently contrasted Davy with
Wollaston, who declined to stand against him for the
Presidency of the Royal Society, and whom Sir Humphry
converted into an expert fly-fisher when he had nearly
reached the age of fifty. Paris has summed up the
difference between them in some telling sentences :

" Davy was ever imagining something greater than he
knew ; Wollaston always knew something more than he
acknowledged. In Wollaston the predominant principle
was to avoid error; in Davy, it was the desire to discover
truth. The tendency of Davy, on all occasions, was to raise
probabilities into facts ; while Wollaston, as constantly,
made them subservient to the expression of doubt."

Sir Henry Holland, in his " Recollections of Past
Life," also touches on Wollaston's sternly logical and
sceptical turn of mind as a hindrance to his career,
and tells how he took calm but careful note of his

own decay, in the functions of the senses, the memory, and the will-power. Wollaston's investigations, therefore, never led him to those broad generalisations on which new systems of philosophy are built. On the other hand, the discoveries to which he devoted his life advanced nearly every branch of science, including "pathology, physiology, chemistry, optics, mineralogy, crystallography, astronomy, electricity, mechanics, and botany." Unlike Davy with his safety lamp, Wollaston kept the secret of pure platinum to himself, and so acquired a considerable fortune. Though his life was mainly spent in his laboratory at Buckingham Street, Fitzroy Square, he took interest in public events, and though reserved about his own affairs, was pleasant to meet. Lockhart heard him describing a coursing match near Abbotsford, when with his "noble, serene dignity of countenance he might have passed for a sporting Archbishop."

Michael Faraday, Davy's greatest pupil, is not included by Princess Liechtenstein in her list of visitors at Holland House, a list which, as it was drawn up for Sir James Mackintosh, must have been compiled before his death in 1832. The omission is probably deliberate, for his correspondence with various members of the family, as printed in Bence Jones's biography, is too formal for any acquaintanceship. They came, however, at the instigation of Sir James South, to the rescue of Faraday after his application for a pension had been treated by Lord Melbourne in a manner which the Prime Minister himself afterwards acknowledged to have been "too blunt and inconsiderate." The aggrieved man of science insisted on a written letter of apology, and it was through the good offices of Miss Fox, or of Lady Mary, General

Fox's wife, that a handsome withdrawal of all wounding expressions was obtained.

The *par nobile fratum*, Alexander and William von Humboldt, were guests of Holland House during their occasional visits to this country. The mission of William, the elder and less famous of the two, was diplomatic. As Prussian Plenipotentiary the statesman-philosopher had a hand in the settlement of Europe after the overthrow of Napoleon. In that capacity he was summoned to London on more than one occasion before the reactionary policy of his Government drove him, in 1819, to abandon affairs and to take up instead the science of language. Alexander von Humboldt knew English society earlier and more intimately, and after he had established himself in Paris to produce his monumental work on the physical geography of South America—between 1805, that is, and 1827—he delighted to return the hospitality of his English friends. "There are few heroes," wrote Sir Charles Lyell of him at this time, "who lose so little by being approached as Humboldt : of Cuvier this cannot be said." The geographer was loquacious, but his own exploits seldom formed the theme. He was equally at home in the laboratory and the salon. Karl Vogt declared that he went to at least five receptions every evening, and on each occasion related the same incident with variations. After he had talked for half an hour he rose, made a bow, and then, retiring with some one for a few minutes' whispered conversation, he slipped away quietly to the door. His conversation was lively, and he was not sparing of sarcasm. "I shall never leave," impatiently said a young lady at a reception, "as long as that gentleman remains ; I should not like to be the object of his remarks." Arago, the astronomer, whose friendship with Humboldt was not unattended with tiffs, used to tease him by recalling this set-down.

The two were companions during a stay in England in 1818, the last of three visits paid by Humboldt, either in the suite of the King of Prussia or as an instructor of diplomacy on its geographical side. When he was finally established at Berlin as " the most besieged inquiry-office in the country " and the dining companion of the King, Humboldt was fond of imparting to English travellers his reminiscences of the men of science and affairs he had met in London when the nineteenth century was young. Yet he was no great admirer of the nation, chiefly, it would seem, because it had never cultivated the free-and-easy manners of the *café*. " This England is a detestable country," he wrote ; " at nine o'clock you must wear your necktie in *this* style, at ten o'clock in *that,* and at eleven o'clock in another fashion."

Natural history was represented at Holland House by Charles Waterton, gaunt of limb, who celebrated his eightieth birthday by climbing an oak-tree in the park of Walton Hall, his estate. It may be that Sydney Smith's facetious review of his "Wanderings in South America" in the *Edinburgh* formed the connecting link, since it did justice to a work which only just misses being a classic, while it aired its author's powers of quizzing.

Nor were distinguished surgeons wanting, like Sir Benjamin Brodie, the elder, President of the Royal Society and Sergeant-Surgeon to William IV., who materially advanced the scientific knowledge of the relations between the brain and the heart. His auto-biography, though chiefly devoted to his profession, records his first visit to Holland House, in the year 1814 or 1815, his brother-in-law, Marsh, having been

Lord Holland's tutor at Christ Church, and Lord Holland having been admitted to the Royal Society on the day that Brodie received the Copley medal. An intimacy of a quarter of a century succeeded, but the great surgeon's description of the circle is commonplace, except for the touch of nature that :

> " I know not how it was that they liked me at first so well as they did, for in general society I was at the time, and for some years afterwards, a shy and deficient young man, contributing but little to conversation, and not feeling myself at home among the politicians and persons of rank who met at Holland House, as I did among my friends of the Royal Society and those of my own profession or of the law."

Sir Henry Holland, whose " Recollections " have been quoted more than once in this volume, must have found entrance into society an easier matter than young Brodie, who had come from a Wiltshire parsonage to the hospitals. Extensive travel gave him a knowledge of the world ; as Sydney Smith's son-in-law he had little chance of allowing his wits to become rusty ; while, on his own account, he cultivated a pleasant bedside manner, or, as he termed it, " the frequent half-hour of genial conversation," with his patients. The Andrew Clark of his day, he must have known many social secrets, and it is to his credit that no scandal, not even about Queen Caroline, appears in his amiable, if rather colourless, autobiography.

CHAPTER XIX

THE NEW SCHOOL OF WHIGS

Serious Whiggism—Dugald Stewart and Bentham—Jeffrey—
Mackintosh's beginnings—The King of Clubs—Mackintosh in conversation—His residence in India—Mackintosh in the House—In
bondage to the Whigs—Ignored and slighted—A literary lotus-
eater—Francis Horner—His arrival in London—Horner in
society—As member for St. Ives—Nominee for St. Mawes—The
Bullion Committee—Horner's illness and death—Romilly and
Dumont—Romilly's parliamentary diary—The criminal law—
Romilly's reforms—A peace-at-any-price man—Romilly's character
and death.

THE years of the Liverpool Ministry witnessed the
affliction of the Whig party, but they also coincided with its regeneration. The politicians who
came to the front on that side—Brougham, with all his
faults, Horner and Romilly—belonged to an altogether
different school from the roystering irresponsibility of
Fox, Sheridan, and Erskine. They meditated seriously
upon serious things, and brought to debate the principles
of humane legislation which they had acquired from the
treatises of Bentham and the habits of systematised
thought which Dugald Stewart had imparted to them.

Neither of those luminaries was intimately associated
with Holland House in the days of the third peer.
Dugald Stewart was established in Edinburgh, where he

formed the minds of more statesmen than any philosopher before or after his day, young Tories like Lord
Palmerston and Lord Dudley resorting to him no less
than Whigs like Lord Lansdowne and Brougham.
Bentham, some years before the beginning of the nineteenth century, had retired to his "Hermitage" in Queen
Square Place, Westminster. There he contented himself
with "anteprandial circumgyrations" of a garden, in
which the poor show of gooseberries and currants
grieved him, and with the society of his secretaries and
his cat, knighted as Sir John Langborn, but renamed in
its sedate old age the Reverend John Langborn. On rare
occasions he entertained *tête-à-tête* at dinner some distinguished man like Talleyrand. From that retreat, however, he conducted a correspondence with Holland House,
in which the fantastic dreams of the recluse contrast with
the good sense of the man of affairs. In 1809, while
travelling in Spain, Lord Holland furthered Bentham's
strange project of settling on the tableland of Mexico—an
idea ultimately dropped in consequence of the remonstrances of his friends—by enlisting the advice of the
Liberal statesman, Jovellanos. But he descended with
vigour on the philosopher's whimsical advocacy of
"Brithibernia" as a title for the United Kingdom calculated to conciliate the Irish. He replied that though
names had unquestionably great influence on mankind,
it was less certain that princes or Parliaments had power
to change them.

The rallying-ground of young Whiggism was the
Edinburgh Review; and whenever its editor, Jeffrey,
visited London he was made welcome. But such
appearances on the part of the hard-working Scots
lawyer and vigorous, if obscurantist, writer were com-

SIR JAMES MACKINTOSH

FROM THE PAINTING BY SIR THOMAS LAWRENCE, P.R.A., IN THE NATIONAL PORTRAIT GALLERY

FRANCIS HORNER

FROM THE PAINTING BY SIR HENRY RAEBURN R.A., IN THE NATIONAL PORTRAIT GALLERY

paratively rare, except during the brief period when he
sat in the Reform Parliament as member for Perth,
Malton, and Edinburgh.   In 1811 his London campaign,
which he closed with a sense of release, included a large
dinner-party at Holland House, where the hostess was
"in great gentleness and softness," and where he failed
to appreciate the charm of Lady Caroline Lamb.   Jeffrey
kept up a constant correspondence with Allen, one of
his reviewers.   He does not appear, however, to have
revisited Holland House before 1840, when he had "a
sweet walk under the cedars and in the garden, where he
listened in vain for the nightingales ; though Lord
Holland and Allen challenged them to answer by divers
fat and asthmatical whistles."   During the same stay in
London he was asked to dine on Sunday *en famille*, but
found sixteen people—foreign Ambassadors and everybody ; and a second dinner followed on the Tuesday—
present, Lord Melbourne, Lord John Russell and Guizot.
Jeffrey kept up his acquaintance with Lady Holland in
her widowhood, and dined with her within four days of
Allen's death.

Mackintosh, who was an *Edinburgh* reviewer, a partial
disciple of Dugald Stewart, and a preacher, with variations, of Benthamite doctrines, combined the three
influences mentioned above.   His vast learning he
picked up while he was ostensibly an idle student at
King's College, Aberdeen, and qualifying as a doctor at
Edinburgh University.   It included a smattering of the
classics, the whole range of history and metaphysics ;
he "had waded through morasses of international law,"
wrote Sydney Smith, "where the step of no living man
could follow him," and he understood, without appreciating, political economy.   By the beginning of the

nineteenth century Mackintosh had made a political reputation by his "Vindiciæ Gallicæ," a reply to Burke's "Reflections on the French Revolution," a polemic containing boisterous Whig opinions, which he soon abandoned for a regret "of having been once betrayed into an approbation of that conspiracy against God and man." Mackintosh had also made a legal reputation by his course of lectures on "The Law of Nature and Nations," delivered in Lincoln's Inn. He was making an income at the Bar, which in 1803, the last year of his practice, exceeded £1,200.

Above all, Mackintosh had discovered his most congenial resource, learned and literary intercourse, in the King of Clubs, which was founded by Bobus Smith and himself at his house in Serle Street, Chancery Lane, in February, 1798. The original members, besides the originators, were Rogers, "Conversation" Sharp, Scarlett, and John Allen. To them were added, amongst others, Lord Holland, Brougham, Porson, Romilly, Sydney Smith, Jeffrey, Luttrell, Hallam, Lord Dudley, and Ricardo. The King of Clubs was a dining club, like the Eumelian and many more, and it first met once a month at the "Crown and Anchor," in the Strand, though it afterwards migrated from hotel to hotel. It long survived Mackintosh's absence in India, from 1804 to 1811, and finally expired, apparently of a superfluity of brilliance, which comes to much the same thing as boredom, about 1823.[1]

Talk at the King of Clubs, at Holland House, or any-

[1] The best account of the King of Clubs, containing some new information, is to be found in a chapter contributed by Mr. W. P. Courtney to "The Pope of Holland House: Selections from the Correspondence of John Wishaw and his Friends," edited by Lady Seymour.

where else in cultivated society, formed the main object
of Mackintosh's life.   Rogers lamented that he had
sacrificed himself to conversation; that he read for it,
thought for it, and gave up future fame for it. He
was not for all time, but of his age.   Still, every man
has a right, within limits, to order his days as he pleases,
and there can be no question as to the pleasure imparted
by Sir James to his contemporaries.   Lord John Russell,
Macaulay, and Sydney Smith have all attempted to
analyse his conversation, and the last of the three
probably comes nearest to the reality.   Mackintosh's
memory was prodigious, and it was always under
command.   He passed, said Tom Grenville, from
Voltaire's letters to Sylvia up to the most voluminous
details of the Council of Trent.   He argued, not for
dialectical victory, but for the elucidation of truth, and
his language might have gone from the fireside to the
press.   Mackintosh, besides, had the power of putting
things so mildly and interrogatively, that he always
gained the readiest reception for his opinions.   He
was too eulogistic, and sometimes clothed common
ideas in over-impressive phraseology.   But Sir Henry
Holland attributes to him, in common with Madame
de Staël, "the power of putting an argument into its
most pithy form—a wit of speech, apart from that gift
of humour to which neither of them could lay much
claim."   On this point Sydney Smith differs.   Mackintosh
had a good deal of humour, and he relates how Sir
James kept up a perfect comedy for several hours at the
expense of a simple Scotch cousin, who had mistaken
him, Sydney, for Sir Sidney Smith, the hero of Acre.
Horner thought less of him than others did, and complained that he did injustice to his own talents for

discursive and descriptive conversation when he forced them out of their way to an imitation of Bobus Smith's smartness and point and sarcasm. Mackintosh often conversed on his legs, and observers remarked, as characteristic of his self-distrust, that he would advance three or four steps forward, and then, as if suddenly recollecting himself, retire again.

Futility, indeed, cannot be dissociated from this benevolent man, whom his generation compared to Burke, but whom posterity has assuredly accepted as Burke *dimidiatus*. He was a child in the common affairs of life, ignorant of the value of money, and totally deficient in the arts of self-advancement. The temptations of a settled income and of a pension that would give him leisure for literature induced him in 1803 to accept from Addington the recordership of Bombay, to the unjust resentment of his political friends. Thirteen years afterwards he returned, as it was said, with all the diseases and none of the wealth of the East. Approached by the Tory Government, he remained faithful to the Whigs, though the mild reasonableness of his politics would have largely palliated a change of sides.

Nevertheless, Dr. Parr's ferocious epigram[1] pursued Mackintosh, and he was an apostate to faction-mongers like Whitbread and Creevey. As member for the county of Nairn, and afterwards for Knaresborough, he failed to gain the ear of the House, making, says Sydney Smith, "rather a lecture or a dissertation than a speech. His voice was bad and nasal; and though nobody was in reality more sincere, he seemed not only not to feel, but hardly to think what he was saying." Mackintosh's propensity to inflict oratorical essays on his hearers

[1] See p. 166.

must be pronounced the more perverse, because he defined the correct style, happily enough, as "an animated conversation on public business." Tierney had some reason for his complaint that Mackintosh could be relied on for a sound opinion "on Cardinal Wolsey or so," but was useless for any matter at hand. He did, nevertheless, carry on Romilly's mission, the reform of the criminal code, until Peel took it up with a more practical grasp.

Mackintosh's son and biographer, Robert James Mackintosh, reflects bitterly but not unjustly on his father's treatment by the Whigs. They never would let him cut himself clear of politics, though Parliament distracted him from the writing of his " History of England." In 1820, when he was holding the professorship of Law and General Politics in the East India College, Haileybury, an appointment worth a meagre £300 a year, he was offered the succession to Thomas Brown in the chair of Modern Philosophy at Edinburgh. "That which six-and-thirty years ago was the object of his ambition," he thought, "might now afford an eligible retirement." Mackintosh was an ideal man for the post, but with weak amiability he yielded to the solicitations of his political friends and renounced the project, greatly to his subsequent regret.

In the result Mackintosh was wholly ignored by the Whigs when they submitted to Canning their candidates for office in his Coalition Government, much to the astonishment of Canning himself ; and in the distribution of appointments in 1830 he was fobbed off with a seat on the India Commission. His health was impaired, no doubt, and indolence and inexperience could be adduced against him as a bar to Cabinet rank. But, when it is remembered that room was found in the Reform Government for Charles Grant and Charles Wynn, the truth of Sydney Smith's reflection becomes manifest that Mackintosh would have acted a great part in life, "if only he had had a little more prudence for the promotion of his interests, and more of angry passions for the punishment of those detractors who envied his fame and presumed upon his sweetness."

What between politics, literature, illness, and procrastination, Mackintosh left nothing behind him that has endured. Throughout the greater part of his life he was oppressed by a want of pence, and, after he resigned his chair at Haileybury in 1824, he availed himself of Lord Holland's hospitality and made Ampthill his home for several years. Yet it needed a stern taskmaster like Dr. Lardner to make Mackintosh produce even such facile hackwork as the "History of England" and "Life of Sir Thomas More" which he contributed to the "Cabinet Encyclopædia" of that vigorous editor. His "Dissertation on the Progress of Ethical Philosophy," a supplement to the "Encyclopædia Britannica," is none too perspicuous, and its inaccuracies gained it a castigation from James Mill. Mackintosh's "History of the Revolution in England" remains a fragment which, though dignified and judicial, is so overloaded with disquisition that its completion on the original scale would have been an impossibility. Lord Holland said that Mackintosh was the only Scotchman he ever knew who felt the delight of lounging. He took four or five days to decide whether "utility" or "usefulness" was the better word, and had not made up his mind when his visitor, Lord Nugent, left him. That is literary lotus-eating indeed; and thus it was

that when Mackintosh was asked on what his reputation depended, he referred his questioners " as usual
to his projects." Among them was an historical account
of Holland House.

Francis Horner was not wanting in those practical
abilities which Mackintosh lacked. If he had lived some
eighteen years longer he might well have become, not
indeed Prime Minister, as some of his friends pardonably
thought, when in 1817 he was snatched away from
them—there his mercantile origin would have stopped
the way—but a much abler Chancellor of the Exchequer
than Spring-Rice, or a firmer Colonial Secretary than
Lord Glenelg. As things were, Horner earned the
enviable memory attaching to talents and integrity pre-
maturely lost to the world. Sydney Smith could not
remember an impression so general as that excited by
his death, and the House of Commons has witnessed
few scenes more affecting than when Canning united
with Romilly in eulogising his virtues.

Horner unquestionably owed not a little to Edinburgh
and Dugald Stewart. He was regarded as having
issued from the right mint, when, in 1802, he resolved
on being called to the English Bar. The compact little
band of Scots in London and their English allies, like
Bobus Smith and Scarlett, received him with open
arms, and his modesty and quiet sincerity won him
their esteem, with the solitary and unworthy exception
of Brougham. He was taken to the King of Clubs,
where he found the presence of Romilly acting as a
restraint, and displays of memory prevailing over discussions of opinion. He scrutinised his brother
barristers, and reported that they were illiberal and
capable only of labouring on a brief.

March, 1803, saw Horner finally established in town, having assisted in the meanwhile in founding the *Edinburgh Review*. Sydney Smith described him as living very high up in Garden Court, Temple, and thinking a good deal about mankind. It is permissible to suggest that Horner was a trifle dull; he put Sir Walter Scott in mind of Obadiah's bull in "Tristram Shandy," and laid no claims to wit, while avoiding what Sydney Smith called the infinitely distressing variety of "wut." But from that same authority we learn that he was affectionate and truthful, "the Commandments were written on his face"; while Lord Dudley lamented him as by far the best and wisest man with whose friendship he was ever honoured. Yet Lord Dudley associated with all the finest spirits in literature and politics.

By the end of the London season of 1805, Horner had made his way to Holland House, and expressed himself to Lord Webb Seymour as delighted with the spirited understandings and sweet dispositions of Lord Holland and Miss Fox, both of their uncle's make. The serious young man of twenty-seven soon became a repository of Whig secrets, and his diary records authentic details of the formation of the "Talents" Administration, together with such characteristic memoranda as—"Use to be made of individual minds, Sharp, Rogers, Whishaw, Smyth, Dumont." He also established himself in Lady Holland's good graces, and after the influence of Lord Henry Petty and Lord Kinnaird had brought him into Parliament as member for St. Ives, she seems to have created him her reporter-in-chief. Horner's comments on debate were pithy; he hit off Windham, when about to speak, sitting

quite absorbed, and growling if any one approached
him ; and characterised Speaker Abbot's praise of the
Ministry, at the close of the session of 1813, for its
resistance to the Catholic claims, as "more like the
panegyrics that the French Government pronounces
upon itself by the mouth of a senator or tribune, than
the propriety and reserve that ought to be adhered to
by the president of an assembly really free."

Horner represented the pocket-borough system on its
most defensible side, a point adroitly made by Canning
in his obituary speech. The independence of mind
which caused him to decline the prospective appointment of Financial Secretary to the Treasury, on the
ground that he had resolved not to take office until
he was rich enough to live at ease when out of office, did
not desert him when he became the Marquis of Buckingham's nominee for St. Mawes. When he voted, after
Napoleon's return from Elba, for Whitbread's motion
directed against a resumption of hostilities, he offered
to resign his seat, but his patron, in an honourable letter,
declined to take him at his word. "Though put into
Parliament by some of the great borough lords," wrote
Sydney Smith, "every one saw that he represented his
own real opinions."

With his invariable good sense, Horner, after Jeffrey
had spurred him on to exert himself, approached the
House on the state of the currency, a topic on which his
Edinburgh training had qualified him to express a sound
opinion. He obtained the appointment of the Bullion
Committee, acted as its chairman, and though the
resolutions he based on its report were defeated, his
exertions eventually led to the resumption of cash
payments. His advocacy of honest finance was the

more creditable because it arrayed the banking interest
against him—a hostility which he disarmed, however,
by his opposition to the Corn Bill of 1815. On foreign
policy he had his full share of the limitation of outlook
that afflicted the Whigs throughout the Napoleonic
period.

Horner, long since a general favourite with the House,
was fast improving as a speaker when, in the summer of
1816, his health, which, with a consumptive's heedlessness,
he had neglected, completely collapsed. The concern
of his friends, Holland House at their head, was
extreme, and if solicitude ever saved the life of a man,
that man would have been Francis Horner. But
eminent doctors were consulted too late, and he went
southward to die at Pisa, leaving behind him a
manuscript volume of " Designs," which embraced
subjects so various as the study of the rhythm of
English prose and questions to be put in the House
of Commons on the sinking fund and debt. The
inscription on Chantrey's monument to him in Westminster Abbey duly comments on the "expectations
which premature death could alone have frustrated."

Sir Samuel Romilly, for whom Horner offered to
stand aside at St. Mawes, belonged to an austerer
school of Whiggism than the friend whom he survived by less than two years. His upbringing among
the gaunt religious surroundings of the French
Protestant colony in London probably deepened the
natural gloom of his disposition, though the arrival
of youth brought cheerfulness with it. Rousseau was
Romilly's first inspiration; Dumont, who was afterwards to be the secretary of Mirabeau and the translator
of Jeremy Bentham, but who was then a student for

the ministry at Geneva, his first important acquaintance. The young barrister was thus drawn within the current of the French Revolution; he gave Mirabeau the original matter of his pamphlet, "Lettre d'un Voyageur Anglais sur le Prison de Bicêtre," and drafted for the use of the States General a statement of the procedure in the House of Commons. But Romilly, like Mackintosh, soon abandoned his zeal for Revolutionary principles, and suppressed "Groenvelt's Letters," a little volume of reflections on French and British institutions written by Dumont and himself. He had sown his political wild oats, and Bentham's treatises on the reform of the criminal code were supplying him with a motive for exertion more practical than the Rights of Man. Practice was coming to him, besides, at first slowly, but afterwards rapidly, and by 1805 he led in the Court of Chancery.

Much to Romilly's surprise the Prince of Wales offered to bring him into Parliament, wishing, no doubt, to introduce an element of respectability into Carlton House politics. Romilly entertained, however, the most rigid ideas on political independence. As a choice of evils he preferred buying a constituency to representing it as the nominee of a great man, and he had accepted the Solicitor-Generalship in the "Talents" Administration before an accommodating M.P. made room for him at Queensborough. Romilly's parliamentary diary is, perhaps, the strongest searchlight that has been thrown on the politics of the pre-Reform epoch. It is the truthful record of a mind overprone to self-examination, dissatisfied with existing conditions, and given to censuring opponents, especially when they happened to belong to the legal profession, but animated by a noble desire to abolish abuses and to advance the condition of the people. Few statesmen, with the shining exception of Brougham, would have written with Romilly in 1807 : "To enable men to read and write is, as it were, to give them a new sense. We cannot prevent those who are in the lowest ranks of life having political opinions ; and few men would venture to avow that they would prevent it if they could."

The "Talents" Ministry had come and gone, and Romilly, besides distinguishing himself by summing up the evidence against Lord Melville, had substantially amended the Bankruptcy Acts, before he set his hand to the work of his life, the reform of the criminal law. The resolve came upon him during a holiday at Cowes in the summer of 1807. That law, though Draconian in the letter, was, on the whole, humanely administered. Juries frequently declined to convict in the face of the clearest evidence ; or, when the capital sentence depended on the value of the thing stolen, they were induced to price the articles at less than a tenth of their real worth. Romilly would not accept Blackstone's theory that such evasions of the law were pious perjuries. Juries, besides, were liable to be swayed by appeals to their commercial instincts, and while he was trying, but in vain, to carry his Shoplifting Bill a boy of ten was lying in Newgate under sentence of death.

Romilly shrank from proposing a general scheme of legal reform, and endeavoured instead to purge the Statute-book by a little here and a little there. Even so the forces of obscurantism, as represented by Lord Eldon, Lord Ellenborough, and Lord Redesdale, were too strong for him, and unceremonious rejection, or at best mutilation, awaited most of his measures. The

abolition of the death penalty for private stealing from
the person, and for stealing from bleaching-grounds,
and in the case of soldiers and sailors who were found
wandering without their passes, comprises the meagre
sum of his accomplishment. He also amended the law
of treason by taking away corruption of blood, under
which the sins of the fathers were visited on the
children, and did away with the hideous punishment
of disembowelling and quartering. These were but
small results; still, Romilly, and Mackintosh after him,
made ready the way for Peel, who between 1823 and
1827 swept away over 250 statutes, mostly obsolete,
but all barbarous.

Romilly might conceivably have succeeded better as
a legal reformer if he had been less thoroughly identified with extreme Whiggism, not only in such legitimate
matters as Catholic Emancipation and the freedom of the
blacks, but also in Whitbread's· fantastic peace-at-any-
price policy after Napoleon's return from Elba, even
while he admitted that the Emperor's disavowals of
ambitious designs were probably insincere. During the
sessions of 1817 and 1818 he was practically the leader
of the Opposition in the House of Commons, and sometimes, it must be confessed, he railed rather than argued.
Thus he was not ashamed to oppose the second restoration of Louis XVIII. on the ground that the Sovereigns
of Europe, including France, might eventually unite, by
way of imitation, in forcing a new form of government
on England. Such unworthy suggestions were, however,
to the taste of a party embittered by long exclusion
from office. He would have been the official leader of
the Whigs in the House of Commons if his practice
had not interfered, and in the year of his death he

was placed at the head of the poll for the City of
Westminster, though, in obedience to his invariable rule,
he kept away from the hustings during the whole of
the election. The Romilly whose diatribes against Lord
Castlereagh's foreign policy won the approval of Creevey
was thus honoured, we may suppose, rather than the
Romilly whose efforts to save children from the gallows,
soldiers from being flogged to death, and to abate the
misery of the Marshalsea, Creevey never troubled so
much as to mention.

As might be expected with a man who tested conduct
by the first principles of philosophy, Romilly seems to
have been regarded with some awe by his intimates. He
carried the austerity so marked on his features into
general society ; and in the case of Perceval, a close
associate at the Bar, he permitted political differences
to break off an old friendship. But he entertained
strong attachments for a few, among whom were Scarlett
and Dumont, and no more devoted husband and father
ever existed. His death, by his own hand, on November 2, 1818, was directly due, in fact, to that of Lady
Romilly, his "dear Anne," in the Isle of Wight, after
much suffering. The blow plunged him into a deep
melancholy, which should have been more carefully
watched by those about him. Had proper precautions
been taken, it is difficult to believe that so upright a
mind as Romilly's would not ultimately have been re-
stored to public and private duties. His diary frequently
refers to the happiness of a life in which every professional object had been attained—he distrusted his
capacity for the office of Lord Chancellor—while he
had still leisure for domestic and even literary enjoyment. A severe illness in 1815 drew from him, indeed,

SIR SAMUEL ROMILLY

FROM THE PAINTING BY SIR THOMAS LAWRENCE, P.R.A., IN THE NATIONAL PORTRAIT GALLERY

LORD DENMAN
FROM THE PAINTING BY JOHN JAMES HALLS IN THE NATIONAL PORTRAIT GALLERY

the gloomy reflection that if it had ended in death it would have been fortunate. But he noted the suicide of Whitbread without any premonition that a similar fate awaited himself ; and, if only he had rallied from his grief, he might well have occupied the woolsack in 1830 instead of Brougham, much to the strengthening of the Grey Administration.

CHAPTER XX

LAWYERS AND RADICALS

Brougham's descent from the North—A breach and its cause
—Brougham in Parliament—His championship of the Princess—
A proposed settlement—Queen Caroline's trial—Brougham as a
reformer—On the woolsack—Brougham's downfall—Lord Mel-
bourne's sentence—Brougham's eccentricities—His good qualities
—The rise of Denman—Solicitor-General to Queen Caroline—His
speech and its sequel—At Holland House—A Whig dinner-party—
Plunket and the Grenvilles—Irish Attorney-General and Chancellor
—Plunket's oratory and puns—John Wishaw—"The Pope" and
"the Mufti"—Hobhouse and Byron—Hobhouse and Burdett—
" Liberty candidates"—Exhausted enthusiasms.

BROUGHAM descended on London from the North
in 1805, and supported himself by indefatigable,
though shallow, contributions to the *Edinburgh
Review.* He came into Whig politics as a pamphleteer,
notably during the General Election of 1807, when, with
slight assistance from Lord Holland and Allen, he produced a prodigious amount of what the Americans call
campaign literature. Three years later, on Lord Holland's
suggestion, the Duke of Bedford brought him into Parliament as member for Camelford. An estrangement from
Holland House followed, and Brougham's correspondence with Earl Grey supplied a reason, namely, feminine
resentment against a rebuff :

" A sagacious friend of mine . . . had heard, I know not how, that some time ago the Hollands made an attempt to call at Brougham on their way South from Scotland ; that my mother ordered the gate of the courtyard to be barred against their entrance, saying that she herself was too old to be hurt by Lady Holland, or anybody of that kind, but she had an unmarried daughter, then living with her, and therefore that no Lady Holland should set foot in her house ! I remember my mother was immovable, and there was nothing to be done but that I should go out to the carriage, make any excuses I could invent, and drive on with the Hollands to visit Lord Thanet, he being then at Appleby Castle—and this I was accordingly compelled to do."

Brougham's stories require confirmation as a rule, but in this instance the conduct attributed to his determined old mother seems credible. He was, however, mistaken in attributing to Lady Holland's animosity his three years' exclusion from Parliament after his defeat at Liverpool, with Creevey for a colleague, in 1815. In spite of such brilliant successes in the House as the repeal of the Orders in Council which he wrung from the Tory Government, and triumphs at the Bar like his first defence of the Hunts, his extravagances and impatience of control damaged his party, and inspired the borough-holders with distrust. Grey, however, stood by him, and persuaded Lord Darlington to accept him as member for Winchelsea. He promptly distinguished himself by a tirade against the Regent, described by Romilly as composed in " Suetonian terms which would not have been too strong for the latter days of Tiberius," and calculated according to Creevey's friend Mr. Western —one of the most successful instances on record of a man living up to his name in literature—to damn him past redemption. Yet within a few days he forced the

Chancellor of the Exchequer to withdraw the unpopular income tax ; while as chairman of the Select Committee on the Education of the Lower Orders he laid the foundation of the Act of 1870 and stirred the public conscience against the misapplication of endowments. His labours stand to his great honour, yet it is undeniable that by adopting suaver methods with witnesses and Lord Eldon he would have materially expedited reform.

Brougham's championship of the Princess of Wales, before she became Queen Caroline, and of Princess Charlotte was, like most of his actions, a strange mixture of baseness and chivalry. His letters to Lord Grey and Creevey show that he regarded mother and daughter as instruments ready to Whig hands after the Regent had identified himself with the Tories. Nothing could be more cynical than his assertion of principle that "little Prinnie" (Princess Charlotte) should be taken along with his friends as far as they both went the same road, and no farther. But Brougham, exulting in his own prodigality of resource, made himself out more of a "Wicked Shifts," as Creevey called him later on, than he really was. His advice to the Princesses was kind and judicious, as when he persuaded Princess Charlotte to return home after her flight from Warwick House, and when he vainly tried to dissuade the mother from quitting the country in 1814.

The conduct of Brougham became far more questionable when, without consulting his client, he took upon himself to lay before the Ministry a proposed settlement of her case on the basis of an ample income in return for an undertaking never to return to England or to assume the title of Queen. His ruling motive was presumably unlimited confidence in his own dexterity, but in the result he was suspected by one side of wishing to betray his client and by the other of plotting to inveigle the Government into concessions which could afterwards be used against it. Brougham, in any case, entirely miscalculated his influence over the headstrong woman who, though she appointed him her Attorney-General, placed more confidence in Alderman Wood, a fussy busybody, and still more in her resolute self. Stung by the omission of her name from the Liturgy, she swept her legal adviser aside when he waited on her at St. Omer, and made her triumphant entry into London in the congenial character of a mob heroine.

Brougham's management of Queen Caroline's case was a marvel of legal strategy. There is no reason for disbelieving his statement that he began by thinking that she must be guilty, but as he went on became more and more convinced of her innocence. The conscientious Denman underwent the same process of conversion. With boundless audacity, he treated the House of Lords as if it were a jury on the Northern Circuit ; his sarcasms reduced the hostile witnesses, particularly Majocchi, of *non mi ricordo* notoriety, to pulp ; his great speech was a masterpiece of invective, though an unsubstantial defence, and we have it on record that Denman considered the peroration sublime. It was written out seven times before he was satisfied with its form ; and, perhaps for that reason, it reads pompously in cold print. There was force, however, in his warning to the Lords on the consequences of passing the Bill of Pains and Penalties ; and when it is remembered that he might have enlisted revolutionary evidence on his client's side, he must be pronounced, on the whole, to have used his vast powers with moderation. But though he frightened the Govern-

ment into dropping the Bill, he could not convert the
Queen into a model of propriety, and when she disregarded his advice and created a disturbance at the
Coronation she discovered that the London mob had
wearied of her. Thereafter she died.

During the remainder of the reign of George IV.
Brougham was politically detached ; his support of the
Canning Government produced a temporary breach
between him and Earl Grey, and Creevey speculated
alternately on his madness and his wickedness. But he
was prolific in schemes of popular education and of
legal reform, in establishing Mechanics' Institutes, in
founding the Society for the Diffusion of Useful Knowledge, and in setting up London University. Viewed
from a distance, he seemed, next to the Duke of Wellington, the greatest man of his time, and when the county
of Yorkshire returned him, free of expense, at the General
Election following the death of George IV., Brougham,
as his latest biographer, Mr. Atlay, justly remarks, was " a
potent force for which there is no parallel save in the
case of Mr. Gladstone after the successful issue of the
first Midlothian campaign." But advancing years had
rendered him more unstable than ever. Lord Grey
expressed the general feeling when he tried to relegate
him to the Attorney-Generalship, though the Premier
misread his Brougham entirely in thinking that he would
put up with a second-class position. He shouldered,
instead, his way on to the woolsack ; and though his
flippancies and sarcasms in debate brought discredit on
the Government, his driving power carried the Reform
Bill, while his clearance of arrears in the Court of
Chancery was regarded as nothing short of a legal
miracle. It is a pity that he has obscured his services

to the cause of popular government by imaginary narratives of his patriotic prowess in the Royal closet, which conscientious historians have been compelled to reject.

The passing of the Act of Reform placed Brougham at the height of his fame. His downfall followed with catastrophic rapidity. He had time, indeed, to create the Judicial Committee of the Privy Council, the most permanently beneficial of his experiments. But his levity in court had become a public scandal, while his restless interference in every department of State vexed his colleagues beyond endurance. " I suppose it must be so," said Lord Holland at Lansdowne House, when the determination was taken to offer him the Seals, " but this is the last time we shall meet in peace within these walls." The familiar history of his meddling in Irish affairs, and concealment of his meddling, which drove Lord Grey, the much-enduring, to resign, his oratorical extravagance at the Edinburgh banquet, which infuriated his Sovereign, and finally his betrayal of the dismissal of the Melbourne Ministry to the *Times* with the gratuitous addition, "The Queen has done it all," can be passed over with a bare allusion. His trickery and his attempt to jockey Scarlett out of the post of Chief Baron of the Exchequer completed his political ruin, and Lord Melbourne pronounced sentence with a dignity that Brougham never approached :

" You domineered too much, you interfered with other departments, you encroached upon the province of the Prime Minister, you worked, as I believe, with the Press in a manner unbecoming the dignity of your station, and you formed political views of your own and pursued them by means which were unfair towards your colleagues."

Brougham had made himself impossible ; still, his fall might have been broken, and the Melbourne Government brought disaster on themselves when, by leaving him to learn of Lord Cottenham's elevation to the woolsack through the public Press, they drove him into unholy alliance with Lord Lyndhurst. He lived on to be an embarrassment to whatever side of politics he chose to attach himself, the target of Harriet Martineau's scathing journalism and the sport of " H. B.'s " malicious pencil.

The plain clue to Brougham's conduct is that he was the maddest man who has taken part in the public life of this country. Close observers like Creevey and Greville entertained but little doubt that the morbid activity of his brain passed the thin partition now and again. The taint was hereditary, but by strength of will and intense application to work he could generally keep it under control. Still, there were times when he suffered from deep melancholy, others when he took refuge in boisterous buffoonery. He can be forgiven for indulging in leapfrog with the little Ponsonbys, but playing hide-and-seek with the Great Seal at Rothiemurchas passed the bounds. So did his pleasantries, if Greville is to be believed ; with Brougham and Lord Sefton in vigorous vein it is intelligible that ladies did not know which way to look. The eccentricity of his appearance and attire corresponded with the oddity of his character. The twitching trumpet-shaped nose and the dingy complexion, " looking like something that had been dug up," as Lady Granville expressed it, have been immortalised by " H. B." At one time it pleased him to dress entirely in black; later came the plaid trousers. He ate like Dr. Johnson, drank like Squire Western, and when at

Edinburgh he called his fellow-citizens to witness that after four years of office his hands were clean, there were those who asserted that they were exceedingly dirty. At one time he was Lord Grey's tenant in Berkeley Square, and he left the house in an indescribable state of neglect.

Yet there must have been much that was likeable about the man. Even after he had tripped up their father he disarmed the hostility of the Greys ; though he wrecked the first Melbourne Ministry, several of his old colleagues pleaded for him with the Premier. Melbourne himself resumed habits of intimacy, and actually appointed Brougham one of his executors. In spite of his impish humour and rasping tongue, he was capable of enduring friendships, and in his " Statesmen of the Reign of George III." he raised no unworthy memorial to one which, after the breach had been once repaired, seems to have stood time and political change, namely, that with the inhabitants of Holland House. In his old age he would often come to spend an hour or two in the familiar rooms, and would sit sadly down, sometimes in tears.

Denman, who as Queen Caroline's Solicitor-General was associated with Brougham in her defence, belonged to the correct school of lawyers. While Brougham, as a student at Edinburgh, was wrenching off knockers and drinking deep, Denman was a blameless Etonian, with a love for music. The contrast continued through their respective lives. Denman married young, and became the father of fifteen children. He worked assiduously at his profession, instead of scattering his energies over the whole field of knowledge. In 1815 he received his first advancement, through the interest of Lord Holland, becoming Deputy Recorder of Nottingham. His defence of the Luddites, and of Brandreth, the "Nottingham Captain" who led a pitifully abortive rising instigated by sheer want, unsuccessful though they were, marked him out as the Whig lawyer likeliest to repeat the triumphs of Erskine. The Duke of Devonshire and Lord Lansdowne in 1818 brought him in at their joint expense for the close borough of Wareham, but, like many another able lawyer, he failed to impress the House of Commons.

His appointment as Solicitor-General to Queen Caroline appears to have been made at Brougham's suggestion. To it we owe his most valuable narrative of her trial, composed in 1821, of much superior authenticity to his colleague's dateless and incoherent recollections. Denman enters into the squabbles that distracted the Queen's advisers and his own uncomfortable position between Brougham, on the one hand, and Alderman Wood on the other. "So now we are in for it, Mr. Denman," was her Attorney-General's gloomy observation after he had unfolded the sinister reports that had reached him as to her morals. There follows the curious confession that Mrs. Denman wished to call on her in Portman Street, but that he begged her to wait until Mrs. Brougham did so, " dreading that such scenes of vice would be proved as would overwhelm with shame any woman who had formed any acquaintance with the criminal." Yet in the House he made his memorable declaration, in answer to the suggestion that the Queen, though omitted from the Liturgy, might consider herself included in the general prayer for the Royal family, that "if her Majesty was included in any general prayer, it was the prayer for all that are desolate and oppressed."

Whatever his feelings at the outset may have been,

Denman soon worked himself up into an ecstatic belief in his client's innocence. His speech was preferred by many to Brougham's because it was more dramatic. The apostrophe to the Duke of Clarence, "Come forth, thou slanderer!" received all the emphasis that a consummate actor could lend it. He raised his voice, says his biographer, Sir Joseph Arnould, to the full measure of its magnificent compass, till the old roof rang again, and a thrill of irrepressible emotion pervaded every heart in the densely crowded assembly. But the peroration contained two astonishing errors of taste. The first was the quotation of a foul passage from Dion Cassius, suggested to him by Dr. Parr, which to most people appeared to impute to the King the vilest vices of the Court of Nero. The second was the conclusion with a reference to the woman taken in adultery—"Go, and sin no more." The phrase came into his head after ten hours' speaking, and gave him some of the bitterest moments of his life.

Those blunders earned for Denman, and naturally, the intense hostility of George IV. Lord Eldon and Lord Lyndhurst were peremptorily forbidden to mention his name for promotion to silk. The latter had to explain to Denman the construction placed by the King upon his unfortunate incursion into the classics, and the great authority of the Duke of Wellington had to be invoked before the King granted his patent. "Mr. Denman," said the Duke, "we have gained this point, but I never had a tougher job in my life." His many friends were delighted. "I do indeed rejoice most warmly," wrote Lord Holland from Brighton, "at an act, however tardy, of justice to you. It comes, I fear, a little too late to be of much pecuniary advantage in your profession; but the sincere satisfaction it gives to so many, and indeed to all honest men, must afford you a gratification of a higher order."

Denman spent his leisure during the Queen's trial at Holland House, where he " luxuriated in an admirable library and the best company in the world, at the same time recruiting his health in good air and delicious gardens." He generally occupied Mr. Fox's chamber and was " as happy as a man could be." His friends belonged mainly to that circle, and included Mackintosh, Sydney Smith, Rogers, Moore, and Thomas Campbell. To the last of them he sent a rhymed reply, when invited to dinner, more remarkable for Whiggism than wit. Denman's political opinions, in fact, continued to be of the advanced order. After some years' absence from Parliament, he made a timely re-entry as member for Nottingham at the General Election consequent on the death of George IV., when he harangued the multitude from the window of the Corn Exchange and attended a meeting of the " Lambs," where he sucked a long clay pipe and sang a comic song. On the formation of the Grey Ministry he became Attorney-General, and braved odium by conducting the prosecutions against the agrarian and Bristol rioters. But the " Mumpsimus " party, Lord Eldon and the Duke of Cumberland, were sorely exercised when, two years later, this strong politician, who had branded his present Sovereign as a " slanderer," was appointed Lord Chief Justice in succession to Lord Tenterden.

Absorbed in circuit and legal reform, Denman does not seem to have seen much of his old friends until May, 1838, when he met Lord Grey and Lord Holland at Lord Clarendon's house.

" Lord Grey not in absolute good-humour with his old

friends ; a little sore on a good many points. . . . The
general asperities not softened by his being seated next
to Lady Clarendon, who required him to carve all the
dishes, especially a roast pig ! Lord Holland more amiable,
good-humoured, and entertaining than I ever saw even him
before—quite aware of Lord Grey's infirmity, but only
amused by it. Both deep in Wilberforce's biography, and
agreed that it raised him in their estimation. Holland said
in addition (but with some nervousness as to how it would
be received) that the work also raised Pitt in his opinion.
This was controverted, but not ungracefully. . . . Grey said
he could not read ' Pickwick.' Holland spoke of it with
discriminating discernment, but mentioned Boz's other
book, ' Oliver Twist,' almost with tears. When Grey
offered to help him to pig, he declined hastily, and gave
me the most comical look, as though he should have come
between the lion and his wrath."

A new generation had occupied Holland House for
many years before Lord Denman laid aside the ermine,
to end his days a paralytic unable to communicate with
others either by tongue or pen.

Plunket, the Irish orator, was reckoned as a follower of
Lord Grenville, who brought him in for Midhurst just
before the dissolution of 1807. He was essentially the
political pupil of Grattan, whose efforts to defeat the
Act of Union he had ably seconded in the Parliament
House on St. Stephen's Green, and to whom he paid
filial attention both in public and private. Though he
made a name and fortune in the Dublin Court of
Chancery, it was not until 1813 that he rose to fame
in England, when, having been returned member for
Dublin University, he made the first of his great speeches
on behalf of Catholic Emancipation. Its effect, we are
told, was very great. Brougham has left it on record

that Plunket lacked only one requisite of a perfect
orator—the power of combining and clothing rapid,
overwhelming declamation with argument ; and that he
surpassed all orators in that there was no interval whatever in his speech, the whole being an exemplification of
clear statement, close reasoning, and felicitous illustration.
The breach between the Grenvilles and the Whigs, however, caused Plunket to lend his voice to Tory measures
like the Seditious Meetings Bill, and Lord Grey is supposed to have aimed at him the bitter reproach that " he
had acted with more than the zeal of an apostate." In
1821 he rehabilitated himself in Whig eyes by his second
great speech on Catholic Relief, the speech which Mackintosh declared to be the ablest he had ever heard in
Parliament, and which was followed by the adoption of
his resolution by a majority of six in a House of four
hundred and forty-eight. This Bill, managed by Sir
John Newport in its later stages, passed the Commons,
but was rejected on its second reading by the Lords.

The Catholics had to wait for seven years longer, and
in the meantime Plunket accepted the appointment of
Irish Attorney-General in Lord Liverpool's Ministry, that
pliant statesman having admitted the principle as an
" open question." He acted in close alliance with the
Lord-Lieutenant, the Marquis Wellesley, who was also an
Emancipationalist, while Goulburn, the Irish Secretary,
represented the opposite pole of political thought. While
Attorney-General, Plunket, in a brilliant flight of sustained
eloquence, supported Burdett's Relief Bill, which passed
its second reading by a majority of twenty-one, only to
be thrown out by the Lords through the conscientious
bigotry of the Duke of York. Plunket during these years
was much in the confidence of Canning, who, in 1827,

made him Chief-Justice in the Irish Court of Common
Pleas with a peerage. The House of Lords, therefore,
was the audience which was privileged to hear his last
speech on Emancipation, the crown of his political career.
It remained for him to receive a tardy reward for his
services from Lord Grey in the shape of the Irish
Chancellorship, and to place his wisdom and experience
at the disposal of three successive Viceroys—Lords Angle-
sea, Wellesley, and Mulgrave—during ten critical years.
In return he was jockeyed out of office in 1841 to make
room for a more pushing politician in Sir John Campbell
by what Brougham, an expert in such matters, regarded
as " the most gross and unjustifiable act ever done by
party, combining violence and ingratitude with fraud."
He lived on to 1854, and died in his ninetieth year.

"There has been nothing like it since Plunket " was in
the " forties" and "fifties " the hall-mark of a political
speech. The standard was a high one, though the age of
Plunket, Brougham, and Canning must be pronounced
the silver age of English eloquence ; that of Pitt, Fox,
Burke, Sheridan, and Windham the golden. A perusal
of Plunket's speeches leads to the conclusion that their
strength consisted in their aptitude to debate rather than
their grasp of political philosophy. As to his other
attributes, Bulwer Lytton wrote in *Blackwood's Magazine*
that with—

"No grace in feature, no command in height,
Yet his whole presence fills and awes the sight.
Wherefore ? you ask. I can but guide your guess—
Man has no majesty like earnestness."

Plunket was a man of long and enduring friendships,
chiefly Irish, though he was always welcome both at

Dropmore and Holland House.   Among the famous men whom he entertained at Old Connaught, his country home, was Sir Walter Scott.   Moore, meeting Plunket at Holland House in 1832, was pleased to disparage his strongly Irish manner, sounding Dublin all over. Pretty cool that for the son of a Dublin tradesman ! Plunket, apart from his manner, was an inveterate punster in and out of court.   When some one praised his waterfall at Old Connaught as quite a cataract, he replied, " Oh, that's all my eye ! "   "Well, you see ——'s predictions have come true."   " Indeed," said Plunket, " I always knew he was a bore, but I didn't know he was an augur."   Brougham has handed down a prettier instance of his wit.   Lord Essex said one day that he had seen a brother of Sir John Leach so like the Master of the Rolls that it seemed as if the manner ran in the family.   " I should as soon have thought," exclaimed Plunket, " of a wooden leg running in a family."

John Wishaw was a connecting link between the Whig politicians of the Regency and the reign of George IV., and may therefore be included in this chapter.   He held a good position as an equity barrister when, in 1806, his Whig friends gave him the comfortable appointment of Commissioner at the Audit Office.   Thus provided for, Wishaw spent his tranquil existence as a confidant of public men, whose advice carried all the greater weight because he was cautious about giving it.   Sydney Smith sought his acquaintance, when he set up house in Doughty Street, as one of the well-to-do barristers of the neighbourhood.   When Horner came to town, Abercromby, afterwards Speaker and Lord Dunfermline, recommended him to cultivate Wishaw as a " very particular friend of mine whom I hold a most excellent critic and accurate in his opinions of character." Romilly, who was a still earlier friend, made Wishaw his executor, and entrusted him with the care of his children, a duty performed with exemplary care. When Brougham was appointed in 1806 Secretary to Lord St. Vincent's mission to the Court of Lisbon, Wishaw offered to lend him any reasonable sum to meet the emergency, and Brougham never forgot the kindness. His hand was frequently suspected in the pages of the *Edinburgh Review ;* but, in reality, his literary performances appear to have been confined to biographical memoirs of Mungo Park the explorer and Smithson Tennant the mineralogist.

How, then, did Wishaw acquire his reputation for wisdom ? By the process, it would seem, of making up his mind with deliberation and holding to it with tenacity. Sydney Smith once wrote that when a new book came out Wishaw gave no opinion for the first week, but confined himself to chuckling and elevating his chin. " In the meantime he drives diligently about the first critical stations, breakfasts in Mark Lane [with "Conversation" Sharp], hears from Hertford College [from Mackintosh], and by Saturday night is as bold as a lion and as decisive as a court of justice." His confidence in his own views won for him the nicknames of " the Pope " and " the Mufti " ; and Lady Seymour, who has edited his correspondence, has borrowed from Creevey the apt title of " The Pope of Holland House." His letters exhibit Wishaw as moderate rather than profound, singularly unruffled by tremendous events like the fall of Napoleon, the trial of Queen Caroline, or the carrying of the Reform Bill, but liable to err in his literary judg- ments. Thus he condemned Benjamin Constant's " Adolphe," the object of Balzac's unstinted admiration,

as an absolute failure. His description of Bentham as
" a schoolman, born some ages too late," is, however, by
no means destitute of point. Wishaw, with his cork leg
and blunt manners—"a puffy, thick-set, vulgar little
dump of an old man" is Carlyle's uncomplimentary
description of him—spent his old age serenely, afflicted
by decayed eyesight, but surrounded by devoted friends.
The news of Lord Holland's death, abruptly broken to
him by Sydney Smith, is said to have given him a
paralytic stroke, and two months later he passed away.

Between the Whigs and the Radicals there was a great
gulf fixed.   It is impossible to conceive Horne Tooke or
Major Cartwright as visitors at Holland House.   Still,
members of that party did cross the threshold, and
among them were John Cam Hobhouse and Sir Francis
Burdett.   The former is best recollected as Byron's companion on the memorable tour immortalised in the first
canto of " Childe Harold," and to him the fourth canto
is dedicated as to one whom its author—

" had known long, accompanied far ; whom he had found
wakeful over his sickness and kind in his sorrow ; glad in his
prosperity and firm in his adversity ; true in counsel, and
trusty in peril ; a friend often tried and never found wanting ; a man of learning, of talent, of shrewdness and of
honour."

The notes contributed by Hobhouse to the canto are the
product of a scholarly and tasteful intelligence.   When
they parted at Pisa for the last time in September, 1822,
Byron eloquently said : " Hobhouse, you should never
have come, or you should never go."   He had behaved
with great tact and loyalty during the poet's domestic

difficulties, and when Byron died he wrote "a full and scrupulously accurate account" of the separation. Lord Holland, a friend of some sixteen years' standing, strongly recommended silence. Lady Byron, he declared, would be far more annoyed if left unnoticed than if, whether wrong or right, she had to figure in a controversy. Hobhouse, whose simple desire was to do duty by the dead, deferred to this opinion, and the manuscript remains unpublished.

Hobhouse's robust Radicalism caused him to be elected in 1820 the companion of Sir Francis Burdett in the representation of Westminster, after he had been defeated two years previously by George Lamb, the Whig candidate, owing to party dissensions. The pair continued to represent the borough until after the Reform Bill had become law, and in many ways they were well fitted to give voice to middle-class aspirations. The exertions of a committee of Westminster tradesmen— Brooke, the glass manufacturer in the Strand, Adams, the coach-builder in Long Acre, and Place, the tailor at Charing Cross—had placed Burdett at the head of the poll in 1807, with Lord Cochrane, afterwards Earl of Dundonald, as a Whig colleague with a grievance against the Government. Canning and Tierney ranked Burdett very nearly, if not quite, at the head of the parliamentary orators of their day. He was tall and gifted with a melodious voice ; his command of language was easy and natural, and he never used a note. Hobhouse wrote of him that in private life "a manly understanding and a tender heart gave a charm to his society such as I have never derived in any other instance from a man whose principal pursuit was politics."

Sir Francis had also a spice of the mountebank in him

which was much to the taste of the uneducated Westminster mob. When the House committed him to the
Tower for breach of privilege, his offence consisting of
the republication of a speech in defence of a brother
demagogue, John Gale Jones, he barricaded himself in
his house in Piccadilly, with Cochrane as a hare-brained
chief-of-the-staff. The troops brought the siege to a
close by effecting a breach on the fourth morning, and
ruined a hastily arranged scene in which Burdett was
teaching his son to translate Magna Charta. Imprisonment being a valuable qualification for Radicalism in
those days, Burdett was thenceforth safe for Westminster,
though an official Whig like Romilly or George Lamb
occasionally contrived to share the representation. As
for Hobhouse, he was a more pertinacious debater than
Burdett, whom wealth—for he had married a Miss Coutts
—made lazy, and who was apt to weary of dividing in
hopeless minorities. He, too, contrived to get into
prison, since he was committed to Newgate in 1819 for a
pamphlet, entitled " A Trifling Mistake." Mr. Graham
Wallas, in his "Life of Francis Place," produces evidence
however, to the effect that the most violent passage,
which it is difficult to construe otherwise than as an
appeal to force, was written, not by Hobhouse, but by
that pragmatic tailor.

If Westminster had never carried its " Liberty candidates " at election after election, and if Place had not
been behind Burdett and Hobhouse to stiffen their
flagging energies, the Whigs might have delayed a
generation or two before they embraced Parliamentary
Reform. Even when the Grey Administration was
formed no room was made in it for the two members
for Westminster, though a curious passage in Hobhouse's

" Recollections of a Long Life" implies that their claims
were considered. However, they played vigorous parts
in the first Reform campaign both inside the House and
out of doors. The Bill once carried, Burdett rested and
was thankful. Westminster grew tired of him, and the
beginning of Queen Victoria's reign found him a supporter of the Conservative Opposition. He could boast
in all sincerity that he had never been a Whig. That
fate was reserved for Hobhouse, who, appointed Secretary
at War in 1832, held various offices without much distinction, and became, in the eyes of an indignant Radical
like Place, " live lumber." When, in 1852, he finally
retired, he had become one of the most Conservative
members of Lord John Russell's Cabinet, and, as Lord
Broughton de Gyfford, had departed from the democratic
ideas he had advocated when " Burdett and Hobhouse
for Westminster" was the cry.

CHAPTER XXI

TORIES AT HOLLAND HOUSE

Wilberforce and Lord Eldon—Lord Stowell—A great character
—Stowell's penurious habits—As Judge of the Admiralty Court—
Lord Aberdeen—His relations with Pitt and Dundas—"Athenian
Aberdeen"—His varied attainments—As envoy abroad—Aberdeen
and Greece—His domestic afflictions.

TORY politicians of the orthodox kind were scarce
birds at Holland House. Wilberforce found
himself there in 1819, and described Lord
Holland in his diary "as truly fascinating, having something of his uncle's good-humour." A more unexpected
guest still was Lord Eldon, who owned to surprised
amusement at his surroundings. He dined at Holland
House in 1822 and reported to his daughter, Lady
Frances Bankes, that he had met Lord Grey, Lord
Lauderdale, and several of the Opposition ; had enjoyed
a good and pleasant party, and had never seen a house
that he thought better worth seeing.

Lord Eldon's brother, Lord Stowell, though a Tory in
politics, moved freely in Whig circles. He is the Sir
W. Scott whom Moore frequently mentions in his
journal as dining at Holland House and other Opposition
resorts. He also kept up a correspondence, character-

ised on his side by courtly archness, with a great Whig lady, the Duchess of Somerset. " He was one of the pleasantest men I ever knew," wrote Sir Walter Scott, when he met Lord Stowell in 1828, frail and even comatose. But then the son of the Newcastle publican and coal-shipper had moved in the best society of his time. At Oxford he formed an intimate friendship with Dr. Johnson, who made him one of his executors, and about whom he supplied much personal information to Croker for his unduly maligned edition of Boswell. He was equally at home with the learned and the frivolous, and could carry his two bottles of port discreetly. " My brother," said Lord Eldon, who was much attached to him, " will drink any *given* quantity of wine," the allusion being to Lord Stowell's penurious habits. He also liked strong meats, and Canning once detected him driving down to his country house with a turtle in the carriage. "Was it not your son who was with you the other day ? " innocently inquired Canning when they next met. Beef-steak pie with layers of oysters was his favourite dish.

Altogether Lord Stowell was a great character, slovenly in his dress, dirty as to his hands, but polished in his manners. By no means an ideal husband for a dowager Marchioness, his second marriage with Lady Sligo, whose acquaintance he made through trying her son for enticing two seamen from the Royal Navy on to his yacht, proved inharmonious. He was grasping ; she openhanded. He could seldom be induced to dine at home or to keep reasonable hours ; she disliked dining out. The ill-assorted union, which Lady Sligo's death ended in little more than four years, occasioned one of the most searching of Jekyll's puns. When Sir William

Scott, as he then was, removed from Doctors' Commons to his wife's house in Grafton Street, he brought with him, in his frugal way, his own door-plate, and placed it under hers. Jekyll condoled with him on having to "knock under." Sir William promptly ordered the plates to be transposed. A few days later he said to Jekyll, "You see, I don't 'knock under' now." "Not now," was the answer received by the antiquated bridegroom, "now you 'knock up.'" His parsimony extended even to his sight-seeing. He visited every show in London which could be entered for a shilling or less; and was once admitted free because the money-taker, an honest North-country lad, confessed to him that the "green monster serpent" of the invitation cards was the old serpent which he had seen six times before in other colours.

As a politician Sir William Scott suffered from the same weakness as his brother : he "doubted." Though he represented Oxford University for twenty years, he did little more than obstruct Romilly's legal reforms. The clergy, however, regarded him as a safe representative of their interests, and his Residence Bill abolished a crying ecclesiastical scandal, none too soon. As Judge of the Admiralty Court he acquired a unique reputation. He found maritime law in a state of uncertainty and with no published records; he left it clear and consistent. Brougham, in his "Statesmen of the Time of George III.," warmly praises the learning, graces, and reasoning powers which Lord Stowell brought to the Bench. "If ever the praise of being luminous could be bestowed on human composition," he adds, "it was upon his judgments, and it was the approbation constantly, and as it were peculiarly, appropriated by those wonderful exhibitions of judicial capacity."

Another steady Tory who frequented Holland House was Lord Aberdeen, the future Prime Minister—a Tory, perhaps, rather by upbringing than inclination. When a boy at Harrow he escaped from the neglectful guardianship of a harsh old grandfather by availing himself of the Scotch law and appointing Dundas and Pitt as his curators, living alternately with both. He was thus educated in the centre of the Tory party; and, being by nature diffident, he submitted during his early manhood to the political tutelage of politicians so circumscribed as Lord Liverpool and Lord Bathurst, the latter a typical product of the "pigtail" school. Lord Stanmore's admirable little biography of his father throws a pleasant light on his relationship with Pitt. The intercession of the curators wrung from old Lord Aberdeen consent to his grandson's matriculation at St. John's College, Cambridge, Pitt tersely informing him that he "did not concur with his lordship in considering that rank superseded the necessity for education." Even after his marriage with Lady Catherine Hamilton the young peer lived in Dundas's villa at Wimbledon, hard by Pitt's residence at Bowling Green House, Putney, and he was one of the first to receive the news of the Prime Minister's death. "I have lost," he wrote, "the only friend to whom I looked up with unbounded hope and devotion."

By 1806 Lord Aberdeen had grown into a studious, cultivated, and modest young man. At Harrow he became a sound Greek scholar, and had read the Italian poets and modern history. Cambridge made him, in addition, an accomplished Latinist and a follower of the by-paths of literature, especially that of the Renaissance. How many undergraduates of the present day, asks Lord Stanmore, have read or heard of Vida, the fifteenth-century author of the "Christiad"? Lord Aberdeen knew his works, and those of Sannazarius and Frascatorius. But it was as "the travelled thane, Athenian Aberdeen," that he appeared in "English Bards and Scotch Reviewers" as "first of the oat-fed phalanx." The title was earned him by two years' journeyings in the Levant, during which he excavated the Pnyx, or ancient meeting-place, at Athens, and visited sites, then almost unknown, of dead cities in Greece and Asia Minor. Lord Stanmore informs us that he made careful copies of inscriptions which have since disappeared. His criticism of Gell's "Topography of Troy" in the *Edinburgh Review*, and still more his "Inquiry into the Principles of Beauty in Grecian Architecture," originally written as a preface to an edition of Vitruvius, prove him to have been a discerning antiquary, though modern research has rendered obsolete many of his conclusions.

Lady Granville, on meeting Lord Aberdeen in 1813, wrote to her sister, Lady Morpeth, "I acknowledge he looks beautiful, and there is something in the quiet enthusiasm of his manner and the total absence of frivolity in his mind and tastes as uncommon as it is captivating." The cast of his features in later life was one of dignified sternness rather than of beauty. But Lady Granville was right in pointing out a seriousness of taste as a distinguishing characteristic of Lord Aberdeen. As a connoisseur of art and antiquary his voice carried weight with his fellow-trustees of the National Gallery and British Museum. By extensive planting he converted his estate at Haddo, which he began by disliking, from a barren wilderness to a well-wooded domain, and the visit of a botanical friend revealed him as learned in plants and mosses. "Nothing," writes his son, "could be more curious than the way in which colleagues and friends, whenever at a loss, came to him for information on the most varied topics, and rarely came in vain. But while ever ready, without any apparent disinclination, to communicate to others the knowledge he possessed, his habitual attitude was one of reticence." A memory stored with art and history caused him to be welcome both at Holland House and Bowood; while at Stanmore Priory, the home of his father-in-law, the Marquis of Abercorn, the Sheridans, Sir Walter Scott, Lawrence, Kemble, and Payne Knight were familiar guests.

Lord Aberdeen carried his stock of quiet enthusiasm into public life. Despatched to Vienna in the spring of 1813, a moment of supreme importance, he succeeded in gaining the complete confidence of the Austrian Emperor and Metternich, no less than of the Russian Minister, Nesselrode; and when the Allies reached the Rhine his influence as representative of England prevented mutual jealousies from blazing forth. Thus he was duly appointed the chief British negotiator at the Congress of Châtillon, when Napoleon, if he had not been too exorbitant in his demands, might have preserved his Empire; and when the restoration of the Bourbons had been decided, he put his hand to the general treaty of peace. But he wisely observed that Louis XVII. had no root and might be upset at any time, though the leverage did not prove to be, as he anticipated, that of a republic. Later on, he allowed himself to be dissuaded by his Tory friends from advocating the cause of Hellenic independence at public meetings. But he was a true friend to the Greeks, and after he had declined a seat in Canning's Cabinet, it fell to him, as Foreign Secretary in the Duke of Wellington's Administration, to deal with their case as complicated by the hostilities begun by Russia against the Porte.

Aberdeen has been accused of crippling the resources of the new kingdom and limiting its extent. But, in the first place, he had to reckon with colleagues who were strongly pro-Turkish; and, in the second, the campaign had disclosed such military weakness in the Ottoman Empire that a big Greece was likely to become a Russian satrapy. Lord Aberdeen instinctively played for safety, both when he averted the disintegration of the Porte and when he declined to intermeddle in the internal affairs of Portugal. His caution brought him into sharp collision with his Whig friends, and particularly with Lord Holland, but he maintained that a showy policy was not necessarily a sound one. Before he went out of office he recognised Louis Philippe as King of the French, and so paved the way for the excellent understanding between the two Courts that prevailed when he became Foreign Secretary for the second time.

Here we must take leave of Lord Aberdeen, with the parting remark that he was the most misunderstood and most undervalued statesman in nineteenth-century politics. His domestic afflictions helped to obscure his talents. For the loss of his first wife, whom he worshipped, he found consolation in a second, the widow of his brother-in-law, Lord Hamilton, though it may be inferred from Lord Stanmore's book that the marriage was rather a matter of arrangement by others than of his own choice. But he became a sad and lonely man after his first family, girls of remarkable beauty, died in rapid succession; and after the second Lady Aberdeen, too, died in 1833, he made but rare appearances in London drawing-rooms. Directly public business permitted it, he sought refuge at Haddo, where he lived in stern patriarchal simplicity, with duties assigned to every hour of the day.

CHAPTER XXII

THE CANNINGITES, PALMERSTON, AND MELBOURNE

The friends of Canning—Palmerston—His slow advance—Palmerston in society—As Foreign Secretary—His marriage—The Syrian crisis—Palmerston's triumph—William Lamb, Lord Melbourne—His marriage—Lamb as a student—A detached politician—As a Canningite—Home Secretary—Lord Melbourne's Premierships—His unconventionality—His character.

THE greater part of the politicians other than Whigs who frequented Holland House belonged to the band over which Canning cast his spell. They all had ability, with the possible exception of Charles Grant, subsequently Lord Glenelg, a worthy, pious man who discussed theology with Rogers, but who, as Grey's Colonial Secretary, was totally unequal to contending with Brougham in debate, and left the mark of his irresolution on the history of Canada and South Africa. Most of them, like Lord Palmerston and Lord Dudley, were Tories who rebelled against the *quieta non movere* principles of Lord Eldon and Lord Bathurst. A few, like Lord Melbourne, were Whigs who recoiled from the unpatriotic extravagance of Whitbread. Enthusiasts for Catholic Emancipation, the Canningites were no believers in Parliamentary Reform, and they joined the Ministry of 1830 reluctantly and of necessity. But the tie was to a considerable extent personal; they were dazzled by the versatile brilliance of their chief, and even submitted to being disbanded by him when it so suited his purpose. The Grenville, Charles Wynn grumbled thus: "Canning always likes to have young men about him who will wonder at and admire him, and they would be flattered at being asked to meet him." Their hero-worship, though it may have been overstrained, was sincere, and fidelity to his memory kept the little band together after his death, until it became absorbed into Whiggism, though they never felt quite at home in that exclusive organisation.

The ablest of the Canningites, Lord Palmerston, retained his leader's principles to the end of his days. He accepted Parliamentary Reform as a disagreeable necessity, and in his later years adroitly thwarted any further instalments of it; he advocated reciprocity rather than freedom of trade; above all, he followed the cardinal point of Canning's system, that is the opposition, under the ægis of England, of Powers with free institutions to despotic Governments like Austria, Prussia, and Russia. Unlike Canning in one respect, he ripened slowly. As Dugald Stewart's pupil at Edinburgh, where he laid "the foundation for whatever useful knowledge and habits of mind" he possessed, and at St. John's College, Cambridge, he gained a character for industry. But for nearly twenty years he was content with the post of Secretary at War in successive Tory Administrations, an office concerned chiefly with finance and not carrying with it a seat in the Cabinet. He refused the Chancellorship of the Exchequer when it was offered him by

Perceval, and the Governor-Generalship of India twice from the hands of Lord Liverpool.

Palmerston was unknown, except as a conscientious departmental administrator, until, in 1828, the Canningites retired from the Wellington Ministry. His interests lay rather in his racing-stable, in country pursuits, and his Irish and English estates, and at Almack's, where he was known as "Cupid" and a great lady-killer, and where, on the introduction of the waltz, he could be seen dancing with Madame de Lieven. Though without any literary instincts, he had a smattering of science, and the squibs he wrote for the Tory papers, in conjunction with Croker and others, mostly parodies of Byron, are tolerable specimens of rough-and-ready political wit. They were collected in a slim volume entitled "The New Whig Guide," and the curious can find in it the origins of some of Creevey's nicknames.

In Opposition, Palmerston found his opportunity, and made comprehensive attacks on the foreign policy of Lord Aberdeen. The two were marked out for rivalry; the former being experimental beyond the verge of rashness, the latter cautious up to the edge of timidity. Palmerston's speeches were oratorical successes ; and, when Lord Grey formed his Administration, he was an acceptable Foreign Secretary. He held the appointment for eleven years, except for the four months of Peel's first Premiership. Lord Grey appears to have exercised some control over him ; Lord Melbourne but little. Virtually Palmerston went his own way, and the creation of the kingdom of Belgium, independent of Holland and yet not subservient to France, was a striking example of his diplomatic skill, even if his various devices for supporting constitutionalism in Spain and Portugal, notably the despatch of the British Legion, were too clever to be dignified.

Palmerston's faults were chiefly those of manner. He treated the representatives of foreign Courts, even a veteran like Talleyrand, too much as if they were fellow-sportsmen in the hunting-field. His despatches, too, often substituted bluster for reasoned argument, and encouraged his subordinates, Sir Henry Bulwer, for example, and Lord Ponsonby, to ruffle it in season and out of season. British meddling in the internal affairs of the smaller States passed all bounds; the Prime Minister was expected to be our creature, and as a natural consequence the leader of the Opposition received direction from France. Still, the ablest of British diplomatists, Lord Granville for one, believed in Palmerston; and Greville, who regarded him with a malignant eye, was forced to the conclusion that when he took his pen in hand his intellect seemed to have full play.

In 1839 Lord Palmerston entered the Whig cousinship through his marriage with Lord Melbourne's sister, the widow of Earl Cowper, who had long been his Egeria. Lady Granville thought that foreign affairs would in consequence be more "come-at-able" than they had been for some time, and that Lord Palmerston's incivilities would obtain a varnish. The prophecy was for the moment none too fortunate; for within a few months his Quadrilateral Treaty, by which England, Russia, Austria, and Prussia agreed with the Porte to combine in expelling the Egyptians from Syria, brought this country to the brink of war with France, whose sympathies were strongly with Mehemet Ali. Here again Palmerston gauged the situation with a penetrating eye. The Government of Louis Philippe aimed at establishing Egypt in the Mediterranean as a second-rate Power under French control, whose fleet might help to destroy our maritime preponderance. He also took the exact measure of the King of the French, who, after preparations for war had been hurried on, suddenly flinched, dismissed his bellicose Premier Thiers, and appointed instead the pacific Guizot, who was re-called for that purpose from the London Embassy. The dash of the Allied Fleet, and more particularly of Commodore Napier, who bombarded the Egyptians out of Sidon and Acre, did the rest.

Palmerston cannot be altogether acquitted, however, of needlessly offending French *amour propre* and of refusing concessions on points of form to Guizot which would have brought about a renewal of friendly relations. The pages of Greville, who throughout the crisis was fetching and carrying news for the French Embassy with unwarrantable zeal, give a lively picture of the perplexities into which the Melbourne Cabinet was thrown by Palmerston's dashing game. Traditional Whiggism, with its French leanings, was arrayed against Canningite confidence in the mission of England.

When Lord Holland attacked the management of the Syrian question, Palmerston completely nonplussed him by producing a letter of warning from Sir Henry Bulwer, the *chargé d'affaires* in Paris, proving that his intention of so doing was already known in the French capital. The bow, as we have already seen, was not drawn at a venture. But "Bear" Ellice and Greville were the chief newsmongers who kept the French Embassy primed with stories of Ministerial dissensions. Within

VISCOUNT MELBOURNE
FROM THE PAINTING BY JOHN PARTRIDGE IN THE NATIONAL PORTRAIT GALLERY

a few days of the trial of strength in the Cabinet Lord Holland died, and Palmerston hastened to acknowledge that though he "felt, or rather thought, strongly on public affairs, he never mixed any personal feeling with his private differences." The Palmerstons, indeed, dined frequently at Holland House during the crisis, and there, on one occasion, Greville busied himself with trying to pick Lady Palmerston's brains. He considered the conversation of importance as showing the state of her husband's mind. We may be sure, however, that she told him just as much and just as little as it was good for him to know.

Lord Melbourne resembled Lord Palmerston, with whom in other respects he had little in common, in that he was slow in coming to the front. Until he was nearly fifty he was known as a man of fashion, with literary tastes, who had not accomplished what his friends expected of him. William Lamb, after breaking a poetic lance with the *Anti-Jacobin*, a contest in which he was signally worsted, had made good the defects of Eton and Trinity College, Cambridge, by studying at Glasgow under Professor Millar. The letters he sent thence to his clever mother are priggish in tone and give little indication of future ability. The death of his elder brother in 1804, when he was reading for the Bar, changed the course of his life. In the following year he was returned for Leominster, and in June he married Lady Caroline Ponsonby. His journal shows him to have paid close attention to politics, but he had made but little mark when, at the General Election of 1812, he fell a victim to the "No Popery" cry, and for four years was absent from Parliament.

During those years occurred the crisis of his domestic life. An easy-going husband and a flighty wife never make a well-assorted couple, and in the Lambs' case their only child, who might have brought them together, was an additional source of unhappiness, since his intellect never developed. "By marrying," commented William Lamb in his commonplace book, "you place yourself upon the defensive instead of the offensive in society, which latter is admitted to be in all contentions the most advantageous mode of proceeding." Still, they seem to have been fairly happy together until Byron came into contact with Lady Caroline's irregular orbit. Enough has already been said of her share in that unhappy story. Her husband's conduct was stigmatised by Greville at the time of his death as "good-natured, eccentric, and not nice." As a matter of fact, he seems to have behaved with much consideration to an elfish being whom it was difficult to regard as responsible, and delayed separation from Lady Caroline until her reason finally gave way.

Lamb turned for consolation to letters, and it was during this period of his life that he accumulated those stores of learning which in after years lent attractiveness to his conversation. His commonplace book shows that his reading ranged freely over the classics and English historians like Clarendon and Burnet; he was versed in patristic theology, a philologist, and a grammarian. He also set down reflections in a cynical vein, which only needed terseness to be genuine contributions to whimsical philosophy.

When Lamb lost his seat, Brougham wrote to Lord Grey that he was as much of a Canningite as J. W. Ward (Lord Dudley), and that his defeat was not to be regretted.

They both had a weakness for "little prize essays of speeches, got up and polished, and useless, quite useless, for affairs." He returned to the House a very detached politician, though still nominally a Whig, who supported the Six Acts and other coercive measures of the Tory Government, approved of Catholic Emancipation, but resisted Parliamentary Reform, which he anticipated would result in the total destruction of freedom of speech. His chance of distinguishing himself came when he was appointed Irish Secretary in the Canning Government, and an efficient Minister he made.

Lamb stuck to his party after their leader's death, though he was the only member of the Whig connection that did so, and resigned with them shortly after the formation of the Wellington Administration because "he had always thought it more necessary to stand by his friends when they were in the wrong than when in the right." Together with the rest of the Canningites, he swallowed his objections to Reform, in his case very strong objections, and became Home Secretary under Lord Grey.

Greville, who at first ridiculed Melbourne as too idle, soon discovered that he had "surprised all about him by a sudden display of activity and vigour, rapid and diligent transaction of business, for which nobody was prepared." He was, in fact, the strong man of the Government, and coped manfully with the violence of trade unionism in the North and rick-burning in the South, while as the Minister responsible to Parliament for Irish affairs he had to deal with an agrarian agitation combined with the new movement for Repeal. His firmness made him most acceptable to William IV.; and, Lord Lansdowne being unwilling, his colleagues were not surprised when

the choice fell upon him as Prime Minister in succession
to Lord Grey. Very characteristic was his saying to his
private secretary, Tom Young, that "he thought it a
damned bore, and that he was in many minds what
he would do—be Minister or no." There came the
unanswerable reply: "Why, damn it, such a position was
never occupied by any Greek or Roman, and, if it only
lasts two months, it is worth while to have been Prime
Minister of England."

Lord Melbourne's two Premierships must be briefly
dismissed. His first lasted, not two months, but four.
The Government was weak when formed; it was still
further discredited by Brougham's vagaries in the North,
and his wrangling on public platforms with Lord
Durham. Disgusted with this and other squabbles, the
Prime Minister practically played into the King's hands
when Lord Althorp's elevation to the Upper House
necessitated a reconstruction of the Ministry, and its
dismissal was far more of a voluntary retirement than an
autocratic ejection on the part of the Sovereign. When
he returned to office, he purged the Ministry of Brougham
and Durham with a decision which proves him to have
been far removed from the *poco curante* figurehead that
he is sometimes represented to have been. But the
Government of 1835 was discredited in English eyes
because it could not dispense with the capricious support
of O'Connell. It had to reckon from the first with the
rooted hostility of the King and with the Tory majority
of the House of Lords, which freely mutilated or rejected
its measures.

The succession of Queen Victoria gave the Government
strength collectively, and to the Prime Minister a new
object in life, because a General Election sanctioned him

and his colleagues as the guardians of their youthful Sovereign. Soon afterwards, however, Brougham's resentment found a convenient target in the Durham mission to Canada, and the Prime Minister, kept in the dark on many points by the haughty High Commissioner, had to make what headway he could against an orator of superior powers to his own. During the Syrian crisis his main idea was to keep his rickety Cabinet together, and the accusations of vacillation brought against him by Greville are not supported by his published correspondence. He may have clung to office too long, but there again he evidently felt that his first duty was to the Queen, and that it would be unkind to desert her until her misunderstandings with Peel had been removed.

Lord Melbourne and Mr. Gladstone are, in all probability, the only two Prime Ministers who have found time to keep themselves posted in new publications during their terms of office. Even under the stress of his Home Secretaryship the former was investigating early dramatic literature, and asked the Principal Librarian of the British Museum for out-of-the-way works like Rainold's "Overthrow of Stage Plays" and Heywood's "Apology for Actors." The passages already given from Greville illustrate the uses to which he put this learning, so persistently acquired. Lord Melbourne was thoroughly at home at Holland House, whither he had constant recourse for political advice, and where he was allowed to lounge and, presumably, to "damn" as he pleased. But, for that matter, his disregard of convention was not to be restrained even at Windsor Castle. "He was often paradoxical," writes Greville, "and often coarse, terse, epigrammatic, acute, droll, with fits of silence and abstraction, from which he would break out with a vehemence and vigour which amused those who were accustomed to him, and filled with indescribable astonishment those who were not." A hearty laugh, with ejaculations of "Eh! eh!" interposed at every burst, and a rubbing of the hands together were tricks of his. At the same time he was easily moved by the expression of a fine sentiment, and seldom mentioned the Queen's name without tears in his eyes.

Melbourne's was really a far more sensitive nature than Greville admits in an otherwise discriminating character; that nature, though essentially open, had been sorely tried by circumstance, and had grown to conceal itself under a mask of reckless indifference. Thus he loved to put off the philanthropic by describing himself as "not a subscribing sort of fellow," and to scandalise artists by declaring that Raphael had been employed to decorate the Vatican, not because he was a great painter, but because his uncle, Bramante, was architect to the Pope. It was at Holland House that he staggered Moore by saying: "I see there is a new edition of Crabbe coming out; it is a good thing when these authors die, for then one gets their works and has done with them." At Holland House, too, he enunciated the proposition that he would rather have men about him when he was ill; it required very strong health to put up with women. "Oh," said Lady Holland, tapping him with her fan, "you have lived among such a rantipole set"—which, by all accounts, was true enough.

CHAPTER XXIII

OTHER COLLEAGUES OF CANNING

Melbourne's advice to Dudley—Dudley as Foreign Secretary—
"Ivy" and Bishop Copleston—Dudley's friendships—His conversation—His relations with Holland House—George Ellis—"The
Rolliad" and the *Anti-Jacobin*—Ellis's friendships—The sixth
Earl of Carlisle—Lord Lyndhurst—A lawyer-politician—"For
'views' read 'prospects'"—Lyndhurst's hospitality—His conversion
to Toryism—Scarlett, Lord Abinger—Scarlett and the Whigs—*Qui
s'excuse*—"Not at Home."

L ORD MELBOURNE was an intimate friend of John
William Ward, Lord Dudley, the most brilliant
intellectually of all the Canningites. When Ward
was offered the Under-Secretaryship for Foreign Affairs
in 1822, he consulted William Lamb, who advised him
to take it, while warning him that he would have to bear
every species of malice and misrepresentation and the
imputation of the most sordid and interested motives.
After painful vacillation Ward declined the appointment,
partly because it was "a completely subordinate situation." Yet office under Canning might possibly have
arrested, through the medicine of hard work, the torpor
that was even then creeping over that over-sensitive
brain.

Five years later, when he became Secretary for

Foreign Affairs in Canning's Administration, it was too late. So long as the Prime Minister lived, all went well, since Canning kept our dealings with Portugal and the Porte under his personal control. But after he died Lord Dudley, left to his own resources, failed to grapple with the perplexing situation created by the usurpation of Dom Miguel and the Battle of Navarino. His chief exploit, if the story is true, was to enclose letters intended for the French and Russian Ambassadors in the wrong envelopes. Prince Lieven returned his with a polite note saying that of course he had not read a word of it, and with suppressed but profound admiration for a Foreign Minister who could set so dexterous a trap. But the Duke of Wellington, when he became Prime Minister, discovered that Lord Dudley's slowness in writing despatches and preparing his speeches disabled him from coping with the current business of the office, and Lord Aberdeen was associated with him as "co-adjutor *de jure successionis.* Within a few weeks the Canningites were out, after Dudley had been painfully divided between his duties to his colleagues and the King. " He would willingly," wrote Palmerston in his diary, " have given £6,000 a year out of his own pocket, instead of receiving that sum from the public, for the pleasure of continuing to be Secretary of State for Foreign Affairs."

A stay at the Foreign Office lasting for little more than a year, some speeches more polished than practical, and some articles of varying merits in the *Quarterly Review* are the sum of Lord Dudley's achievement. Yet at the outset of his career the world seemed at his feet. He was rich, highly educated, and original. Unhappily, he had grown up, at the same time, a hothouse plant, his mind forced at the expense of his body by tutor after tutor, to whose charge his thoughtless and free-living parents committed him. It was not until he was placed under the care of Dugald Stewart in Edinburgh that he had a real home, and found in Mrs. Stewart, the "Ivy" of the letters given to the world in 1905 by Mr. S. H. Romilly, a gifted companion whom he worshipped with an affection half filial and half romantic. Oriel College, Oxford, followed in 1799, and there he formed a friendship with his tutor, Copleston, afterwards Bishop of Llandaff, but not of such an intimate character.

Lord Dudley's correspondence with the Bishop, published by the latter in 1840, was characterised by Greville at the time of its appearance as artificial, and it is, no doubt, the composition of a pupil writing to a literary superior, and never quite at his ease. To Mrs. Dugald Stewart he poured out his whole soul, and, though gaps occur in the correspondence, he appears, almost to the last, as a playfully amiable, modest, and simple gentleman. His friendships, too, were numerous, and, in addition to Canning and other politicians of his way of thinking, included Whigs like Brougham and Sydney Smith and Rogers, except when the thrust of the review was met by the parry of the epigram. Though he lived carefully and looked after his affairs, he was liberal in entertainment. "Those who did not dine with him," wrote a friendly hand in the *Quarterly Review*, "asserted that his days were spent in writing dinner invitations." From the same authority it may be gathered that, though he never married, he "was always in a sort of love; and when he did set his Platonic affections on other men's wives, he never did so by halves. It was difficult to determine whether he admired them or their husbands the most."

From fits of intense dejection, which culminated in insanity, Lord Dudley sought refuge in travel, though he took but little interest in art and was signally insensible to natural beauties. He stood with Sir Henry Holland on the roof of Milan Cathedral without a single phrase of admiration for the wonderful view. But he studied city-living mankind, whether London or Vienna was the place, with an observant eye, and no better summary exists of the results of the French Revolution, good as well as bad, than is to be found in his letters to the Bishop of Llandaff. In society he had tricks of abstraction and of muttering to himself in two voices, one gruff, the other shrill, which latterly became disconcerting to his friends, and the sources of ill-natured stories spread abroad by the unthinking. He is the Lord Dallas of "Glenarvon," described by Lady Caroline Lamb as

"diminutive and conceited, had a brilliant wit; spoke seldom and studied deeply every sentence he uttered. He affected to be absent, but in fact no one ever forgot himself so seldom. His voice, untuned and harsh, repeated with a forced emphasis certain jests and *bons mots* which had been previously made and adapted for certain conversations."

This is, of course, a gross caricature of a man praised by Madame de Staël as the only true cultivator of the art of conversation in England. Withal, there does seem to have been a certain artificiality about Lord Dudley's talk. Moore complained of it, and Creevey declared that he could be put down by the more nimble wit of Jekyll. He dealt sometimes in direct personal sarcasm, as in his reply to Rogers, who was quoting the lines :

> " The robin, with his furtive glance,
>   Comes and looks at me askance."

" If it had been a carrion crow," said Dudley, " he would have looked you full in the face." Then there is his crushing retort to the Viennese lady who complained of the wretched French spoken in London : " It is true, madame, but we have not had the advantage of having the French twice in our capital." He could, however, be gay enough. Thus, as befitted an accomplished scholar who preferred an old classic to a new publication, he answered, when asked if he had read one of Scott's novels, " I am ashamed to say I have not, but I am in hopes that it will soon blow over." All the same, he criticised current authorship with point.

Lord Dudley's association with Lord and Lady Holland was not altogether harmonious. He seems to have accompanied them in 1808 on part of their journey through Spain. But she was to him a feminine Dr. Fell, and some scornful remarks on her character and past, confided to " Ivy " as they were waiting to start at Falmouth, did not argue well for the peace of the expedition. Eventually—about the year 1812 it would seem—a downright breach occurred, because, as has been already mentioned, Lord Dudley could not put up with Lady Holland's dictation. The quarrel endured until 1832, when, as his mind was fast giving way, the town was astonished to hear that he had

called at Holland House; that a reconciliation dinner
was to be given, to include Luttrell, against whom he
also bore a grudge, and that the Duke of Wellington
and Lord Lyndhurst were invited to meet the party.
The odd assortment did not take place because, when
the guests arrived, they found that their host was too
ill to receive them, an incident improved by Croker into
a statement that he was dining elsewhere. Two days
afterwards Sir Henry Halford placed him under restraint, and the world knew no more of a gifted and
unhappy man.

While Lord Dudley held the reputation of one of the
acutest talkers of the day, his friend, and Canning's
friend, George Ellis, was confused and unintelligible
in conversation. He is not the only man of letters who
has found the pen a readier instrument than the tongue.
In the House of Commons Ellis sat silent during the
Parliament of 1796 as junior member for Seaford, with
his cousin Charles Ellis, afterwards Lord Dover, another
frequenter of Holland House, as his colleague in the
representation of that small borough. He also accompanied Lord Malmesbury on some of his diplomatic mis-
sions, and when he took part in that to Lille, William
Lamb satirised his "sapient prominence of nose."
Ellis could afford to take the joke in good part, since he
had a hand in "The Rolliad," which scarified the Tories,
and, after he had cut himself clear of Whiggism, in the
Anti-Jacobin, which threw ridicule on Fox and the Duke
of Bedford. To the former he contributed the burlesque
heraldry of the introduction and the fierce attack on
Pitt, beginning, "Pert without fire, without experience
sage"; in the latter he played a worthy third to Frere
and Canning.

But Ellis is chiefly remembered, perhaps, as an attached friend of the great. Canning delighted in his society, and his papers may one of these days disclose the extent to which he leant on Ellis for advice. In 1801 came another important intimacy, for in that year he met Sir Walter Scott. They had tastes in common, besides being fellow-contributors to the *Quarterly*. Ellis showed himself, by his "Specimens of the Early English Poets" and "Specimens of Early English Romances in Metre," to be a discriminating cultivator of the fields to which Sir Walter first turned his attention. Their correspondence, as published in Lockhart's "Life of Scott," abounds in critical discussion, and the majority would probably agree with Ellis when he pronounced against an unexpurgated edition of Dryden, with the proviso that if omissions must be made they should only affect the passages in which the poet became dull. Scott, by the way, declared Ellis to be the best converser he had ever known, in flat contradiction to the general opinion. The explanation may possibly be that he did himself justice in a *tête-à-tête*, but was unequal to contending in a general *mêlée* of wits.

George, sixth Earl of Carlisle, was an amiable Whig who entered Canning's Cabinet as First Commissioner of Woods and Forests, and subsequently became Lord Privy Seal under Lord Grey. He was the son of the better-known Lord Carlisle who, in his youth, unwisely became responsible for Fox's gambling debts, and had in consequence to intern himself at Castle Howard, and whose "paralytic puling" was attacked by Byron in "English Bards and Scotch Reviewers," because of his neglect to take any trouble in introducing his ward to the House of Lords. The sixth earl had an earlier period of Toryism, since he was, as Lord Morpeth, a contributor to the *Anti-Jacobin*, turning his attention to Citizen Muskein, and a hearty supporter of the Union. A wavering politician, he performed the duties of friendship in admirable taste when he paid an affecting tribute to the memory of Francis Horner; while Lady Granville's correspondence with her sister, his Countess, gives glimpses of a pleasant home-life. His son was the Lord Morpeth who distinguished himself as Irish Secretary in Lord Melbourne's second Administration—the most successful, perhaps, among the many occupants of that difficult post.

Lyndhurst, Canning's Lord Chancellor, and Scarlett, his Attorney-General, began as Liberals and ended as Tories. The former incurred, during the early years of his public career, the bitter reproaches of his political opponents as an apostate from Whig principles. Lord Campbell, in the " Lives of the Chancellors," elaborated the charge in the elongated libel which purports to be a biography of Lord Lyndhurst. In reality he was a detached lawyer-politician who, throughout his life, argued to his brief. As the son of the American painter, Copley, he could claim no hereditary connection with either of the English political parties. In his early days at the Bar he may have aired democratic sentiments on the Midland Circuit, and he seems to have attended Radical debating clubs. If, as advocate, he identified himself with extreme opinions one month, by defending Watson, one of the ringleaders in the Spa Fields riots, he was ready the next to accept a retainer from the Crown to prosecute Brandreth, the leader of the pitiful stocking-maker's rising.

When Serjeant Copley entered the House of Com-

mons as member for the Treasury borough of Yarmouth, Isle of Wight, in 1818, he evidently looked on
Parliament as a means of pushing his fortune at the Bar.
Politics were with him a matter of business; and to that
extent there is force in Mackintosh's emendation when
he exculpated himself from the charge of inconsistency
on the ground that "he had seen nothing in the views,
the policy, or the conduct of the gentlemen opposite to
induce him, as a true friend of the Constitution, to
join them." "For 'views' read 'prospects,'" whispered
Mackintosh to Lord John Russell. The Attorney-
Generalship, in 1824, and the Mastership of the Rolls,
two years later, were successive steps on the ladder of
promotion ; and he accepted the Chancellorship from
Canning, though only a few weeks before he had been
castigated by that emotional statesman for a declaration
against the Catholic claims.

Holland House probably saw most of Lord Lyndhurst during his first Chancellorship. Essentially broad-
minded in the disposal of his patronage, he appointed
Sydney Smith to a prebendal stall in Bristol Cathedral.
His private friends included quite as many Whigs as
Tories ; Brougham was among them, and Earl Grey, and
even the Radical Burdett. Lord Lyndhurst was essentially a society man, delighting in dining and being dined,
in driving a cabriolet, to the scandal of Lord Eldon,
and in dressing like a cavalry officer, to the scandal of
the stricter Bar. His wife, the widow of a colonel in
the Guards, has come down to us as one of the most
handsome of Lawrence's matrons. She recruited her
drawing-room in George Street from many sources
besides the legal profession, and the generous profusion
of Lord Lyndhurst's *régime* stood in the strongest con-

trast with the thrift of Lord Eldon's. The pair lived up to the Lord Chancellor's salary of £14,000 a year, and possibly beyond it. They migrated to Paris for the winter, and there mixed with politicians and diplomatists, going frequently to the British Embassy. It was in Paris that Lady Lyndhurst died in 1834. She had been her husband's best adviser, and no small portion of his political success was due to her social influence.

By the time of his wife's death Lord Lyndhurst had become definitely associated with Tory politics. The Act of Reform had created a dividing line which he was never to recross. But up to that date he had been regarded as a politician who might join either side without much loss of character—another way of saying that he had not much character to lose. While Peel never lived down his conversion to the cause of Catholic Emancipation, nobody thought much the worse of Lyndhurst for his change of front, though it was equally abrupt and far less sincere. In the last days of the Wellington Ministry he laboured to bring Lord Grey into the Government, and approximated success. When the Whigs came to their own it seemed quite likely that he would be retained as Chancellor, but a demonstration from Brooks's resulted in the dropping of the idea. Again, he made ·no bones about receiving the appointment of Chief Baron of the Exchequer as a gift from his old friend Brougham. After Lyndhurst had placed himself at the head of resistance to Reform, the Whigs regarded him with a very different eye. His blistering sarcasms galled them sorely, and his obnoxiousness increased as time went on. It was in answer to Lord Holland's angry lamentation against his mutilation of the Government Bills that he delivered, in 1836, the first of those scathing reviews of the session which were the chief cause of the Whig *débâcle* in 1841.

For such a considerable person, James Scarlett, Lord Abinger, has left a very meagre record behind him. The son who undertook his biography was evidently at some loss for materials. An unfinished fragment of recollections touches on his intimacy with Romilly, his companion in long walks after the courts had risen about two o'clock—a different state of affairs from the present. Scarlett reveals, too, the secret of his success as a matchless verdict-winner, which consisted in studying the shifting feelings of the jury and never talking above their heads. He would open a case in five minutes, understating rather than overstating his facts, against the half or three-quarters of an hour occupied by others.

Scarlett brought his cross-questioning habits with him out to dinner, and Sydney Smith used to say that " Do you know, Sydney, you are not altogether in the wrong," was the highest compliment ever paid him by his friend. In spite of his disputatiousness, the Whig leaders apparently set store by Scarlett, who refused more than one appointment from the Tories, and he consulted Lords Grey and Fitzwilliam before accepting the Attorney-Generalship from Canning. Though he left office when Wellington became Premier, he felt free to join the Administration in its last days as Attorney-General for the second time, and again the Whig leaders encouraged him to accept the appointment, and even, according to his own account, pressed him to take it. Nevertheless, when the Government was changed he was dismissed *sans phrase.*

Post hoc and possibly *propter hoc,* Scarlett vigorously opposed the Reform Bill. An attempt to explain himself at Lord Holland's carriage window produced a good-natured letter from that nobleman, signed " Ever truly and unalterably yours," and expressing a hope that when the business of Parliamentary Reform was over, Scarlett might be reckoned a Whig once more. The reply was a long and acrimonious citation of past services to the party, of Tory lures refused and of fidelity to Whig principles preserved. Too much on the lines of *qui s'excuse,* the letter is, nevertheless, a protest typical of many that must from time to time have disturbed the repose of the Whig chiefs. Its writer was "too proud and perhaps too calm " for resentment, but——

At any rate, Scarlett was finally and decisively un-Whigged, and directly the Tories came in they made him Chief Baron of the Exchequer. Even before that he complained that the Hollands and all connected with them had forgotten his existence. There came a day when Lady Holland was " not at home," the explanation being that she was engaged with the Russian Minister, Count Pozzo di Borgo. *Tantæne animis!* Wiser in his generation than Scarlett, Sir James Graham, after he had become a convert to Conservatism, declined all further invitations on the ground that his presence was disagreeable in the eyes of the friends of Holland House. The Whigs could make their resentments felt.

CHAPTER XXIV

FOREIGN REFUGEES AND VISITORS

Ugo Foscolo—A "tremendous" companion—"From a lion to a bore"—Blanco White—His reception at Holland House—A melancholy tutor—With Archbishop Whately—White becomes a Unitarian —Calonne—His exit speech—Louis Philippe—Etienne Dumont and Mirabeau—Dumont's worship of Bentham—Madame de Staël —"The perpetual motion"—A welcome outstayed—Washington Irving—George Ticknor—His impressions of Holland House.

HOLLAND HOUSE cultivated the political refugee, not always to its comfort. Sydney Smith's letters afford a fleeting glimpse of an Italian, Pecchio by name, who drifted up to Yorkshire through its gates and there married an heiress. Another and more famous Italian, Ugo Foscolo, was not equally amenable to English influence.[1] That purifier of his country's language made England his resting-place, if rest can be associated with his name, in 1816. Foscolo had hailed Napoleon as deliverer of Italy, and served under him in 1806 at St. Omer and Calais as an officer in the Army of Invasion. He had covertly attacked Napoleon's rule, and had been evicted in consequence from his professorial chair in the University of Padua ; and

---

[1] He was born on the island of Zante, of Venetian parentage.

after 1815 he had made Zurich too hot to hold him by a satire directed against the restoration of the Austrian Government in Lombardy. His "Essays on Petrarch," written in excellent English, soon won him a literary reputation.

Foscolo was invited to Holland House, probably on Rogers's introduction, and, in a letter to Horner, Lord Holland declared that "his learning and vivacity are wonderful, and he seems to have great elevation of mind, and to be totally exempt from affectation, though not perhaps equally so from enthusiasm, violence, and resentment." His vivacity, unfortunately, assumed exuberant forms. Under the excitement of contradiction he would rise from the dinner-table and stamp about the room, his knife in his hand. Thus Sir Henry Holland ; Jekyll was equally graphic. "With all his learning and talents he is what Dr. Johnson would call a 'tremendous' companion, uttering, with the clamour of a speaking-trumpet, a jargon composed of every language under heaven and never combined before since the Tower of Babel. At Holland House they grew dead sick of him." In fairness it must be said that their weariness does not seem to have been aggravated by the fact that in 1821 the essayist, having borrowed three MS. letters of Petrarch from the library, contrived to lose them, though, after they had been advertised for in vain, they were eventually discovered in the pages of a folio book. Lord Holland took the mishap in the best of tempers, and warmly defended the genuineness of the letters against the strictures of the Abbé Meneghelli.

It was Ugo Foscolo's misfortune, however, to alienate all his friends. Sir Walter Scott remembered him as haunting Murray's publishing house and as sinking in two seasons from a lion to a bore. Though he made considerable sums by his contributions to the *Quarterly*, and, it is said, as much as £1,000 by his lectures on the Italian poets, he squandered his gains in beautifying Digamma Cottage, St. John's Wood ; tormented Murray with impracticable statements of his affairs, and sponged for "loans," which he haughtily declined to regard as "gratuities." There came the debtors' prison, and death from dropsy at Turnham Green when he was only in his fiftieth year. He lies, not as he had proposed, under a plane-tree on English soil in a tomb designed by himself, but in Santa Croce, the Westminster Abbey of Florence, between the tomb of Alfieri and the monument of Dante ; nor is the honour unmerited.[1]

Ugo Foscolo, the ebullient, suggests, by a contrast of ideas, Blanco White, the depressed. That erratic theologian, the son of an Irish merchant of Seville and an Andalusian lady, made the acquaintance of the Hollands in 1809, when they were travelling in Spain, about the time that he was emerging from his first religious phase, membership of the Roman Catholic priesthood. The process was complete by the following year ; and, with scepticism strong within him, Blanco White availed himself of the Spanish Revolution to cut himself clear of his country and his calling. Having escaped the vigilance of the local government at Cadiz by "damning the eyes" of an official in good round English, he landed safely on English soil, and soon after his arrival in London pre-

---

[1] Foscolo was buried at Chiswick, but in 1871 his remains were transferred to Florence by the Italian Government. A cenotaph by Marochetti marks the spot where "the wearied citizen poet" rested for forty-four years in Chiswick churchyard.

sented himself at Holland House. "My reception by Lady Holland," he writes in his autobiography, "was not encouraging. Perhaps Lady H.'s manner originated in the too sanguine notions which she and most of her friends entertained at that time of the prospects of Spain: according to such notions I ought to have remained at Cadiz." However, she relented, and Blanco White pays a warm tribute to the qualities of her heart and mind and to the steadiness of her friendship, while of Lord Holland he declares that every one who approached him must have loved him.

It was impossible, on the other side, not to like the gentle and shrinking man of letters, cast adrift in troublous times. Lord Holland and Allen helped Blanco White with constant advice when he started the *Español*, a periodical supporting the Revolutionary cause, which, however, embroiled him with patriots of different ways of thought. It continued until the expulsion of the French from Spain, when the British Government granted him a pension of £250 a year. By that time Blanco White had embraced Anglicanism, and had settled at Oxford to qualify himself for orders. He was recalled to London, much against his will, to be tutor to Lord Holland's son, Henry, the heir to the title. The melancholy man "suffered dreadfully"—to use his own expression—during his two years' residence at Holland House, though kindly allusions to him occur in the correspondence of Sydney Smith and others. He practised asceticism under a roof which cannot have sheltered many sympathisers, and repeatedly requested to be released from an occupation to which his health and spirits were totally unequal. He declined to accompany the Hollands to Belgium, and on June 17, 1817, the day they left town, wrote resigning his charge. Lord Holland's reply is printed in Blanco White's autobiography; it could not have been better calculated to soothe a hypersensitive spirit.

The kindness of Holland House did not end with Blanco White's departure. Sir William Scott was consulted on the possibility of a Roman priest entering Anglican orders. In spite of heretical views on Catholic Emancipation, Blanco White was permitted to quote Lord Holland as fully satisfied of the honour and integrity of his conduct both in Spain and in England. He kept up a fairly regular correspondence with his patron, especially after he had sought refuge from the slights, probably imaginary, inflicted on him by the Fellows in the Oriel Common-room—the Common-room of Newman and Charles Marriott—by becoming tutor to the son of Whately, the Archbishop of Dublin. The efforts of that broad-minded states-man-ecclesiastic to compose the religious differences in Ireland were, of course, in keeping with Whig traditions.

Holland House, where scepticism prevailed, was far from expressing resentment when Blanco White, at the expense of a breach with the Archbishop, executed his fourth theological somersault and landed on Unitarianism. On the contrary, as has already been mentioned, Lord Holland applauded the move. Through the influence of that powerful friend Blanco White obtained a grant of £300 from the Civil List, and the fortunes of his son, Ferdinand, were pushed in the army. When the news of Lord Holland's death reached him at Liverpool his grief was intense, and he poured forth his soul in letters to General Fox and Allen. Blanco White sur-

vived "that kind, benevolent, affectionate man" less
than a year, leaving behind him much controversial
theology, lively descriptions of Spain and the Spaniards
in the "Letters by Don Leucadio Doblado," and the
resonant poem, "Night and Death," which the partiality
of Coleridge and Frere reckoned as the finest and most
grandly conceived sonnet in the English language. It is
hardly that.

To enumerate all the distinguished foreigners who, at
one time or another, enjoyed the hospitality of Holland
House would be to write, not a chapter, but a volume.
Mention must be made, however, of Calonne, the lively
Minister who gambled away the finances of France in
the reign of Louis XVI. and so rendered the Revolution
inevitable, transacting business in the corner of a
drawing-room or the recess of a window. He made
London his city of refuge on two occasions—the first
after his dismissal by the French Court, the second
when, having returned to France, at the peace of 1802,
he was exiled a second time for caballing with Fouché
and the Jacobins to supplant Talleyrand in the Ministry
of the First Consul. "*Comment, Calonne, tu aimes donc
la retrait?*" was Talleyrand's banter after the order of
his expulsion had been signed. After a short banishment he was allowed to return, and died within a few
days of pleurisy and a bad doctor. "*Tu m'as assassiné,*"
he scribbled when he could no longer speak, "*et si tu es
honnête homme, tu renonceras à la médecine pour jamais.*"
The old *régime* excelled in its exits. Lord Holland, who
saw much of Calonne during the last three years of his
first residence in England, asserts that his contemporaries
did not malign him when they admired his sprightliness
and perspicuousness of statement, but deplored his

levity, imprudence, untruthfulness, and almost incredible ignorance.

Another refugee who visited Holland House was Louis Philippe, Duc d'Orléans, afterwards King of the French. This was presumably while he was living at Twickenham with his two brothers, the Duc de Montpensier and the Comte de Beaujolais, waiting for a turn in the tide of Royalism which the establishment of the Consulate seemed to have indefinitely deferred. After the Revolution of 1830 Lord Holland wrote, in answer to an irate lady whose name is not given in the " Foreign Reminiscences," a thoroughgoing defence of Louis Philippe. It does justice to his virtues as *père de famille*, but it is inclined to blink the tortuous paths by which he reached the throne.

Etienne Dumont, the Swiss publicist, was a more regular frequenter of Holland House. Romilly, as has been already said, made his acquaintance at Geneva in 1781, and five years later, after he had left that city through becoming involved in revolutionary troubles, he was appointed tutor, on Romilly's recommendation, to Lord Henry Petty. At Lansdowne House Dumont made the acquaintance of the Whig leaders, and formed the second great friendship of his life, with Jeremy Bentham. In 1788 he and Romilly went to Paris together, and there he met Mirabeau. Thus began the association between " the great Frenchman and the little Genevese," as Carlyle calls them, to which the world owes the diverting "Souvenirs sur Mirabeau." Dumont " devilled," as lawyers-phrase it, for the mighty orator ; he fetched and carried, got up facts for his speeches, and possibly wrote some of the reports published under his name. But this hod-work by no means justified

Dumont in persistently representing Mirabeau as, to
quote Carlyle, "a thing set in motion mainly by him
[M. Dumont]." Lord Holland, discussing the point in
his "Foreign Reminiscences," admits that his "excellent
friend," though veracious and fond of anecdotes, was,
by his own admission, a very unobservant and, by the
experience of others, a very credulous man. Among the
subjects with which he cultivated an imperfect acquaintance was evidently his own position in the scheme
of existence. Yet Macaulay good-naturedly wrote of
Dumont in the *Edinburgh* that "he was not solicitous to
proclaim that he furnished information, arguments, and
eloquence to Mirabeau." Not at the time, it is true;
secretaries who boast that their employers are their
creatures are apt to get discharged. But he certainly
wished posterity to believe that their relations in theory
were reversed in fact.

By a piece of singular good fortune Dumont was
attached to Chauvelin's mission, and so reached this
country before the revolutionary hurricane burst in its
full violence. He remained "contemplating from a
peaceful spot the storm in which he would have been
immersed" until 1814, living chiefly with Lord Lansdowne, attending the King of Clubs, enjoying the friendship of Romilly and Horner, and worshipping Bentham.
In common with James Mill, Francis Place and other
disciples of that philosopher, Dumont loyally drudged at
reducing the *disjecta membra* of his speculations to order
and lucidity. To his industry are due the "Théories des
Peines et des Récompenses" and other works, which he
brought out of chaos into well-proportioned speculations,
without suppressing such eminently utilitarian suggestions as that coiners should be punished by being

branded on the cheek with hot half-crowns, and women
guilty of infanticide by being compelled to wear the
leaden images of their murdered babies at their necks.
Dumont carried his learning and vivacity into society,
though Moore caught him tripping over Bayle's attitude
towards Catholicism, and was a much-appreciated reader
of Corneille and Molière. Even after he had settled at
Geneva, where he gullibly swallowed a most astounding
narrative of Byronic vice and retailed it to the indignant
Moore, he paid visits to his old friends in England. He
was at Bowood in 1818, and again in 1824, three years
before his death, bubbling over with anecdote and information. A learned oddity, indeed, was the little Genevese,
with his beady eyes and humorous mouth.

Another Swiss by origin, though French by adoption
and Swedish by marriage, captured the town in the
summer of 1813, when Madame de Staël, in the course
of her wanderings, took up her abode in George Street,
Hanover Square. In her train came her eldest son, her
daughter Albertine, and an unacknowledged second husband in M. de Rocca, the young French cavalry officer.[1]
Her second son, the scapegrace Albert, was killed in a
duel, fought in Mecklenburg-Schwerin, soon after her
arrival, and Byron grimly predicted that she would write
an essay on the incident. Madame de Staël refrained from
doing so ; but the prompt publication of her book, "On
Germany," made her the literary lioness of the season.
Besides, as the victim of Napoleon's persecutions, she
came into high favour with the Regent and the Ministry,
and was, in consequence, looked upon politically with
dubious eyes by Byron and other Whigs.

[1] For Campbell's gibe see p. 222.

With much astuteness Madame de Staël selected Mackintosh, who had excellent French, as her convoy, and that amiable man described himself as "ordered with her to dinner, as one orders beans and bacon," to the houses of all the Cabinet Ministers. Rogers submitted to her sway with less docility. When she made him take her to Lansdowne House he remarked how she so placed herself that she could display the beauty of her arms. The Dandies unmercifully quizzed her and her daughter. Still, Madame de Staël's success was prodigious, even though Hallam cynically suggested that she might find English curiosity soon yielding to English prejudice. "She is," wrote the kindly yet discriminating Mackintosh, "one of the few persons who surpass expectation; she has every sort of talent, and would be universally popular, if, in society, she were to confine herself to her inferior talents—pleasantry, anecdote, and literature—which are so much more suited to conversation than her eloquence and genius." Byron, whom she alternately flattered and lectured—on his ignorance of *la belle passion* amongst other things—also complained that her tongue was the perpetual motion, and that she wrote octavos and talked folios, though in later years he admitted her kindness of heart.

Madame de Staël certainly gave herself astounding airs, as when she sent for Curran and cross-examined him as to his character, which left a good deal to be desired in some respects, with the view of discovering if she could afford his acquaintance. Yet Byron asserted that she met her match in Sheridan, with whom, however, she seems to have been compelled to converse in English—a heavy handicap. Mackintosh saw Lord Wellesley fight a good battle with her at Holland House over the Swedish

treaty, parrying her eloquent declamations and unseason-
able discussions with politeness, vivacity, and grace.
Madame de Staël took a house at Richmond for the early
autumn, and there uttered the sententious observation
that the view was "*calme et animée ; ce qu'il faut être, et
ce que je ne suis pas.*"   She then went a triumphal tour to
Bowood, whence Mackintosh returned early in November
from "a rather fatiguing week," the party including
Romilly, Dumont, and Ward ; and to Coombe Wood,
Lord Liverpool's place, where Croker detected her passing off as her own an epigram of Camille Desmoulins'. By
December she was dining at Holland House again, and,
observed Byron, "less loquacious than heretofore."   She
seems, indeed, to have slightly outstayed her welcome,
when in the following May she returned to Paris in the
wake of the Bourbons, complaining, on her part, of the
nothingness of London conversation—a condemnation
elaborated in her "Considérations sur l'Angleterre."
Altogether, it is possible to sympathise with Sir Walter
Scott, who made no attempt to see Madame de Staël,
and even with stout old Jeremy Bentham, who called her
a "trumpery magpie" and flatly refused her admittance
to the Hermitage.

Rogers made much of Americans, and it was probably through him that distinguished statesmen and
diplomatists like Van Buren, Daniel Webster and
Monroe visited Holland House.   They seem, however,
to have been little more than birds of passage. Washington Irving was a more regular guest during the
three years of his stay at the American Embassy, in
1829 and onwards, as Secretary of Legation. "The
Sketch-book," including as it did the immortal Rip van
Winkel, had by that time made his name a household

word in this country; Oxford honoured him with the honorary degree of LL.D., and the Royal Society of Literature with its gold medal. Moore at one time considered him too American, which was unkind, as Irving took some trouble about negotiating the sale of the " Life of Byron" in the United States.

George Ticknor, the historian of Spanish literature, was a closer intimate. In 1819, and again in the thirties, that accomplished and modest man spent many evenings at Holland House. He did not at first like Lady Holland, but they became friends after a passage of arms, in which Ticknor countered her assertion that New England was originally colonised by convicts by saying that some of her family, the Vassalls, were early settlers in Massachusetts. His impressions of the circle do not vary greatly from those that may be gathered from other sources, except that he pays Brougham the unexpected compliment of attributing to him kindness of heart, and describes him as commonplace on common topics, but original when excited. He relates, however, with some surprise, that Lord Melbourne commented freely on the oratorical tendencies of his Sovereign, William IV.—fourteen toasts and a quantity of speeches at one dinner. The easygoing conduct of public business also struck him: the Bill for admitting Dissenters to the Universities was down for the following Tuesday, but as Lady Jersey had a grand party she would probably succeed in getting it postponed. In 1857 Ticknor revisited Holland House under its new ownership, and found it much altered and made very luxurious, but he missed things he would have been glad to see in the library, the dining-room, and the drawing-room.

CHAPTER XXV

CONTINENTAL DIPLOMATISTS

Metternich—Pozzo di Borgo and others—Van der Weyer—
Princess Lieven—A *"très grande dame"*—Her intimacies—The eyes
and ears of an Embassy—The Lievens' recall—Madame de Lieven's
last years—Talleyrand at Holland House—His appearance and conversation—His affection for England—Count Montrond—A salaried
clubman—His relations with Talleyrand—Count Flahault—A Paris
salon—A figure of the Second Empire—Guizot's mission—His
stories of Lady Holland—Holland House and the Syrian crisis.

THE year of Madame de Staël's advent, 1813, also
witnessed the arrival of Metternich—the profound,
as Lord Beaconsfield called him, the reactionary,
as others. The Austrian statesman had just witnessed
the signature of the Treaty of Paris, and came to sound
the British Government on the negotiations about to be
opened at Vienna. He attended the Czar and the King
of Prussia, and brought to the Prince Regent, who had
personally invited him, the excuses of the Emperor
Francis. He thus took part in the premature celebra-
tions of peace, and renewed an acquaintance with the
Whig aristocracy formed when, as a young man of
twenty-one, he had visited England in 1794. On that
occasion Metternich came to the conclusion that the
Prince of Wales was one of the handsomest men he

had ever seen, and most agreeable, but that he kept
very bad company. His "Mémoires" are reticent as
to the impressions derived from his second visit, but
he cannot have had much in common with the Whigs.
In spite of hospitality received, he refused Lord Holland
admission to Austrian territory in 1824 as "a person
notoriously of very bad sentiments, and known to be
an enthusiastic adherent of Radicalism."

The continental diplomatists who, at one time or
another, made their *entrée* at Holland House may, for
the most part, be briefly dismissed. Among them were
Count Pozzo di Borgo, the little Corsican, who carried
on a family vendetta against Napoleon by entering
Russian service and labouring untiringly to bring about
his overthrow, and who, after several stays in this
country, was Ambassador here from 1835 to 1839; the
Duke of Palmella, the witty Portuguese, who upheld
the constitutionalist cause against absolutism as represented by Dom Miguel; and Sylvain van de Weyer,
the first Minister sent by independent Belgium to this
country. The last of the three, a cultivated man of
letters, it is worth recording, put down Lady Holland
with some decision. When the King of the Belgians
was new to the throne he was dining at Holland House.
"How is Leopold?" asked Lady Holland with her usual
abruptness. "Does your ladyship mean the King of the
Belgians?" "I have heard," she rejoined, "of Flemings,
Hainaulters, and Brabanters; but Belgians are new to
me." She was calmly referred, as a woman of wide
reading, to Cæsar's "Commentaries." Van de Weyer,
says Hayward in an obituary essay on the diplomatist,
became an established favourite at Holland House.

Princess Lieven, the wife of the Russian Ambassador,

identified herself more completely with English society than any of these. Her husband, a quiet, laborious man, whose nickname, " Vraiment," seems to stamp him, appears to have immersed himself in diplomatic business, and to have allowed her to go her own way. Greville ungallantly gives a list of her lovers, Palmella among them, adding that she never seriously attached herself to any one. The Lievens, on the evidence of Lady Granville, understood one another fairly well, and when the Prince died at Rome in 1839 she lamented him on her knees in torrents of tears. But her affections were centred in her children, of whom her son Paul became very popular.

The Lievens arrived at the Russian Embassy in 1812, Pozzo di Borgo having paved the way for their reception, at a moment when friendly relations with Russia, interrupted temporarily by the Treaty of Tilsit, were about to be renewed. No cleverer female politician ever made her drawing-room the manœuvring ground of international affairs than Madame de Lieven, and none was more fitted by nature and training for the task. She was, writes the partial Greville, "a *très grande dame*, with abilities of a very fine order, great tact and *finesse*, and taking a boundless pleasure in the society of the great world and in political affairs of every sort." As such she almost immediately took her place in the cream of the cream of English society, figured at Almack's, and was frequently a guest of George IV. at the Pavilion. Her closest friend was Lady Cowper, afterwards Lady Palmerston ; and therefore the ill-natured took upon themselves to say that she was the making of Lord Palmerston, but the insinuation had nothing behind it.

The externalities of Madame de Lieven are easily reproduced. She was fascinating and vivacious rather than a beauty, very thin, an accomplished pianist, illiterate, except for one book, the " Letters of Madame de Sévigné," and devoted to whist. Lady Granville reports various scraps of her conversation ; drollery rather than epigram seems to have been her strong point, and she could suppress bores with good breeding. Delighting in the game and devoured by political curiosity, she formed confidential intimacies with the leading English statesmen, from Castlereagh to Lord Aberdeen, and kept up a vigorous correspondence with several of them. Greville warmly defends her from the charge of making mischief, declaring that she was too much attached to this country to abuse her position.

The facts remain that Madame de Lieven acted as the eyes and ears of the Russian Embassy, and that the information she extracted from Lord Grey—his babbling, as she called it—and others was regularly communicated to the Imperial Court and the Chancellor Nesselrode. More than that, the Duke of Wellington and Lord Palmerston, neither of them suspicious men, accused her of trying to upset them ; and her published correspondence shows this much, that when she discovered the first of them to be hostile to the claims of Greece, she let no chances of ridiculing his Government slip by her. With similar motives she constantly praised Lord Holland ; thus, in 1828, she wrote that " he would be glad to see the Emperor arrive at Constantinople, that he might do as he liked with it, that we might have a port on the Mediterranean—in a word, the only difficulty is to restrain him." The recall of the Lievens came with some abruptness in 1834. They had come to sharp issues with Palmerston, of whom Madame de Lieven wrote that "he would never be more than a schoolboy, and not brilliant as that," over Russian designs in the Levant and elsewhere ; and the appointment of Sir Stratford Canning, whom the Czar Nicholas hated, as Ambassador to St. Petersburg, gave a finishing touch to their discomfiture.   She was rejoicing over the awkward position in which the French Ambassador, Talleyrand, "an unprincipled rascal," was placed owing to the antagonism of the British Foreign Secretary, only a few days before they were summoned to St. Petersburg, nominally to fill appointments in the Imperial household.

Madame de Lieven submitted with barely concealed mortification ; but the death of her two youngest children soon rendered St. Petersburg insupportable to her, and she established herself in Paris, where she spent the remainder of her days in social and political alliance with Guizot, maintaining correspondence the while with her friends in England.   A difficult character to define in a phrase, Madame de Lieven may best be described, perhaps, as a survival of the political woman of the seventeenth and eighteenth centuries, sent abroad to lie for her country.   She did it very well up to a certain point.

Greville declares that, when Talleyrand took up the appointment of French Ambassador in London after the Revolution of July had placed Louis Philippe on the throne, Madame de Lieven was at first hostile to him, but soon yielded to the charm of his society and that of his niece, Madame de Dino.   But her correspondence shows that her amity was only skin-deep ; she accused him, amongst other things, of picking up

Cabinet secrets at Holland House. Talleyrand, at any rate, made himself thoroughly at home by the fireside of his friend of nearly forty years' standing—for Lord Holland first made his acquaintance in the course of a visit to Paris in 1791, when Talleyrand was still Bishop of Autun. During his residence at the French Embassy Talleyrand spent his evenings at Holland House, whenever Madame de Dino repaired to France, staying as long as they would let him. The company looked on while he devoured his single meal in the day, when, Sir Henry Holland tells us, " wholly absorbed in the pleasure of eating, he spoke little during dinner and little during the early stages of digestion."

Talleyrand must have been a formidable person to meet. Creevey, never overburdened with modesty, shrank from the encounter, and even Sydney Smith and Macaulay seem to have stood in some awe of him. His appearance was weird, what with his club foot, his head shrunk between his shoulders, his cork-screw curls, piercing eyes, and masklike face. Lady Granville described him as gliding by her at a public reception like a lizard. His talk, too, was difficult to catch in his later days, owing to a habit of pumping up his words from the bottom of his stomach. But for good listeners he was unequalled. " By a happy combination," writes Lord Holland in his " Foreign Reminiscences," " of neatness in language and ease and suavity of manner with archness and sagacity of thought, his sarcasms assumed a garb at once so courtly and so careless, that they often diverted almost as much as they could mortify even their immediate objects." That opinion might conceivably have been modified had he known that when on leave of absence in France Talleyrand said of him : "*C'est la bienveillance même, mais la bienveillance la plus perturbatrice, qu'on a jamas vue.*" Of Lady Holland he remarked, "*Elle est toute assertion, mais quand on demande la preuve, c'est là son secret.*" Another anecdote, with which she was concerned, relates how to please her Talleyrand dined at a certain London house. His reward was that the lobster sauce was upset on the centre of his head, exactly where the long white locks were parted. Talleyrand did not move a muscle while the servant was scraping the sauce up with a spoon, and only remarked on leaving, "*Il n'y a rien si bourgeois que cette maison B——.*"

Still, Talleyrand should not be judged by an occasional asperity, more especially as his powers of sarcasm were unlimited. There can be no doubt that he was much attached to his English friends, and enjoyed the consideration paid to him in society as the Nestor of European diplomacy. Though he chafed under Lord Palmerston's offhand manner, he was deeply grateful when, in reply to a blundering personal attack made upon him by Lord Londonderry in the House of Lords, the Duke of Wellington, who was leader of the Opposition, joined Lord Holland and Lord Goderich, who were members of the Government, in repelling the assault. The prints of the day represent him as a well-known figure in the Park, and he frequented the British Museum. By the public at large he seems to have been regarded as an ogre, and the papers told strange stories of how his pulse intermitted at the sixth beat, whereby he was enabled to thrive on two hours' sleep, and how his bed had a deep slope in the middle, rising equally at the head and the

feet. His mission came to an end, at his own request, in
November, 1834, and bickerings with Lord Palmerston
were probably a contributing cause, though his guiding
reasons were age and infirmity. He had acute differences
with the Foreign Secretary over the Belgian question;
but when they put their hands to the Quadruple Treaty,
guaranteeing Spain and Portugal from external interference, each imagined that he had outwitted the other.

Talleyrand was inseparable from his crony and foil,
Count Montrond, a survival, like himself, of the old
régime. That wonderful individual was not unfrequently
to be seen at Holland House, though Creevey, who
recorded his appearances, could never quite succeed in
spelling his name correctly. "*Qui ne l'aimerait pas ?*"
mused Talleyrand. "*Il est ci vicieux.*" The compliment
is reversed in another version, and it applied, no doubt,
with about equal truth to either worthy. Montrond was
a typical *roué* of pre-Revolutionary days, witty, cynical,
an epicure and an exquisite in dress and manner. The
young men of Paris and London formed themselves on
him, and a caricature by Count d'Orsay has preserved for
us the immensity of his collars and the elegant set of his
coat, with its obvious suggestion of stays. The sources
of his income, other than cards, were a mystery after he
had devoured his wife's fortune, and the hypercritical
declared that he called in skill of an unorthodox kind to
strengthen his chances at the tables. "*C'est possible,*" was
Montrond's answer when accused of cheating, "*mais je
n'aime pas qu'on me le dise,*" and threw the cards in his
critic's face. A duel naturally ensued, and Montrond was
left for dead on the field. "*Il vit de son mort,*" said
Talleyrand.

After the Revolution of July Montrond accepted a

PRINCESS LIEVEN

FROM THE MINIATURE BY UPTON IN THE POSSESSION OF
SIR J. G. TOLLEMACHE SINCLAIR

COUNT MONTROND

pension of 20,000 francs a year from Louis Philippe, the condition being that he should praise the Citizen King at the clubs and in England. As he was on intimate terms with Lord Sefton, Lord Alvanley, and other social lights, it is possible that he earned his salary. He formed one of the dinner-party of recon- ciliation given by Lord Sefton when Brougham accepted the Great Seal, and raised a laugh by asking the Chan- cellor when he was going to mount his bag of wool. Not only was Montrond thoroughly at home on the pavement of St. James's Street, but his confidences to Tom Raikes show, too, that when primed with infor- mation from Talleyrand, he was an effective agent for the conveyance of a political hint. The Prince de Bénévent probably valued Montrond more, however, as his guest at Valençaye, with Motteux, the gourmand, as a frequent third. Besides being witty himself, he was the cause of wit in others. Unfortunately, the most famous repartee attributed to Talleyrand at Montrond's expense—" *Déjà ?* " in reply to his " *Ah, je sens les tour- ments de l'enfer"*—has been traced to Bouvard, the physician of Cardinal de Retz. But authenticity appears to attach to the story that as Montrond lay on the floor in an epileptic fit, scratching the carpet with his hands, his benign host remarked, " *C'est qu'il me paraît, qu'il veut absolument descendre."* Such were their peculiar relations, and it remains to add that Montrond, who opposed Talleyrand's deathbed reconciliation with the Church, himself made a most edifying end. He had never made jokes against religion, he explained to the Abbé Petitot, because he had always lived in good company.

Another *protégé* of Talleyrand, and, some said, a very

near relation, was Count Flahault, the son of the talented
lady better known as Madame de Souza, and the author
of the once popular romance "Adèle de Senanges."
He, too, like Montrond, was a citizen of two countries.
An *emigré*, as a child with his mother, he received his
early education in England, and returned to France to
become a favourite officer of Napoleon, whom he accompanied on most of his campaigns, that of Waterloo
included.   The Bourbons exiled him from France, and
the Tory Government were disposed to exclude him from
England under the Alien Act.   He was permitted, however, to evade its provisions by the purchase of shares in
a Scots bank.   A hero of romance in Whig eyes, handsome and gifted with a beautiful voice, M. de Flahault
won, in 1817, the hand of an heiress, Miss Mercer, who
eventually became Lady Keith in her own right.   She
was the girl whom Byron remembered with gratitude as
having stood up for him when the town was ringing with
the news of his separation from his wife.   The Flahaults
established themselves in Scotland, where he became
proficient in the management of an estate, though his
drinking capacity fell short of the local standard.

   In 1827 the Flahaults made Paris their headquarters,
and Lady Granville describes with some humour the
difficulties of the staid Madame de Flahault in holding
a *salon* for ladies who thought it an outrage that she
should be on such excellent terms with her husband.
The discerning Raikes declared that the house showed
a happy combination of French and English habits,
and that, though the Count was no longer young, few
people were endowed with such advantages of manner
and person or so captivating in their address.   He
made the best of two worlds, since he accepted the

post of equerry to the Duc d'Orléans and a diplomatic
appointment from the Monarchy of July, while he
displayed his fidelity to the Napoleonic tradition by
acting as guardian to the young Duc de Morny, the
natural son of Queen Hortense. During the Syrian
crisis of 1840 he appears to have supplied Louis
Philippe with useful information as to the state of
public feeling in London. He made Holland House
his headquarters during this flying visit, and only left
it a day or two before Lord Holland's death. Count
Flahault became one of the diplomatic mainstays of
the Second Empire, and in that capacity was for a
brief period French Ambassador to the English Court
and the recipient of a grave warning from Palmerston.
His death was removed by a few days only from the
downfall of Napoleon III. at Sedan.

Guizot has left a faithful description of his short but
important mission in the fifth volume of his Memoirs.
As a student of English history and social phenomena
he was familiar with the outside show of our life
when he landed at Dover on February 27, 1840.
Hertford House was then the French Embassy; and
while driving to it he was struck by the monotony
and insignificance of London buildings, though he
admitted that the whole impressed by its vastness, and
that neatness prevailed though taste was absent. He
discovered the aristocracy to be subservient to popular
opinion, and concerned rather with following than
directing it. He was struck by the constraint of the
Court, where, by the way, he committed, to the con-
sternation of Greville, the blunder of insisting on being
placed next Queen Victoria at dinner. But he was
heartily received by the Hollands in South Street; and

after their return to Kensington he records his delight in the historic associations of the Gothic building, the literary wealth of the library, and the various interests of the portraits. Lord Clarendon and Luttrell were asked to meet him, and after the conversation had turned on the great French writers and orators of the seventeenth century, it was concerned with Fox and his contemporaries, whom Lord Holland imitated with much spirit.

Guizot portrays his host as combining in himself the ideas of an English Whig and a French Liberal, a European intelligence and a Saxon physiognomy. Lady Holland he regarded as much more English than her husband ; she was often imperious, sometimes gracious ; she was cultivated, and, though essentially an egoist, abounded in polite attentions. She set herself to correct his English ; and when he quoted the proverb, " Hell is paved with good intentions," she informed him, in friendly rebuke, that it was not good tone to mention that region except in quoting Milton— epic poetry was the only excuse. The Ambassador made his way to Lady Holland's good graces by placing Talleyrand's *chef*, the celebrated Louis, at the head of his cuisine ; he imperilled his position by keeping dinner waiting until half-past eight for Lord and Lady Palmerston. She passed through the three stages of bad temper, genuine discomfort, and fainting ; finally she had to be helped to table by Lord Duncannon. Guizot illustrated her superstitiousness by a story that she warned Canning in 1827 against going to stay with the Duke of Devonshire at Chiswick, because Fox had died in the house. Canning himself was struck by the coincidence, and asked her to keep it a secret.

"And he died at Chiswick," was the triumphantly logical conclusion.

Guizot passes the society of Holland House under rapid and discriminating review. Macaulay talked his books, but brilliantly; Sydney Smith was rather overpowering and given to jesting at his cloth; Hallam, softened by age and domestic losses, was a pleasant and instructive companion; Jeffrey vigorous but inclined to despair of the times. He confirms to the full the complaints of Palmerston that Holland House made no disguise of its sentiments during the Syrian crisis, though a member of the Cabinet—possibly Macaulay—warned him, more diplomatically than truthfully, that such indiscretions must not be taken as evidence of Ministerial differences. Though Guizot thus obtained considerable inkling of what was going on behind the scenes, his representations had made no impression on the resolute Foreign Secretary, when he was recalled in October to succeed Thiers in the troubled position of Prime Minister of France. A few days previously he had heard of Lord Holland's death, and noted the impassiveness with which the news was outwardly received by his friends of thirty years' standing. The English were always a puzzle to Guizot, deeply though he pondered on their history.

CHAPTER XXVI

THE GREY AND MELBOURNE MINISTRIES

Old and young Whigs—Spring-Rice and Abercromby—Lord Duncannon—A healer of differences—The Duke of Richmond—Lord Althorp's early years—His rooms in the Albany—The leadership of the House—An indispensable man—Neighbour and country gentleman—Lord John Russell and Holland House—His literary efforts—The coming man—The Reform Bills—Lord John upsets the coach—As leader of the House—Whig legislation—Lord John at home—The Fox Club—John George Lambton—"Radical Jack"—"A victim of temper"—A mission to St. Petersburg—The Edinburgh banquet—The mission to Canada—Brougham's revenge—The spoilt child of society.

THE last ten years of Lord Holland's life almost coincided with the period of Whig ascendancy, before Peel came to his own in 1841. His house was the Ministerial headquarters, and Lady Holland's divorce having been long since condoned, the Whig peeresses frequented her receptions. To give its history during that full decade would be to re-tell the familiar and not particularly inspiring tale of the Grey and two Melbourne Administrations. Many of the Whigs, besides, had long borne the burden of the day in Opposition, and have figured accordingly in the earlier chapters of this work, while some, like Lord Clarendon and Labouchere, were only beginning to assume prominence, and their careers lie outside the scope of this book. Others can be dismissed with brevity, as comparatively unimportant except for their membership of a compact political organisation.

Spring-Rice, for example, can hardly be said to have won a prominent position for himself on the page of history. He had considerable grasp of detail, and made an efficient Secretary to the Treasury. Gifted with a fluent tongue, he was sometimes put up to answer O'Connell, and stated the anti-Repeal case with much ability but more prolixity. As Chancellor of the Exchequer in Lord Melbourne's second Ministry, he failed to grapple resolutely with a series of deficits, and rashly introduced the penny postage at a moment when the revenue was unequal to an additional strain. Spring-Rice incurred the bitter hostility of the Radicals, and after the session of 1839 he was persuaded to accept a peerage with the Comptrollership of the Exchequer as a consolation prize. Abercromby who, thanks to his popularity with the extreme Whigs, was preferred to Spring-Rice for the Speakership in 1835, was an equally colourless politician. As "Young Cole," a nickname borrowed from the drama, Creevey heaped ridicule on him in conjunction with Tierney, "Old Cole." Abercromby was, it would seem, a bustling Whig barrister, who won his way to the chair less by ability than by a Scot's capacity for turning opportunities to account. He proved a weak Speaker when passions ran high, though equal to the ordinary routine of business.

Lord Duncannon, Lord Melbourne's brother-in-law, was a different kind of man, less pushing, more trustworthy. He was afflicted with a catch in his speech,

and so cut no figure in debate. But his knowledge of
men made him a successful Opposition whip, though in
" Tommy " Holmes he had a most astute and unscrupulous opponent. When the Whigs came into
office Lord Duncannon's services were ignored, but he
did not desert his party, and formed one of the committee
of four which drew up the Reform Bill. In 1832,
however, he became Chief Commissioner of Woods
and Forests, and in the following year was admitted
to the Cabinet.

" Nothing could be done without Duncannon," wrote
Greville, when he died. He arranged difficulties and
adjusted rival pretensions. King William, though he
hated the rest of the Whigs, held Duncannon in
regard; and another formidable personage with whom,
by sheer straightforwardness of dealing, he contrived to
keep on good terms was O'Connell. Lord Duncannon,
writes Sir Denis Le Marchant, "was the directing
spirit, if not the soul and mainstay, of Lord Melbourne's Irish policy, the chief title of that Administration to credit from posterity." As Privy Seal he
contrived to carry Bills through the House of Lords
without making the semblance of a speech. Residing
for a good part of the year on his well-managed
Irish estates, he undertook the Lord-Lieutenancy, when
the Whigs came back to power in 1846, with universal
approval. He died at his post, his days having undoubtedly been shortened by the Irish famine, and,
when almost too weak to be intelligible, dictated a
letter to Lord John Russell, the Prime Minister, warning him of the dangers that would confront his
successor.

Before we pass to the three prominent members of

the Grey Administration—Lord Althorp, Lord John Russell, and Lord Durham—a sentence or two may be devoted to the fifth Duke of Richmond, the Post-master-General.   He was one of the ultra-Tories who revolted when Wellington introduced the Catholic Emancipation Bill, and who actually tried, but failed, to form a Government of their own.   Greville pictures him as "having a certain measure of understanding ; prejudiced, narrow-minded, illiterate, and ignorant, good-looking, good-humoured, and unaffected, tedious, prolix, unassuming, and a duke."   Rather than be balked of his revenge, he went over to the Whigs, taking with him Sir E. Knatchbull and the Marquis of Blandford.   His appointment as Postmaster-General was not made until he had been discovered to be unacceptable to the army as head of the Ordnance Department and had next declined the Mastership of the Horse.   The Duke threw himself with energy into his new duties, and, to Greville's astonishment, Lord Melbourne reported that as a Cabinet Minister he was "sharp, quick, the King liked him ; he stood up to Durham more than any other man in the Cabinet, and altogether he was not unimportant."   Richmond, however, soon exhausted his devotion to Liberal prin-ciples : in 1834 he joined Stanley, Lord Ripon, and Sir James Graham, the first batch of seceders from the Government, and eventually identified himself with the Protectionist interest, the side that naturally appealed to him as a great landowner and practical farmer.   Even after his breach with the Whigs he was to be seen at Holland House, patting Lord John Russell on the back and treating him like a little schoolboy.

Lord Althorp, of whom it was said that by his fine

temper he carried the Reform Bill, resembled Bute's
Lord Rockingham, in that the strength of his character redeemed the slowness of his intellect and the
hesitation of his speech. At Harrow he was backward, though at Cambridge he distinguished himself in
the college examinations. He was out of his element
at Spencer House, where his brilliant mother, a daughter
of the first Earl of Lucan, entertained all that was
conspicuous in politics and fashion; and, as the wife
of Pitt's First Lord of the Admiralty, became the
powerful friend of Nelson and Collingwood. Althorp's
engrossing interests for years lay in the prize-ring,
shooting, racing, and the management of the Pytchley
Hunt. He entered the House of Commons as a
matter of course, and was second on the poll at the
election for Cambridge University which ensued on
the death of Pitt, when Lord Henry Petty came in
first and Lord Palmerston was last. But he was slow
to emerge from the lower ranks; though, breaking
away from the traditions of Spencer House, which
were Tory, he attached himself to Whitbread, and
took some part in the proceedings against the Duke
of York. He married in 1814 Miss Arklom, the
heiress of Wisedon Hall, Nottinghamshire, and devoted
himself to the improvement of her estate. Though
introduction of the oppressive "Six Acts" stimulated
him to attend the House regularly and join the
Radicals in a vigorous opposition, the death of his
wife in 1818 drove him into retirement from society.
He became a recluse in the Albany and at Wisedon,
devoting himself to political economy, statistics, and
the "Parliamentary Debates," actually plodding through
that voluminous collection.

The medicine of work saved Lord Althorp from misanthropy. He busied himself, though vainly, with Bills for the recovery of small debts, and resisted the increase of the corn duty. Thus he became, before the retirement of Lord Liverpool, an unacknowledged leader of the Opposition, who frequently brought Whig support to the economic plans of Huskisson. But, after the death of Canning, he declared that he knew of no party to which he belonged and saw no immediate prospect of becoming again a party man. As an individual he supported the repeal of the Test and Corporation Acts and Catholic Emancipation. Still, his rooms in the Albany were the rallying point of the Opposition ; and, Brougham being considered impossible, he was induced to accept the leadership of the Whig party in the House of Commons in the course of the session of 1830. Peel started when he announced his new position by giving notice that " *we* intend to take the sense of the House" on a certain question. A few months later the Wellington Government fell.

Thus Lord Althorp passed in one stride to the Chancellorship of the Exchequer and leadership of the House of Commons. The plain country gentleman, awkward and almost rustic of speech, acquitted himself to the general admiration. He hated office, and was painfully conscious of his deficiencies. When the crisis of the Reform Bill was at its height he told Hobhouse that he had removed his pistols from his bedroom, fearing that he might shoot himself. Nor is it to be denied that he committed numerous blunders. He introduced his first Budget in a confused speech, and was compelled to withdraw provision after provision. His simplicity frequently placed him at a

disadvantage in dealing with cunning men.   He could
manage Attwood and the Birmingham Union, but his
mishandling of the difficult negotiations over the
renewal of the Irish Coercion Act, in which slippery
individuals like Brougham and O'Connell were concerned, brought down the Grey Administration.   But
Greville, who censured him, not without cause, for
numerous nightly shortcomings, could eulogise him
when he died with equal propriety as "the very best
leader of the House of Commons that any party ever
had." With practice his speaking improved, and his
knowledge of the provisions of the Reform Bill caused
him to be its most effective advocate.   After Lord
John Russell's health gave way, he steered the Bill
through Committee, and met with imperturbable good
temper the angry remonstrances of borough-holders
who regarded themselves as being robbed of their
own. It was during the debates of March, 1832, on
the measure in its third form that he made his memorable reply to Croker, who had belaboured the Bill with
statistics.   Althorp retorted that he had made some
calculations which he considered as entirely conclusive
in refutation of his opponent's arguments, but, unfortunately, he had mislaid them, so he could only say
that if the House would be guided by him they would
reject the amendment—which they did.

   "There was no standing against such influence as
this," said Sir Henry Hardinge, when telling the story.
Lord Grey was anxious that Althorp should accept a
peerage and take charge of the Bill in the Committee of the Lords, but his successor as leader of
the Commons could not be found.   In spite of his
mismanagement of Irish affairs and consequent resig-

nation, he was equally indispensable when the Grey Ministry collapsed, and Lord Melbourne was charged with its reconstruction. Althorp was, said the new Premier, "the tortoise on whom the world reposed."

When his father's death removed him to the Upper House, William IV. paid him the oblique compliment of getting rid of the Ministry on the ground that he could not be replaced as leader of the House of Commons. Once he had retired to his beloved Wisedon, no entreaties from former colleagues could induce him to resume office, or to make more than rare appearances in the House of Lords. "Your presence alone, without a word," wrote Lord Holland in February, 1835, "may prevent things being said which, if said in your absence, would render future attendance, explanation, and even controversy unavoidable." But Lord Spencer was not to be moved by Whigs like Lord Holland or Radicals like Joseph Hume, any more than by Lord Melbourne when he pressed upon him in 1838 the Governorship of Canada, with the Lord-Lieutenancy of Ireland as an alternative. He remained constant to his duties "as a relation, as a neighbour, and as a country gentleman." He rescued his heavily encumbered estates from their embarrassments, and rendered permanent services to stock-raising by keeping up herds of pedigree shorthorns and contributing papers to the "Transactions" of the Royal Agricultural Society, a body originated by himself in conjunction with the Duke of Richmond. Lord Spencer had been politically extinct for some years before his death, but he handed on as a legacy the epithet of "honest" to statesmen who have been fortunate enough to be christened John.

Lord John Russell, as the nephew of Fox's Duke of Bedford, made his bow at Holland House when he was fourteen. As has already been stated, he accompanied the Hollands to Spain in 1808, and made with them an adventurous journey across the peninsula, while Sir John Moore was conducting his famous retreat to Corunna. Thus he witnessed the hopeful beginnings of the Spanish revolution and its temporary overthrow, and, much to his credit, returned home disgusted with the Whigs, who in the interests of the party were denouncing the war. On the advice of Lord Holland and Allen he was sent to Edinburgh University, and thus broadened his education, besides trying his oratorical strength as a member of the Speculative Society. In after years he owned to deep obligations to Edinburgh and more especially to Professor Playfair.

Though he entered Parliament as member for Tavistock in 1812, Lord John Russell took some time to shape into a strenuous politician. Weak health rendered travel expedient, and in the course of his journeyings he had an interview with Napoleon at Elba, discovering the ex-Emperor to have "fat cheeks and rather a turn-up nose." He also wrote prolifically, but without making any permanent additions to literature, though his "Essays and Sketches," purporting to be by "a gentleman who has left his lodgings," are agreeable, and his "Essay on the English Government and Constitution" is an able exposition of Whig doctrine. But his tragedy, "Don Carlos," is terribly pedestrian, and Lord Holland trounced as it deserved a translation in the Spencerian metre of the fifth book of the "Odyssey."

During his early manhood Lord John made Holland House his second home, and entered into close friendships with Sydney Smith, Rogers, and more particularly with Moore, the association being accompanied by a touch of condescension on the one side and of obsequiousness on the other. In 1819 he identified himself with the cause of Parliamentary Reform by proposing the disfranchisement of corrupt boroughs, and notably of Grampound. From that moment he was the coming man, and his influence widened when to the advocacy of an improved representative system he added that of religious liberty by surprising the Government into the repeal of the Corporation Act. If he could have had his way, a fellow-agitation to O'Connell's would have hastened on Catholic Emancipation in England, but the prudence of Grey and Althorp restrained him. He had stepped, nevertheless, into the front rank of Whiggism when the Duke of Wellington's memorable declaration against Reform precipitated the fall of the Tory Government.

Lack of experience and feebleness of health presumably excluded Lord John Russell from the Cabinet of Earl Grey. He became Paymaster-General, in which capacity he is remembered as having given the Chelsea pensioners their gardens. He naturally formed one of the committee who drew up the plan of Reform, and was chosen by the Cabinet to introduce the Bill. Speaking as he did to an audience which was wholly unsympathetic and sometimes openly derisive, Lord John hardly rose to the occasion. But he became genuinely eloquent when he brought in his second and third Bills, and throughout the weary debates his discretion and temper were second only to Lord Althorp's. Prudence deserted him, however, when he penned the letter of reply to the address of the Birmingham Reform Union pronouncing it an impossibility that "the whisper of a faction should prevail against the voice of a nation."

Lord John Russell was headstrong, and after he had been promoted to the Cabinet he raised unnecessary difficulties. His insistence in debate upon the devotion of the surplus revenues of the Irish Church to secular purposes, after Lord Holland's fatherly advice had with difficulty prevented him from throwing up office on the point, not only "upset the coach" by driving four of his colleagues to resign, but also committed the Whig party to a principle which they were ultimately forced to abandon after suffering ignominious defeats. He had lost ground when King William declared that he would make a "wretched figure" as leader of the House in succession to Lord Althorp, and thereupon dispensed with the services of the first Melbourne Ministry.

The King's prophecy was disproved by events, for Lord John Russell's "best days" were undoubtedly those of his leadership, with Lord Melbourne as Premier once more. He had to reckon with the angry hostility of the Court at the outset, and converted it before long into steady regard. The Opposition were compact and guided by the finest tactician of the day. Lord John Russell's motley host consisted of mutually suspicious Whigs and Radicals, while the support of O'Connell, though useful in divisions, was far from a source of strength in the eyes of the English people. In one respect he failed: his manners were frigid and, as Bulwer Lytton wrote, "played the deuce with votes." The hostility of the Radicals was to a large extent personal, and they lost no opportunity of avenging supercilious treatment in private by public floutings of their icily calm chief. But he was a supreme manager of public business, he conducted debate with much tact and temper, bearing the whole of the burden, except for occasional assistance from Lord Howick, against an Opposition including such formidable speakers as Peel, Stanley, and Graham. The diminutive stature and thin voice could not annul the dexterity with which his points told, nor his tendency to platitude obscure the elevation of his mind. Sydney Smith paid him no more than his due when he declared that " a decent good-looking head of the Government might easily be found in lieu of Viscount Melbourne. But, in five minutes after the departure of Lord John Russell, the whole Whig Government would be dissolved into sparks of Liberality and splinters of Reform."

When the slenderness of the majority and the wrecking propensities of the House of Lords are taken into account, Russell must be allowed to have accomplished great things before the Bedchamber crisis occurred : the Corporation Act, the Tithes Commutation Act, the Marriage Act, the University of London Act, and the Irish Tithe and Municipal Acts made up a good round sum of legislation. After the Government had returned to office, discredited by their resignation, the record showed a lamentable decline, and his conduct during the Syrian crisis will not bear analysis.

Lord John Russell's austerity of manner in public was, like that of Pitt, laid aside in private. He was the life and soul of Grillion's, where he played many pranks with Stanley and other political opponents. Though but few sayings of his have been placed on record, he discloses himself in his prefaces to Moore's journals as a capital judge of humour, and his light verse is tolerable. He took for his first wife a widow, Lady Ribblesdale, and became a most affectionate stepfather to her four children. He repeated poetry to them, told them stories of his travels and of the great men whom he had met, and read to them aloud from Moore, Scott, and Dickens. His second marriage, to Lady Fanny Elliot, occurred in 1841, and so barely falls within the period with which this volume is concerned. It was one of great happiness, though, as his biographer, the late Sir Spencer Walpole, points out, it was to his political disadvantage that his weak health should have forced the pair to retire to the seclusion of Pembroke Lodge, Richmond, when they might have been entertaining in Chesham Place.

In general company Lord John Russell, though rather reserved, could give and take, and unaffectedly enjoyed the brightness of others. Though Holland House watched over his political apprenticeship and rejoiced over the triumphs of his Reform period, it could not be said to have exercised much influence over his beliefs. The four toasts at the Fox Club are drunk to the memory of Charles James Fox, Earl Grey, Lord Holland, and Lord John Russell. But the patriotism inspiring the last of the four when he made the great speech of 1850 on the Colonies would have been unintelligible to the insular Whigs of the generation before his own.

Lord Durham, John George Lambton, was four months older than Lord John Russell, and if he had followed his guardians' advice would have joined him as a student at Edinburgh University. The headstrong youth preferred instead a commission in the 10th Dragoons, followed by a Gretna Green marriage. Through an unexpected vacancy in the representation of the county of Durham he entered Parliament in 1813, and three years afterwards a second marriage with Lord Grey's daughter, Lady Louisa, brought him within the Whig pale.

But Lambton was far from being content with the orthodox doctrine. His impatient spirit could brook neither the irresolute leadership of Tierney nor his father-in-law's reluctance to identify himself with Radical measures. So early as 1819 Lambton declared himself in favour of a drastic measure of Reform, including the destruction of the rotten boroughs and the repeal of the Septennial Act. Lord Holland expostulated, whereupon the resolute youth declared that he was ready to face complete separation from the party and excommunication by Holland House. Lambton rapidly became a power in the North, where he was known as " Radical Jack " and the " King of the Colliers." The Whig aristocracy continued to regard him with alarm, and he made little attempt to conceal his resentment. It was probably to spite them that he lent support to Canning and accepted a peerage from his successor, Lord Goderich. They had little in common with a man who approved of the ballot and triennial Parliaments, and hailed the Revolution of July as "glorious."

Creevey has left a high-coloured description of the splendid discomforts of Lambton Castle, where the brilliant lighting by gas, the new illuminant, apparently served mainly to display the shortness of the provisions and the rarity of servants. The domestic disorder was typical of Durham's imperious and capricious mind. At the same time, he was deeply attached to his home and children, and when his eldest boy, the " Master

Lambton " of Lawrence's delightful picture, was carried off by consumption, his grief was terrible to witness. There was a tender side to the man who was "King Jog" and a "poor victim of temper" to Creevey. Unfortunately, his colleagues saw it but seldom. As Lord Privy Seal in the Grey Administration he was at constant loggerheads with Stanley and the other moderates in the Cabinet, and treated his father-in-law with positive brutality. "If I had been Grey," said Lord Melbourne, after a violent outburst on Durham's part, "I would have knocked him down."

The fact was that domestic misfortune pursued him throughout the crisis. "In eight months," he wrote to Grey, "I have lost son, mother, and daughter. When and where is it to end ? I live little in the world. I have few or no friends out of my family. My children are taken from me one after the other." To divert his thoughts he accepted a diplomatic mission to St. Petersburg, which he discharged with much ability, and soon after his return sent in his often-threatened resignation, nominally on the score of health, though he was also much out of sympathy with the Government's Irish proposals.

The Radicals undoubtedly looked to Lord Durham to succeed Earl Grey, and he, on his side, had cultivated close relations with active local politicians like Francis Place of Westminster and Joe Parkes of Birmingham. He also attracted the fitful admiration of Disraeli the Younger. It was as the advocate of a further instalment of Reform that he figured at the Edinburgh banquet in honour of Lord Grey, and so came into public collision with Brougham. Lord Durham's oratorical campaign through the Lowlands resulted in the silencing of his rival and the focussing of the popular gaze upon himself as the leader of the future. But it also angered the King and frightened the Premier.

Durham was passed over when Melbourne formed his second Ministry, and, feeling that his time had not yet come, went to St. Petersburg again as British Ambassador. All the while he kept touch with home politics through Parkes and other correspondents, and as he was on confidential terms with the Duchess of Kent and Princess Victoria, he had everything to hope of a new reign. Yet he threw up the brightest of prospects to accept the "most arduous and difficult task" of pacifying Canada. His motives were undoubtedly those of an unselfish patriot. But he made mistakes in choosing his staff, and when an outcry arose against the appointments of men of damaged reputations in Turton and Gibbon Wakefield, he took refuge in haughty silence. Nor did he keep the Government well informed as to his motives when he issued his much-discussed ordinance banishing the Canadian rebel leaders to Bermuda. Though really an act of clemency, it bore the appearance of high-handedness, and was of doubtful legality.

A Front Bench deplorably weak in debating power was thus left weaponless against the envenomed rhetoric of Brougham. Lord Durham was thrown over—"sacrificed" was his own expression; he resigned, and came home to write his famous report and to die. The malignity of Brougham actually attempted to deprive him of the credit of that empire-making treatise: it owed its "matter to a felon," Wakefield, and its "style to a coxcomb," Charles Buller. Durham's biographer, Mr. Stuart Reed, has disproved the slander, without perhaps laying sufficient stress upon the unevenness of temper and inability to act with others which stultified, to a considerable extent, his splendid abilities.

Guizot, a close observer of English society, described Durham as he appeared after his return from Canada. He was

"the spoilt child of society, imaginative, popular, still young and handsome, bored by the successes and irritated by the trials of life. We talked of Russia, the East, and Canada ; the conversation animated him for a little while ; but he quickly relapsed into silence, tired even of that which had attracted him, and submitting with a sad and languid pride alike to the illness that was sapping his strength and to the political checks and domestic sorrows which had overtaken him. He would have interested me much, if I had not perceived in his haughty melancholy a strong imprint of egotism and vanity."

LORD JOHN RUSSELL

FROM THE PAINTING BY SIR FRANCIS GRANT, P.R.A., IN THE NATIONAL
PORTRAIT GALLERY

LORD MACAULAY

FROM THE PAINTING BY SIR FRANCIS GRANT, P.R.A., IN THE NATIONAL PORTRAIT GALLERY

CHAPTER XXVII

A MISCELLANEOUS COMPANY

Jock Campbell—Elected to Brooks's—Visits to Holland House—
Norton *v.* Melbourne—The Irish Chancellorship—Macaulay enters
Holland House — Tears and a scene — A Cabinet Minister—
Macaulay as a talker—Charles Greville—A political factotum—
The friend of many—Poodle Byng and Albany Fonblanque—
The Grotes at Holland House—Monckton Milnes—Charles Dickens
—The next generation—Conclusion.

AMONG the smaller fry of Whig politicians who
haunted Holland House during the Reform
period was the future Lord Campbell. Sheer
industry raised him to the Solicitor-Generalship, after
he had long "grubbed obscurely at chambers in the
Temple." There have been many worse men than
"Jock" Campbell, albeit that in dealing with his professional contemporaries he was economical of the
truth. The sickly son of a Scottish minister at Cupar
had no influence to back him when he established himself in Tavistock Row, Covent Garden, in the year 1800,
with an engagement on the *Morning Chronicle* as a
parliamentary reporter for his chief means of sub-
sistence. He paid 9s. a week for his two rooms,
which seems moderate, and 2s. 2d. for his dinner,
which must be pronounced excessive. A secret voice

the while assured him that he would be as great as
Law, or Gibbs, or Erskine.

Jock Campbell carefully studied the conventions, and
informed his father that a card with Lincoln's Inn upon
it was as genteel for a young man as Grosvenor Square.
But he permitted himself frugal evenings at the Cider
Cellar in Maiden Lane, and an occasional " booze "
on port and claret. He was also an ardent volunteer.
Briefs came but slowly, but in 1816 he could afford to
set up a groom and two horses, and to dine daily at the
Verulam, a legal club in Lincoln's Inn Fields. Five
years later he married Miss Scarlett, who had previously declined what seems to have been a somewhat diffident suit, and in the following twelvemonth
enlisted as a Whig by being elected to Brooks's.

Campbell's initiation at Holland House occurred soon
afterwards, but he sagely considered eminence at the
Bar to be a useful preliminary to success in the *salon*,
and went there at first but rarely. He attended, however, one of Lady Holland's Sunday morning receptions,
and described with some humour how she received her
subjects on her throne, a pony chaise on the lawn. It
was a much more formidable ceremony than going to
kiss the King's hand. By that time he had taken silk,
on Lord Lyndhurst's recommendation, a favour he
subsequently repaid by calumniating the Chancellor's
memory, and he was returned for Stafford at the
General Election of 1830. Though he was passed over
on the formation of the Grey Administration, he became
Solicitor-General in November, 1832, and Attorney-
General two years afterwards. Active behind the scenes,
he enjoyed the confidence of his chiefs, and was favoured
by Brougham, whom, nevertheless, he heard " very much

discussed" at Holland House, just before the Chancellor's vagaries upset the first Melbourne Ministry.

Campbell showed spirit in debate, so much so that the Premier had to rebuke him for the warmth of his language when the House of Lords rejected his Bill for abolishing imprisonment for debt. He also harried Lord Melbourne when Bickersteth was preferred before him as Master of the Rolls, and was with difficulty dissuaded from resigning by the bestowal of a peerage on his wife. But they continued excellent friends, and the defence of the Prime Minister in the celebrated case Norton v. Melbourne was entrusted to the Attorney-General. The retainer caused him more professional anxiety than he ever before experienced, but the verdict was a triumphant acquittal. It was, he thought, the most brilliant event in his career.

The beginning of the new reign found Campbell basking in the society of Royal dukes and recording that the little Queen was "as merry and as playful as a kitten." He was also held in great regard at Holland House, where, in 1839, he heard the first whisper of the suggestion that Plunket might be induced to retire, and so create a vacancy in his favour for the Irish Chancellorship. The rumour took some time in becoming fact, and shortly before he died Lord Holland was employed in pressing Campbell's claims on the Prime Minister. "I have received more personal kindness from him," was the grateful record, "than from any other public man." That particular kindness, however, came perilously near to being a job, since, as has already been mentioned, Plunket was sorely unwilling to lay down his appointment. But as Campbell was unaware of his predecessor's chagrin, and refused a retiring pension when the defeat of the Government brought his brief glories to an end, his conduct in the matter appears to have been blameless. The remainder of his protracted career falls outside the scope of this volume.

Greville considered that Macaulay was the most fitting person to have written the history of Holland House, while admitting that he knew it too late to do justice to the subject as a whole. Macaulay had already made a literary reputation as an essayist in the *Edinburgh Review* and his speeches on the Reform Bill had caused Mackintosh to class him and Stanley together as " the chiefs of the next, or rather of this generation," before he entered the circle. In March, 1831, he was presented to Lady Holland, "a large, bold-looking woman, with the remains of a fine person and the air of Queen Elizabeth," at Lansdowne House. An invitation followed, and he was soon accepted as the great acquisition that he undoubtedly was. Macaulay found Lord Holland amusing and good-natured from the first ; by and by he came to appreciate the resources of his conversation in knowledge, narrative, and mimicry, and to admire the uncomplaining cheerfulness with which he endured his sufferings. Lady Holland he regarded with mixed feelings, alive to her talents, but amused by her affectations, and inclined to resent her dictation. He ridiculed her terror of lightning, the cholera, and a howling dog; for an *esprit fort* she was the greatest coward he had ever seen. He made fun of her annoyance when the French cook was ill and she kept up a continual lamentation over the dinner. An invitation to take up his quarters at Holland House almost completely was declined, because he preferred his chambers and independence.

Macaulay knew his worth, and the result was that he received every attention and profuse compliments on his essays in the *Edinburgh*, except when it pleased Lady Holland to display temper, for some unknown reason, against his article on Horace Walpole. When, in the early winter of 1833, he decided on going out to India as a member of Council, there were tears and a scene. Dear, dear Macaulay had sacrificed himself for his family; they were always making a tool of him. This interference he very properly resented, whereat she became profusely penitent. But she stormed at the Ministers for letting him go, and finally provoked her patient husband to the outburst: "Don't talk such nonsense, my lady. What the devil! can we tell a gentleman who has a claim on us that he must lose his only chance of getting an independence in order that he may come and talk to you in an evening?" Such was, evidently, the underlying theory.

So Macaulay went on his way to India, and returned in February, 1839, to become member for Edinburgh, and to enter the Cabinet as Secretary at War. His advocacy of the ballot was scarcely to the taste of Holland House, still less his Palmerstonian attitude during the Syrian crisis. But he was no less of a favourite on that account, and when Lord Holland died he feelingly remarked, in a letter to Macvey Napier, that a whole generation had gone to the grave with him. Custom seems to have reconciled Macaulay to Lady Holland's rule, since Greville represents him as enduring with exemplary meekness her prohibition of various topics of conversation, Sir Thomas Munro for one and St. Chrysostom for another, when she had had enough of them.

Such discipline was really salutary, for it was a subject of not uncommon complaint that Macaulay exhausted his audiences before he had exhausted his subject. Sir Henry Taylor said of him with truth that "his memory had swamped his mind"; lacking originality, his talk lacked charm, though it was inexhaustible in the variety and extent of its information. Greville made up his mind about the "common-looking man in black" at their first meeting and never altered it. Macaulay did not usurp conversation or assume superiority, but somehow he did not please. His voice was unmusical, his face not merely inexpressive, but positively heavy and dull. "If he could tread less heavily on the ground, if he could touch the subjects he handled with a lighter hand, if he knew when to stop as well as he knows what to say, his talk would be as attractive as it is wonderful." There is no getting away from an opinion so obviously unbiassed, more especially as Greville did not dislike the man, and placed an exaggerated estimate on him as a writer. "He gave more than society requires and not exactly of the kind"—that was where he failed. One wonders what Luttrell, a person of supreme social tact, made of him when he took Macaulay on a tour of inspection round the Holland House grounds. But, though the historian may have been heavy in hand when he went abroad, he was a model of generous affection at home, and no man has ever maintained a more undeviating standard of literary and political independence. Of the various elements that go to make Sir George Trevelyan's biography of his uncle one of

the most fascinating in our language, skill in present-
ment counts for much, but the essential moral dignity
of the subject for more.

Of Charles Greville it was written by Lord Derby or
another that

> " For forty years he stood behind the door
> And heard some secrets, but invented more."

His eagerness for information was insatiable, and though
posterity has reason to thank him for gossiping with the
valet of George IV., it does so with the feeling that he
ought to have kept off the back stairs. Again, though
his journal is far from answering to the caustic epigram
that it was " the Lives of the Apostles written by Judas
Iscariot," it does monstrous injustice to individuals,
notably to Palmerston, and, though in a smaller degree,
to Melbourne. At the same time, Greville's editor, the
late Mr. Reeve, justly claimed for him that the leading
qualities of his mind were the love of truth and the love
of justice. He subsequently modified many of his
harsher opinions, and there is no reason to quarrel with
his definition of a good, true, and interesting journal,
as his undoubtedly is—that it should be written
" without the slightest reference to publication, but
without any fear of it."   He always contemplated the
possibility that his Memoirs would be read, and to that
end erased passages relating to private persons and
affairs, and dwelt but little on his own private life,
beyond indulging in lamentations over hours wasted
on the turf and an ignorance of books more imaginary
than real.

Greville's weakness consisted in overrating his own

political importance, and in occasionally departing from the impartiality that should properly belong to a Clerk of the Council, a position he held for nearly forty years. He was a good deal in the confidence of various statesmen, notably of Lord Clarendon and Sir James Graham, and his advice always made for moderation. But his pamphlet on Ireland is by no means a masterly production, though he regarded it with an author's complacency. On two occasions he developed an abnormal activity behind the scenes, and in both he chose the wrong side. The first was during the crisis of the Reform Bill, when he abetted the " Waverers " in their ill-considered attempt to patch up a halfway house between the old system and the new. Again in 1840 he set himself to thwart Palmerston's Syrian policy, and carried his zeal so far that he became to all intents and purposes a French agent. It is amusing to discover that Guizot did not consider his officious advice worth placing on record. Greville put his abilities to better purposes as a negotiator during political changes, as when Palmerston was dismissed in 1851 ; but Sir Henry Taylor's estimate that "he was more fitted, if not more likely, to have been First Minister than at least three of the First Ministers of his generation," must be accounted an extreme instance of friendly partiality.

Socially, " Punch " Greville, as he was called in his prime, or the "Gruncher," as he came to be known in his later years, when deafness drove him back on himself, was decidedly a power. He delighted in good offices, and must have been quite in his element as manager of the training stables of the Duke of York, though his racing partnership with Lord George Bentinck ended in a difference of opinion. Sir Henry

Taylor describes him as "avowedly epicurean," and averse from the expression of ardent affections, but "a friend of many and always most a friend when friendship was most wanted." Little need be added about his intimacy with Holland House, which was already in existence in 1818, when the opening of his diary reveals him as a wise young man of twenty-four, and which continued, though not without periods of estrangement, to the end. The "insolence" of Lady Holland is the cause assigned to one of his revolts, but the story is guardedly told, and may well have had two sides. When Lord Holland died, he was proud to be reckoned, not as an old friend, but as "among the first of the second class of those who were always welcome."

Among the minor figures that appeared at Holland House during the period of Reform were "Poodle" Byng of the curly hair, who went everywhere, talking in a style described by Lady Granville as "a word for the wise"; also Albany Fonblanque, of the *Examiner*, one of the first men to bring earnest convictions to newspaper journalism.[1] A more incongruous element appeared in 1840, when Grote the historian, and Mrs. Grote, much to the amusement of Sydney Smith, were induced to rub shoulders with aristocratic Whiggism. The negotiation was conducted *sous les formes*, and the invited evidently regarded their acquiescence as a serious unbending of principle. They "even went so far"—such is Mrs. Grote's illuminating phrase—"as to accept friendly over-

[1] After Lord Holland's death Lady Holland offered Albany Fonblanque one of his books as a memento. On his choosing Dryden, she wrote : "As you preferred Dryden, I send you the copy my dear lord always liked. You will find some of the volumes in bad condition, as he never went on any excursion without taking one or two with him."

tures from Lord and Lady Holland, and to commence intercourse with Holland House, whither Grote would never have consented to go in past times." So stiff-backed was Philosophic Radicalism. Grote, however, had outlived his earlier prejudices against rank and society, and was, besides, annoyed for the time being with his political associates because of their apathy in the sacred cause of the ballot. It must have been a meeting of the prophetesses, since Mrs. Grote, as well as her hostess, possessed a grand and haughty manner and was totally exempt from shyness. However, " the evening made a deep impression on the imagination " of the gifted pair, Charles Buller, who, in addition to being a most brilliant talker, was thoroughly sound on the ballot, having conceivably acted as a harmonising influence.

The literary traditions of the place were fittingly sustained by two recruits secured towards the close of the period in Monckton Milnes and Charles Dickens, while Bulwer Lytton was also an occasional guest. The first of the three took London by storm in 1836, after he had made a name for himself by the slim " Memorials " of his tour in Greece, and had acquired through residence in Southern Europe a vivacity of manner which, by all accounts, took old stagers of the formal school consider-ably aback. Rogers appreciated him, and the young man returned the compliment by giving breakfasts at his chambers in Pall Mall in imitation of those of St. James's Place. At Holland House he is said to have earned his best-known nickname by entering the room one very hot night, when Lady Holland and a large party were suffer-ing from the stifling atmosphere, and general dulness had crept over the company. " Ah ! here comes the cool of the evening," cried Sydney Smith, and they all revived. In reply to a remonstrance from Milnes, however, Sydney Smith denied that he had coined the names of the "Cool of the Evening," "London Assurance" or "In-I-go Jones," after the boy Jones famous for his invasions of Buckingham Palace. He added, in words which Lord Houghton afterwards admitted to be those of just rebuke : "Never lose your temper, which is one of your best qualities, and which has carried you hitherto safely through your startling eccentricities. If you turn cross and touchy, you are a lost man."

Dickens approached Holland House in much humbler mood. He appears to have been introduced to its mistress by Sergeant Talfourd in 1838, the year of his expedition to Yorkshire with Hablot K. Browne to collect the information reproduced in "Nicholas Nickleby." He hoped to make his appearance under Talfourd's wing, and in a letter to his friend expressed alarm at the prospect of a solitary visit. Hampered by the diffidence natural to one making his first advances towards polite society, Dickens appears to have fallen an easy victim. Lady Holland forced him to disclose the plot of "Nicholas Nickleby," and when he was about to visit America she remonstrated thus : "Why cannot you go down to Bristol, and see some of the third and fourth class people, and they'll do just as well."

With this highly typical observation my attempt to reproduce the figures of a society without its parallel in English life must be brought to a conclusion. Holland House was the centre of yet another circle in the days of Henry Edward, fourth Lord Holland, and his accomplished wife. Dinners gave way to afternoon receptions, when, to quote Hayward once more, "the far-famed Countess of Castiglione moved through the brilliant throng with the air of a goddess ; when the leaders of both Houses were interchanging grave courtesies on the lawn ; when Lord and Lady Russell and Lady Palmerston were talking to the Comte and Comtesse de Paris in a group which the Prince of Wales had just quitted to engage in animated conversation with Longfellow." Hoppner and Leslie were more than replaced by G. F. Watts, who in 1843 made the acquaintance of Lord Holland, then Minister at the Court of Tuscany, in Florence, and so began an intimacy to which Holland House owes much redecoration and some of its best portraits. But the time for writing that page in its history has not come, and—to be truthful—the materials are wanting.

THE END

INDEX

ABERCROMBY, James, Lord Dunfermline, 286, 349
Aberdeen, George Hamilton Gordon, Earl of, 146, 244, 295–299, 311, 338
Adair, Sir Robert, 25, 30, 97, 101–103, 123
Addington, Henry, Viscount Sidmouth, 25, 26, 136, 152, 260
Addison, Joseph, 9, 10, 91 *and note*, 175
Affleck, Lady, 237
Allen, John, 73, 81–89, 91, 95, 222, 237, 238, 258, 327, 360
Althorp, John Spencer, Viscount, 18, 145, 308, 350, 351–355, 357, 358
Alvanley, Lord, 185, 229–232, 343
Anglesey, Henry William Paget, Marquis of, 285
Arago, D., 252
Arnold, Benedict, 103
Auckland, George Eden, Earl of, 93

BANNISTER, John, 243
Bathurst, Henry, Earl of, 39, 295, 300
Beaumont, Sir G., 239
Bedford, Francis, Duke of, 104, 272
Bedford, John, Duke of, 146
Bentham, Jeremy, 79, 166, 228, 255, 256, 266, 288, 333

Brodie, Sir Benjamin, 253–254
Brougham and Vaux, Henry, Baron, 21, 37, 45, 61, 81, 84, 120, 122, 135, 138, 140, 155, 158, 212, 254, 255, 258, 266, 272–279, 283, 294, 300, 306, 308, 313, 319, 320, 333, 353, 362, 366
Brummell, G. B., 97, 230
Brunel, Sir I. K., 69
Buckingham, George Grenville, Marquis of, 133
Buller, Charles, 363, 374
Burdett, Sir Francis, 34, 216, 284, 288–291, 319
Bute, John, Earl of, 10, 11, 123
Byng, F. (" Poodle "), 373
Byron, George Noel Gordon, Lord, 29, 43, 72, 110, 117, 153, 155, 159, 161–163, 166, 168, 177, 186, 189, 208, 209, 211–217, 222, 224, 234, 288, 306, 330–332
Byron, Lady, 214, 215, 289

CALONNE, C. A. de, 30, 328
Camelford, Thomas Pitt, Baron, 106
Campbell, John, Baron, 110, 228, 285, 365–368
Campbell, Thomas, 176, 177, 215, 220–223, 281
Canning, George, 17–18, 34, 47, 48, 99, 102, 117, 135, 137, 145, 149, 151, 153, 154, 159, 171, 260, 264,

284 ,289, 292, 296, 307, 311, 316,
321, 346, 361
Canova, A., 239, 241–242
Carlisle, Charles Howard, first
Earl of, 17
Carlisle, Frederick Howard, fifth
Earl of, 14, 16, 213, 317
Carlisle, George Howard, sixth
Earl of, 17, 43, 47, 317–318
Caroline, Queen, 44–47, 112, 165,
274–276, 288, 289
Castlereagh, Robert Stewart, Vis-
count, 18, 135, 143, 191, 338
Cavendish, Lord George, 154
Chantrey, Sir F., 234, 240, 241, 264
Charlotte, Princess, 274
Chatham, John Pitt, Earl of, 154
Clarence, Duke of. See William
IV.
Clarendon, George Villiers, Earl
of, 54, 282, 346, 348, 372
Cleyn, Francis, 6, 15
Cochrane, Thomas, Earl of Dun-
donald, 289, 290
Colchester, Charles Abbot, Baron,
35
Coleridge, S. T., 80, 128, 180, 248
Collins, William, 241
Constable, J., 241
Cope, Sir Walter, 5, 6
Cottenham, Charles Christopher
Pepys, Earl of, 278
Croker, J. W., 47, 116, 316, 333,
353
Creevey, Thomas, 34, 35, 45, 119,
121, 152, 153, 155, 156–157, 158,
260, 273, 276, 278, 287, 314, 340,
349, 362
Cromwell, Oliver, 7
Cumberland, Ernest, Duke of, 282
Curran, John Philpot, 121, 148,
158, 161–163, 333

Davy, Sir H., 247–250

Davy, Lady, 249
Denman, Thomas, Baron, 64 and
note, 228, 275, 279–283, 289
Deffand, Mme. du, 97
Devonshire, Georgiana, Duchess
of, 126–128, 150
Dickens, Charles, 176, 360, 375
Doyle, Colonel, 209
Dudley, John William Ward, Earl
of, 71, 179, 181, 184, 188, 201,
205, 256, 258, 263, 300, 311–316,
333
Dumont, Etienne, 81, 266, 270,
329–331, 333
Duncannon, J. W. Ponsonby, Vis-
count, 346, 349–350
Duncombe, Thomas, 51
Dundas, Henry, Viscount Melville,
32, 112, 154, 217, 266
Durham, John George Lambton,
Earl of, 137, 308, 309, 350, 360–
364

Edgar (servant), 55, 77
Egremont, William O'Brien
Wyndham, Earl of, 235–236,
237, 244
Eldon, John Scott, Earl of, 37, 46,
131, 217, 228, 266, 281, 282, 292,
293, 300, 319
Elgin, Thomas Bruce, Earl of, 236,
241
Ellenborough, Edward Law,
Baron, 32, 266
Ellice, Edward ("Bear"), 156, 304
Ellis, Charles, Lord Dover, 317
Ellis, George, 98, 316–317
Elliston, R. W., 212, 217
Erskine, Thomas, Baron, 22, 44,
108–113, 119, 140, 161, 198, 229,
256, 366

Fairfax, Thomas, Baron, 7
Faraday, M., 251, 252

Fitzgerald, Lord Edward, 210
Fitzherbert, Mrs., 119
Fitzpatrick, Richard, General, 13, 25, 95–99
Fitzwilliam, William Wentworth, Earl, 35, 321
Flahault, A. C. J., Count, 344–345
Flaxman, J., 175, 234, 241
Fonblanque, Albany, 373
Foscolo, Ugo, 323–325
Fox, Charles, General, 21, 69, 76, 81
Fox, Charles James, 10, 12, 14, 20, 23–25, 27, 32, 33, 55, 78, 103, 122, 127, 130–132, 135, 165, 176, 221, 238, 241, 255, 360
Fox, Elizabeth, Mrs., 17
Fox, Henry. See Holland, first Baron
Fox, Henry, 12
Fox, Mary, Miss, 14, 33, 78–80, 160, 251, 264
Fox, Sir Stephen, 1–3, 91
Fox, Stephen. See Holland, second Baron
Francis, Sir Philip, 101, 118–121, 156
Frere, John Hookham, 17, 82, 125, 151, 169–173, 185, 316

GAINSBOROUGH, Thomas, 126, 128
George III., 10, 33, 34, 112, 131, 142, 145
George IV., 27, 34, 116, 119, 122, 127, 136, 149, 164, 188, 200, 207, 228, 240, 266, 276, 281, 330, 336, 337
Gifford, William, 189, 238
Gillray, James, 106
Glenelg, Charles Grant, Baron, 262, 263, 300
Goderich, Frederick John Robinson, Viscount, 47, 91, 341, 361
Gordon, the Duchess of, 99, 154, 284

Graham, Sir James, 52, 322, 351, 359, 372
Granville, Harriet, Countess, 41, 47, 48, 60, 61, 64, 69, 105, 179, 185, 186, 200, 278, 296, 300, 337, 338, 340, 344
Grattan, Henry, 158–161, 162, 283
Grenville, Thomas, 150–151, 258
Grenville, William Wyndham, Baron, 32, 34, 125, 128–134, 145
Greville, Charles, 50, 54, 65, 75, 81, 92–95, 147, 150, 157, 169, 193, 230, 234, 235, 278, 303, 304, 307, 313, 345, 349, 353, 371–373
Grey, Charles, Earl, 22, 34, 35, 50, 51, 53, 55, 71, 131, 132, 134–139, 145, 146, 151, 153, 156, 158, 179, 198, 240, 272, 276, 278, 282, 289, 300, 306, 321, 338, 360
Gronow, Captain, 157, 230, 231
Grote, George and Mrs., 373–374
Guizot, F. P. G., 54, 76, 147, 257, 304, 339, 345–347, 364, 372

HAMILTON, Charles, 13
Hamilton, Emma, Lady, 125
Hare, James, 97, 99–100, 122, 127, 128
Haydon, B. R., 234, 235–241, 242
Hayter, Sir A., 91
Hayward, Abraham, 62, 67, 175, 182, 198, 199, 375
Hallam, Henry, 40, 183, 224–226, 258, 332, 347
Heathcote, Lady, 213
Herries, J. C., 149, 146
Hobhouse, John Cam, 209, 242, 288–291, 353
Holland, Elizabeth Vassall, Lady, marriage, 21 ; travels, 25–27 ; story of, 35 ; and Murat, 39 ; and Napoleon, 41–43 ; and Queen Caroline, 46; on Canning, 48 ; dissatisfied, 49 ; on

the Reform Government, 52; characteristics, 61–77; letters, 69–72; death, 75; and John Allen, 82–85; her portrait, 91; mentioned, 117, 121, 158, 187, 198, 201–203, 207, 213–216, 221, 222, 223, 229, 237, 240, 242, 272, 310, 315, 322, 326, 333, 336, 341, 346, 366, 368, 375

Holland, Henry Fox, first Baron, 3–4, 10–14

Holland, Henry Edward Fox, fourth Baron, 19, 30, 375

Holland, Henry Rich, first Earl of, 6–7

Holland, Henry Richard Vassall Fox, third Baron, birth, 14; minority, 15, 16; at Eton, 17; at Christ Church, 17–18; travels, 18–21; marriage, 21; takes his seat, 21; travels, 25–27; literary works, 27–31; Lord Privy Seal, 33; his protests, 36–39; at Naples, 38; on Queen Caroline's trial, 46–47; prospects of office, 47–49; on the Eastern question, 50; Chancellor of the Duchy of Lancaster, 50–52; in Opposition, 52; Chancellor of the Duchy again, 53; death, 55; as a statesman, 55–57; characteristics, 57–71; conversation at Holland House, 90–96; mentioned, 113, 122, 126, 134, 136, 151, 160, 165, 176, 198, 202, 206, 208, 210, 211, 212–216, 217–219, 220, 236, 237, 238, 240, 256, 258, 262, 264, 276, 279, 281, 288, 298, 315, 322, 326, 329, 330, 338, 340, 341, 345, 346, 354, 356, 360, 361–369

Holland, Sir Henry, 38, 62, 68, 69, 178, 250, 254, 258, 313, 324, 340

Holland, Mary, Lady, 14, 15, 16

Holland, Stephen Fox, second Baron, 12–15

Hoppner, John, 91, 92, 238–239, 241, 375

Horner, Francis, 40, 70, 71, 81, 89, 183, 197, 215, 225, 226, 255, 258, 263–266, 286, 316, 330

Horton, R. Wilmot, 209

Houghton, Richard Monckton Milnes, Baron, 203, 374–375

Humboldt, Alexander von, Baron, 70, 252–253

Humboldt, William von, Baron, 252

Hume, David, 16, 96

Hunt, James Henry Leigh, 77, 91

IRVING, Edward, 105

Irving, Washington, 333

JEFFREY, Francis, Lord, 177, 203, 217, 256–257, 258, 264

Jekyll, Joseph, 49, 226–229, 293, 314, 324

Jones, Inigo, 6

KEAN, Edmund, 242, 243

Kemble, Fanny, 68, 147, 200

Kemble, John, 242, 243–245, 297

Kensington, William Edwardes, Baron, 10

Knight, R. Payne, 235–236, 297

LABOUCHERE, Henry, Lord Taunton, 348

Lamb, Lady Caroline, 72–74, 213–215, 257, 305, 306, 314

Lamb, George, 211, 289, 290

Lansdowne, Henry Petty, Marquis of, 144–148, 154, 176, 204, 208, 256, 264, 286, 307, 329–330, 352

Lardner, Dr. D., 262

Lauderdale, James Maitland, Earl of, 60, 81, 103–106, 289

Lawrence, Sir T., 91, 127, 147, 163, 175, 236, 238, 241, 295

Leigh, Augusta, Mrs., 209

Lennox, Lady Sarah, 10, 11

Leslie, C. R., 234, 236, 237, 375

Lewis, Sir George Cornewall, 169, 172

Lewis, Matthew Gregory (" Monk "), 63, 95, 118, 167–169

Liechtenstein, Princess, quoted, 10 *note*, 91, 243, 251

Lieven, Princess, 70, 137, 300, 312, 336–339

Lilford, Lady, 237

Liverpool, Charles Jenkinson, first Earl of, 40, 47, 295, 300, 353

Lockhart, J. G., 169, 251, 317

Longman, T. N., 209, 211

Lowe, Sir Hudson, 42, 71

Luttrell, Henry, 59, 60, 61, 66, 73, 91, 95, 174, 178, 183, 184–194, 195, 196, 209, 316, 370

Lyndhurst, John Singleton Copley, Baron, 198, 276, 316, 318–321, 366

Lytton, Sir E. Bulwer, 285, 358, 374

MACARTNEY, George, Earl, 123–124

Macaulay, T. B., Baron, 3, 39, 57, 59, 60, 67, 83, 92, 147, 178, 183, 201, 215, 258, 330, 347, 368–371

Mackintosh, Sir James, 58, 60, 80, 81, 95, 160, 178, 180, 257–263, 266, 269, 281, 283, 287, 318, 332, 333

Majocchi, 275

Malmesbury, James Harris, Earl of, 142

Martineau, Harriet, 158, 278

Medwin, Thomas, 43, 213, 214

Melbourne, William Lamb, Viscount, 47, 52, 53, 55, 60, 90, 93–95, 122, 168, 200, 213, 215, 251, 257, 276, 278, 300, 305–310, 311, 333, 358, 361, 366

Melville, Viscount. *See* Dundas.

Metternich, C. W. N. L., Prince, 335–336

Minto, Gilbert Elliot, Earl of, 15, 59, 119, 124–126, 130, 133, 134

Mirabeau, H. G. R., Count de, 266, 329

Moira, Francis Rawdon, Earl of, 33, 119, 131, 148–150, 206

Molé, L. M., Count de, 70

Monroe, James, 333

Montrond, Count, 342–343

Moore, Thomas, 43, 59, 61, 66, 72, 91, 95, 117, 147–148, 163, 166, 170, 180, 183, 193, 203, 206–211, 216, 240, 249, 281, 285, 310, 313, 330, 334, 357, 259, 360

Motteux, A., 67, 343

Mulgrave, Henry Phipps, Earl of, 239, 288

Murray, John, 29, 208, 209, 212, 216, 219, 325

NAPOLEON I., 25, 30, 39–43, 87, 130, 136, 142, 356

Nelson, Horatio, Viscount, 125, 238

Newcastle, Thomas Holles, Duke of, 4, 11

Nollekens, Joseph, 97, 111, 241

Northcote, J., 238

Norton, Caroline, Mrs., 68, 179, 366

North, Dudley, 100

Nugent, Lord, 262

O'CONNELL, Daniel, 50, 52, 53, 159, 231, 350, 358

Orléans, Louis Philippe, Duke d', 329, 343

Orsay, Charles, Count d', 69, 342

Ossory, Earl of, 14, 16

PALMELLA, Pedro, Duke of, 336, 337

Palmerston, Emily, Lady, 303, 337, 375

Palmerston, Henry John Temple, Viscount, 50, 53, 93, 103, 125, 146, 256, 300, 301–305, 340, 342, 346, 347, 352

Parr, Dr. Samuel, 80, 88, 95, 164–167, 183, 235, 281

Pecchio, 322

Peel, Sir R., 232, 320, 353, 358

Penn, William, 8

Perceval, Spencer, 132, 135, 143, 149

Perry, Henry, 119, 212, 220

Pitt, William, 23, 26, 32, 111, 122, 125, 130–132, 142, 143, 151, 159, 238, 295

Place, Francis, 289, 290, 330, 362

Plunket, William Conyngham, Baron, 49, 283–285, 367

Ponsonby, George, 34, 152, 154

Poole, T., 250

Porson, R., 258

Pozzo di Borgo, Count, 322, 336, 337

RAIKES, Thomas, 238, 344

Redesdale, John Freeman Mitford, Baron, 268

Regent, the Prince. See George IV.

Reynolds, Sir Joshua, 10 and note, 91, 101, 113, 126, 128, 238, 241

Ricardo, David, 258

Rice, Thomas Spring-, 93, 263, 349

Rich, Lady Diana, 8

Richmond, Charles Gordon-Lennox, Duke of, 351, 355

Rigby, Richard, 4, 11, 12

Rogers, Samuel, 17, 28, 60, 65, 68, 71, 81, 91, 95, 97, 109, 121, 160, 163, 166, 174–183, 185, 189, 195, 209, 210, 218, 240, 245, 249, 258, 259, 281, 313, 315, 324, 360

Romilly, Sir Samuel, 58, 166, 215, 255, 258, 263, 266–271, 290, 321, 329, 333

Roos, Henry de, 193

Rose, George, 152

Rousseau, Jean Jacques, 96, 266

Rumford, Benjamin Thompson, Count, 246–247

Russell, Lord John, 25, 39, 48, 50, 54, 69, 76, 91, 146, 177, 195, 200, 209, 210, 215, 257, 259, 291, 318, 350, 356–360, 375

SCARLETT, James, Lord Abinger, 227, 263, 270, 276, 318, 321–322

Scott, Sir Walter, 167, 168, 169, 181, 217–219, 227, 243, 249, 263, 285, 295, 317, 324, 333, 366

Sefton, Earl of, 83, 157–158, 193, 278, 343

Selwyn, George, 4, 12, 60

Seymour, Lord Webb, 225, 226, 263

Sharp, Richard ("Conversation"), 180, 183–184, 215, 258, 286

Shee, Sir M. A., 91, 242

Shelburne, William, Earl of, 3, 11, 12, 79, 144

Sheridan, R. B., 22, 34, 96, 99, 103, 111, 113–118, 152, 155, 160, 208, 255, 333

Shuttleworth, Bishop, 28, 95

Smith, Robert Percy ("Bobus"), 17, 58, 80, 93, 203–205, 238, 258, 260, 263
Smith, Rev. Sydney, 17, 27, 60, 80, 81, 95, 195–203, 204, 221, 224, 226, 237, 249, 257, 258, 259, 260, 263, 281, 286, 287, 288, 313, 318, 319, 321, 340, 347, 360, 375
South, Sir James, 251
Southey, R., 181, 223–224
Staël, Madame de, 94, 118, 170, 222, 249, 314, 331–333
Stanley, Edward Geoffrey Smith, 51, 52, 358
Stanhope, Charles, third Earl, 106
Stanhope, Lady Hester, 107
Stanhope, Philip Henry, fourth Earl, 107
Stewart, Dugald, 81, 255, 257, 263, 301, 313
Stothard, Thomas, 175, 215
Stowell, William Scott, Baron, 292–294, 327
Sully, Max de Béthune, Duke of, 6 and note

Talleyrand, Charles Maurice de, Prince of Bénévent, 19, 25, 41, 205, 229, 256, 300, 328, 339–342, 343
Talma, F. J., 244
Taylor, Sir Henry, 93, 178, 370, 372
Taylor, John, 120
Tenterden, Charles Abbot, Baron, 282
Thiers, Louis Adolphe, 55, 300
Thorpe, John, 5
Thurlow, Edward, Baron, 121–123
Ticknor, George, 334
Tierney, George, 20, 34, 151–153, 260, 289, 349–361
Tooke, John Horne, 111, 121, 288

Townshend, Lord John, 99, 100
Trotter, Mr., 25, 30
Tullamore, Countess of, 210
Turner, W. M., 233

Van Buren, M., 333
Vere, Aubrey de, 5
Vere, John de, fourteenth Earl of Oxford, 5
Victoria, Queen, 240, 345, 363, 367

Wales, Prince of. See George IV.
Wales, Princess of. See Caroline, Queen
Walpole, Horace, 4, 10, 12, 13, 29, 91, 124, 175, 369
Warwick and Holland, Countess Dowager of, 9
Warwick and Holland, Earl of, 9, 10
Waterton, Charles, 253
Watts, G. F., 376
Webster, Daniel, 333
Wedderburn, Sir Alexander, 122
Wellesley, Richard Colley, Marquis, 134, 284, 285, 333
Wellington, Arthur Wellesley, Duke of, 31, 176, 191, 229, 232, 276, 281, 312, 316, 320, 341
West, Sir Benjamin, 238, 242
Westmacott, Sir R., 241
Westmorland, Lady, 213
Weyer, Silvain van der, 67, 336
Whately, Richard, Archbishop, 327
Whitbread, Samuel, 34, 118, 135, 136, 153–156, 212, 239, 260, 269, 270, 300
White, Joseph Blanco, 88, 325–328
Wilberforce, William, 37, 282, 289
Wilkie, Sir David, 147, 237, 239–241, 243

William IV., 51, 138, 240, 281, 307, 350, 358, 363

Williams, Charles Hanbury, 4

Windham, William, 30, 125, 130, 139–143, 264

Wishaw, John, 225, 286–288

Wollaston, W. H., 250–251

Wood, Alderman, 275

Wynn, Charles Williams, 224, 262, 300

YARMOUTH, Francis Seymour-Conway, Earl of, 105, 231

York, Frederick, Duke of, 154, 207, 231, 284, 372

York, Duchess of, 167, 231